RESUME POWER
Selling Yourself on Paper

Tom Washington

Mount Vernon Press
Bellevue, Washington

Mount Vernon Press
1750 112th Northeast C-247
Bellevue, Washington 98004

This book was edited, designed, and produced by Walking Bird Publication Services, Seattle, Washington.

ISBN 0-931213-05-3

Library of Congress Cataloging in Publication Data:
Washington, Tom, 1949 –
    Resume power.
    Bibliography: p.
    1. Resumes (Employment)   I. Title.
HF5383.W316   1984   650.1'4   84-20779

ACKNOWLEDGMENTS

To my parents I owe more than words can state. Their love and support, demonstrated in so many ways at so many times, made this book possible.

Advice for improving the book came from many sources. Each person who reviewed the manuscript not only provided ideas for improving it, but also a dose of encouragement. The rough edges were knocked off and many significant improvements resulted. For their advice, encouragement, and friendship, I thank Michael Badger, Jody Burns, Diane DeWitt, Richard French, Michael Grubiak, Roxanne Legatz, Ivan Settles, and Nat Washington, Sr., my advisor and confidant. Jody Burns, Charles Clock, and Jack Porter were particularly helpful with the resume research.

While obtaining a masters degree in counseling at Northeastern Illinois University, I received a great deal of help and support, especially from two outstanding professors, Jim Fruehling and Mac Inbody.

To Laurie Winfield of Walking Bird I am very grateful. Her editing strengthened the book immensely, and her book design produced a visually appealing product.

Betty Pappas, Judy Callen, and Luella Littleton of Secretel put up with me and my idiosyncracies as they typed several hundred resumes. Their good humor and patience made our relationship most enjoyable. Carolyn Lacy of The Word Shop typed the manuscript drafts on her word processor and somehow kept everything straight.

And Mabel. Mabel Thompson made me a writer. Her love of conciseness and hatred of dead verbs had a profound impact on me.

Finally, a deep thank you to my dear wife Lois, who put up with more than anyone should have to. She read, critiqued, and offered help when I needed it. I love you.

—Tom Washington

FORWARD TO THE THIRD EDITION

Since **Resume Power** first came out in 1985, I have been encouraged by the many favorable comments people have made. It seems to have met a need. I worked very hard to identify the areas where people have the most trouble in writing a resume, preparing for interviews, and conducting a job search. I then tried to write in such a way that people would find practical answers to these issues.

As I considered how **Resume Power** could most be improved and updated, it seemed that interviewing was the key area. Since **Resume Power** was first published I have conducted several hundred practice interviews. I have observed where people most frequently stumbled. This third edition has been expanded in the interviewing area, and represents the insights I have gained in the last five years. I trust it too, will be well received—and helpful.

A TOP-QUALITY RESUME

The eye is drawn quickly to your name to establish your identity.

A clear objective reveals that you are focused and creates a positive impression.

PAUL PRESCOTT
1121 Sturla Drive
San Jose, California 95148
(408) 754-2631

Effective layout invites employers to read your resume thoroughly.

OBJECTIVE: Manufacturing Management

QUALIFICATIONS

The Qualifications section sells you in ways that the job description alone can't do. The section summarizes your strengths and experience and sets the tone for what the reader will discover about you.

Strong background in all phases of production supervision in the electronics industry including job scheduling, quality assurance, inventory control, purchasing, customer relations, and supervising and training up to 35 production workers. Consistently able to increase on-line deliveries while increasing quality and reducing rejections.

EDUCATION

B.A. - Business Administration, University of San Francisco
(1976-1980)

Training demonstrates growth and proficiency.

TRAINING

Increasing Productivity, Castleman Group, 20 class hours (1983)
Implementing Quality Circles, John Hagimoto, 24 class hours (1982)
Supervising Problem Employees, George Mitchell & Assoc., 8 class
hours, (1981)
Blueprint reading, Circuits West, 16 class hours (1980)

EMPLOYMENT

Both job descriptions are filled with results. Results sell you to an employer and reveal much more about your potential than duties alone.

Circuits West, San Jose, California, 6/80-present.

PRODUCTION MANAGER 7/82-present. Supervise 30 shop personnel in the production of prototype circuit boards. Handle cost estimating, job scheduling, production control, and inventory control. Reduced turnaround time on orders from three weeks to one week without adding staff or increasing overtime. Quality increased substantially as rejections were reduced 55%. Significantly reduced purchasing costs through a more effective inventory control program.

The job descriptions are short and concise, highlighting key points. Short job descriptions invite the employer to read thoroughly and help maintain interest.

SHOP LEAD 6/80-7/82. Assigned jobs to 14 production personnel in the drilling, screening, plating, fabricating and camera departments. Supervised programmers and did some programming of numerically controlled machinery. Developed a maintenance program which reduced production losses due to breakdowns, 70%.

ACTIVITIES

Enjoy photography, river rafting, soccer, and hiking

CONTENTS

HOW THIS BOOK CAN HELP YOU GET A JOB

A top-quality resume can net you interviews at a rate ten times greater than your competitors. This book will help you write that resume. *Resume Power* not only will help you write an interview-getting resume, it also provides practical and effective advice covering all phases of the job search. Nowhere can you find a book so packed with proven strategies which have enabled people to find better jobs, at higher pay, and in less time than they had thought possible.

Developing a top-quality resume is dependent not on writing ability but on knowledge and time—knowledge of how to write a resume and market yourself, and time to write, revise, and write again. A mediocre resume takes most people three to six hours to write. An outstanding resume requires six to ten hours. Those three or four extra hours could be the best investment you ever make.

A top-quality resume not only leads to more interviews, but will also produce more job offers. By taking the extra time to review your work experience and accomplishments, you'll be sharper in interviews and appear more confident. Your resume can actually guide the interview and enable you to answer questions that help make you look good. An effective job search begins with a top-quality resume.

Since 1981 I have been researching what makes effective resumes. During that time I have completed some of the first scientific research to determine what really attracts employers to applicants. To date the studies have covered secretaries, engineers, and recent college graduates. The studies have exploded such myths as the belief that resumes must be only one page in length. While more studies are needed, the results of the studies already completed will enable you to write a top-quality resume. For example, having your resume professionally typed is just about the most important thing you can do. There's more: your resume should describe accomplishments and results, not just duties, should be printed or photocopied on ivory-colored paper, and must contain no misspellings or typographical errors.

Additional findings will be described throughout the book.

RESULTS YOU CAN EXPECT

Writing a top-quality resume is not difficult, but it does take time and careful thought. This book is designed so that you can quickly absorb the information you need to write a resume that gets results. It takes you through the process step by step and answers your questions as they arise. It covers key points that are not even mentioned in other resume-writing books, points that can make the difference between getting or not getting an interview. If you follow my advice and take enough time to write and edit, you can obtain interviews at a rate ten times greater than competitors with typical resumes. This figure is based on actual surveys of former clients, most of whom receive one interview for every five to seven resumes sent through the mail. This compares to the national average of one interview for every fifty to one hundred resumes mailed out.

Once you have completed your resume, you may still want professional advice. Career Management Resources can edit and help you strengthen your resume.

Happy writing!

WHAT MAKES A
TOP-QUALITY RESUME?

EYE APPEAL

A resume must be visually appealing. Lasting impressions can be formed during the first five seconds your resume is read. That's how long it takes someone to view the layout, observe the quality of the typing and printing, and note the color and quality of the paper. Of course most of this takes place on an unconscious level. Resumes are usually scanned the first time through. If the reader detects misspellings, smudges, poor-quality typing or printing, clumsy or verbose writing, or a confusing layout, the resume may be set aside after just ten or twenty seconds. The result—no interview.

WELL WRITTEN

The effective resume provides valuable information quickly and is easy to read. Each sentence expresses a fact, impression, or idea which will help sell you. All unnecessary words and phrases have been removed. Concise writing is appreciated by all employers and reveals much about your ability to communicate.

POSITIVE

The top-quality resume presents you in the best light possible, yet does not exaggerate your qualifications. Every item is selected carefully to promote you in the eyes of the employer. Unflattering facts are not hidden, they either are simply left unmentioned or carefully turned into positives. The resume that concentrates on strengths helps you obtain interviews.

IMPACT

Write with impact. Impact is achieved with tight, concise phrases using action verbs. Impact is achieved when you accurately describe *and project* your desired image. Your full potential will come across only when you write with impact. Writing and rewriting is required—something even best-selling authors must do.

HOW TO BEGIN

Before your resume is completed, you will have made dozens of important decisions. This book is designed to help you make those decisions quickly and easily. Examples are provided throughout to explain and demonstrate points more clearly. Read through pages 12 to 101 quickly, then return to study each section. Highlight points or examples that are especially applicable to you. Within one to two hours' reading time, you will have all the knowledge necessary to write a top-quality resume. From that point on, how much time you spend on writing and rewriting will determine your success.

Each section of a resume is explained in detail. *Resume Power* explains when and how to use each section and how to write it. Examples and options are provided. You'll know what will work best for you.

EDITING

If you think you may want editing assistance, Career Management Resources can strengthen your resume in ways that can increase your interviews by 30% or more. For more information, read pages 89-92. Be sure to follow the instructions very carefully, especially concerning the writing of job sketches, which are discussed on pages 27-32. Writing thorough job sketches will enable you to write a better resume in less time.

THE OBJECTIVE

Before starting your resume, write out your objective. Later you can change it or delete it, but having an objective will keep you focused while you write. Objectives such as "Bookkeeper," "Chemist," or "Construction Superintendent" can be very effective.

Objectives demonstrate focus. People naturally respect you if you know what you want. A resume that says, "I'll do anything, just give me a job" will get you nowhere. If your objective states "Sales Manager" but you have never been one, everything that follows must demonstrate your *potential* for that position.

Simple objectives usually work best:

Computer Programmer
Senior Accountant, CPA Firm
Flight Attendant
Secondary Teacher—Drama, English, ESL
Sales Representative

In the above cases, the people knew exactly what they were looking for and so used an exact job title. If this is your case and the title is recognized by all people in your field, use a specific job title. However, if you are considering one of several positions which are all closely related, you might try something like this:

OBJECTIVE: Office Manager/Administrative Assistant/Executive Secretary

I'll use this person as an example to demonstrate a principle. All three types of positions—Office Manager, Administrative Assistant, and Executive Secretary—are similar in nature. A person who is qualified for one is often qualified for all three. In fact, what one company calls Administrative Assistant, another might call Executive Secretary. This person just wants a good job with a good company and would enjoy any of the three types of jobs. But, if only "Office Manager" is listed, a company with an Executive Secretary opening might overlook the resume.

You should never pair such job titles as "Secretary/Sales Representative," "Teacher/Real Estate Agent," "Flight Attendant/Bookkeeper." It's okay to be looking for both positions at the same time, but you would need two resumes with two different objectives to do so.

Sometimes an exact job title is *not* advised. This is particularly true in management. If you are currently a Personnel Manager but are considering positions such as Training and Development Specialist, Director of Training and Development, and Vice President of Human Resources, you might choose, "OBJECTIVE: Human Resource Management." Using the term *management* does not limit you to a specific job title, while "Human Resource" is just specific enough that it is clear you have focus.

TO HAVE OR NOT TO HAVE AN OBJECTIVE

Use an objective if your goal can be easily stated with a job title or a descriptive phrase. Occasionally you will find it better to omit an objective and let your cover letter and the tone of your Qualifications section indicate your goal. I use an objective for approximately eighty-five percent of the resumes I help people write. I frequently recommend multiple versions of a resume where the only change is the objective. If you were interested in both Sales and Marketing, you could have two versions, one with a "Sales" objective, and the other "Marketing." One would be directed to sales managers and the other to marketing managers.

QUALIFICATIONS

A Qualifications section is, in a sense, a summary of your background and strengths. If well written, your Qualifications section can greatly strengthen your perceived worth. It includes positive statements about you that would be difficult to express in any other section of a resume. Since it is designed to sell your most marketable abilities and experiences, the statements must catch and hold the reader's attention or the section will be skipped. Studying some examples will help a great deal. A job or two has been included with the examples of Qualifications below to help you see how they fit together.

Example #1

OBJECTIVE: Marine Sales

QUALIFICATIONS

Outstanding sales record. Highly knowledgeable in all facets of sail boats, power boats, commercial fishing vessels, and marine hardware. Strong ability to introduce new product lines to distributors, dealers, and boat builders. Number-one rep in the country for four major marine manufacturers.

EMPLOYMENT

Bellkirk Marine, San Diego, California 5/79 to Present

MANUFACTURERS' REPRESENTATIVE—Represent 27 lines covering California, Nevada, and Arizona. Increased the number of accounts with distributors, dealers, and boat builders from 35 to 96 and increased sales 85%. Since 1980 have been the number-one rep for four major manufacturers.

Qualifications Section Example #1 includes a summary and an accomplishment. It starts off with a simple but bold statement: Outstanding sales record. It then goes on to describe the areas of expertise. The top accomplishment (being the number-one representative in the country for four manufacturers) has been included twice—in Qualifications and the job description. It is a valuable statement worth repeating.

The next person has a degree in fine arts and wants to support himself through carpentry or outdoor work while he develops his talent in painting.

Example #2

QUALIFICATIONS

Enjoy working with my hands—indoor and outdoor work.

Learn tasks and the use of new equipment very quickly.

Take strong pride in the high quality of my workmanship.

Skilled in carpentry, including finish work, framing, roofing, siding and foundations.

Skilled in woodworking. Experienced in making fine handcrafted furniture.

Experienced with most power tools—radial arm saw, band saw, jigsaw, skillsaw, router, power sander, planer, chainsaw.

Hard working and reliable. Easy to get along with. Cooperative.

EMPLOYMENT

Sportland, Tyler, Texas 6/81 to 10/81

DESIGNER—Designed cartoons and logos for printing on T-shirts. Also did hand lettering, color separation and process camera work.

Green Construction, Rossland, Texas 6/80 to 9/80

CARPENTER—Roofing, framing, foundations, clapboard siding and finish work.

The last line of Qualifications Example #2 states, ''Hard working and reliable. Easy to get along with. Cooperative.'' Such a statement could only be made under Qualifications; it would be inappropriate in any other section. These kinds of statements are usually used by young people (age sixteen to twenty-five) and others with little work experience. You might be asking, ''How does an employer know this person is really hard working, reliable, and cooperative? Where's the proof?'' Actually there *is* no proof. These are statements the person believes to be true about himself and has so stated. If employers want proof, they'll have to interview the person. Of course, in a face-to-face meeting the applicant must be prepared to back up every statement in the resume with evidence.

Example #3

OBJECTIVE: Grocery Store Management

QUALIFICATIONS

Over seventeen years' experience in upper-level retail grocery management as district manager and grocery store manager.

Planned, organized and coordinated the construction and opening of two new locations. Each has been extremely profitable.

Successfully planned and implemented one of the nation's first complete scanning systems at the retail level. Profits immediately increased as a direct result of the system.

Took over a six-year-old store with the lowest volume in the twenty-one-store chain and in fourteen months built it to the second highest.

EMPLOYMENT

Fine Food Centers, Tulsa, Oklahoma 5/68 to Present

DISTRICT MANAGER 8/75 to Present. Responsible for profit and loss analysis, wage and salary administration, merchandising, store layout, advertising and buying. Installed NCR scanning systems throughout the twenty-one-store chain. Supervised the remodeling and construction of seven stores and developed in-house cleaning and repair services which saved the company $150,000 annually.

Qualifications Section Example #3 begins with a summary: "Over seventeen years' experience in upper-level retail grocery management as district manager and grocery store manager." The reader realizes immediately that this is a highly qualified person. Of course, just a lot of experience in a field is not enough. An employer looks for results. The next three statements prove that she was successful.

Write your Qualifications section last. It is the most difficult to write and requires the most care. Once you have the Employment section completed you will know better what needs to be included in your Qualifications.

Before you begin writing your Qualifications, determine what you most want an employer to know about you. Start by listing the concepts you want to get across. That could include length and type of experience, personality characteristics, or special areas of experience. Once you know what ideas you want to convey, the actual writing will come fairly easily.

The length of your Qualifications section will depend on the strength of the rest of your resume. If you have a very strong background that is well demonstrated by education and employment, you will want a brief Qualifications section so the reader can quickly get to the heart of the resume. Career changers or those with weaker backgrounds usually will need longer Qualifications sections.

A more detailed description of how to actually write a Qualifications section is covered in pages 83 to 86.

EDUCATION

Education should usually appear on the first page right below Qualifications. If you have a college degree or a certificate in a technical field, it should be obvious why you would want Education to appear early in the resume. You can design the section so that just a glance will tell the reader what degree(s) or certificate(s) you hold. Perhaps you don't have a college degree or a certificate but have very strong experience in your field. In that case, you would still place Education right after Qualifications because you'll want the reader to see quickly that while you don't have a great deal of education, you have a wealth of qualifying experience.

I find that employers are curious about education. If education does not appear on the first page they will often flip immediately to the second page. This can give the impression that you are ''hiding'' or ''burying'' your education. For these reasons, I rarely place education at the end of the resume.

EDUCATION

    B.A.—Business Administration, University of Texas (1978)

The above example represents the most typical way of describing a college degree. ''B.A.''—instantly a reader can see that you hold a degree. The next most important fact is your major, then your school, followed by the year of graduation.

Some bad examples will help here:

EDUCATION   Butler University, Indianapolis, Indiana.
        Received a B.A. in Business Administration in December,
           1979. Curriculum emphasized Marketing and Finan-
           cial Management, with field of specialization Real
           Estate. Grade point average 3.21.

EDUCATION

Central Michigan
University

    Mount Pleasant, Michigan

September 1975 Bachelor of Arts, Majored in
       to   Sociology with a minor in Psychology
   June 1980

Both are hard to read. They take time just to find out whether the person has a degree.

The following section reveals the best way to show your education, depending on just what your educational background is.

Let's look at special cases. Highlight or place a mark by the one that matches your situation.

HIGH SCHOOL GRADUATE, NO COLLEGE

EDUCATION

> Graduated—Roosevelt High School,
> Chicago, Illinois (1976)

SOME COLLEGE, NO DEGREE

If you have attended college, there is rarely a reason to include your high school.

EDUCATION

> University of Arizona, Business, 136 credits (1974-1977)

In this example, credits were included to show that although a degree program has not been completed, the person was at least a serious student, accumulating 136 of 180 quarter credits necessary to graduate. A major is given to show the emphasis of study. When determining what major to include, try to make sure it is related to the type of work you're seeking. If you have twenty or more credits in each of three fields, pick the one that will help sell you the most.

CERTIFICATE FROM A TECHNICAL SCHOOL

EDUCATION

> Certificate—Computer Programming, Sims Business College (1972)
> Graduated—Norcross High School, Norcross Pennsylvania (1969)

NO DEGREE, ATTENDED SEVERAL COLLEGES

Some people have acquired credits at four or more schools. If this is your situation, you need not list all schools on your resume; it may give the impression of instability.

EDUCATION

Cheboit Junior College, Castlerock Community College, Riverside Community College, 98 credits.

In this example, four other colleges, where just a few credits were obtained, are not mentioned, but the credits are included in the total. Attendance was very sporadic over a ten-year period, so no dates are given. As in this case, there is usually no need to mention the cities and states where the colleges were located.

NO DEGREE, ATTENDED TWO COLLEGES

EDUCATION

Northeastern Illinois University, Business, 70 credits (1974-76)
University of Southern Illinois, Business, 30 credits (1972)

DEGREE, ATTENDED ONE OR MORE COLLEGES

Unless you have a special reason for including all of your schools, list only the college you graduated from. If you got an Associate of Arts (A.A.) and then moved to a four-year college, still mention only the four-year college. Everything else is extraneous. Since you did not attend four years at the college mentioned, state only the year of graduation.

EDUCATION

B.S.—Physics, Rhode Island University (1976)

BACHELOR'S DEGREE PLUS GRADUATE STUDIES, BUT NO GRADUATE DEGREE

EDUCATION

Graduate Studies, Public Administration, University of Georgia (1976-78)
B.A.—Political Science, University of Georgia (1971-75)

M.S. Program, Psychology, Washington State University, 30 credits (1977-1979)
B.A.—Psychology, Eastern Washington University (1972-1976)

RECENT COLLEGE GRADUATE, LITTLE WORK EXPERIENCE

You may want to include some of your coursework to demonstrate the extensiveness of your training. If you are a liberal arts graduate seeking a management trainee position, you could list economics, accounting, and business courses. The person with a technical degree is also often benefited by listing courses. Although the reader knows your major, that information alone is not always adequate. For the person with very few summer or part-time jobs, listing coursework will make your resume, and therefore your experience, look fuller. For other examples, see pages 131, 132, and 133.

EDUCATION

B.A.—Journalism/Advertising, University of Oregon (1985)

Specialized Courses: Advertising Copywriting, Public Relations Writing, Media Planning, Media Representation, Production Graphics, Advertising Layout and Design, Media Aesthetics, Principles of Design, Principles of Color

This person was looking for an entry-level position in advertising.

The person below wanted to become a technical writer.

EDUCATION

B.A.—Botany, University of Colorado (1976-1980)

Technical Writing (20 credits) Technical Writing, Bio Scientific Vocabulary, Magazine Editing—4.0 GPA

Writing (18 credits) English, Report Writing, Expository Writing—3.7 GPA

Sciences (92 credits) Biology, Botany, Zoology, Chemistry, Physics, Astronomy—3.6 GPA

Mathematics (15 credits) Calculus, Geometry, Statistics—3.1 GPA

Programming (10 credits) BASIC, FORTRAN—3.0 GPA

GRADUATE DEGREE(S)

EDUCATION

M.A.—Counseling, UCLA (1972-1974)
B.A.—Psychology, Oregon State University (1966-1970)

❋

EDUCATION

Ph.D.	Industrial Psychology, Stanford University (1975-1977)
M.A.	Psychology, Northwestern University (1972-1973)
B.A.	Sociology, Northern Illinois University (1967-1971)

LISTING MAJOR AND MINOR

In some cases you may want to list both your major and minor if you believe the minor will also help to sell you. In the case below the person wanted to become a labor relations negotiator and felt the economics minor strengthened her credentials.

EDUCATION

B.A.—Major: Industrial Relations. Minor: Economics
Syracuse University 1971

DEGREES

If you hold a B.A., B.S., M.A., M.S., or Ph.D., it is best to abbreviate since everyone knows what they stand for. Many people are not familiar, however, with B.F.A. (Bachelor of Fine Arts), so it is better to spell out the term. The same is true of M.P.S. (Master of Professional Studies), B.B.A. (Bachelor of Business Administration), and others. Almost everyone knows A.A. stands for Associate of Arts, but many do not know A.S. stands for Associate of Science or that A.T.A. stands for Associate of Technical Arts. If you think some people will not know what your degree stands for, spell it out.

DECISIONS TO MAKE ABOUT EDUCATION

Use the following guidelines to help you decide if you should include grade point average, honors, the location of your school, or fraternal organizations.

When to Use Grade Point Average (GPA)

Since the late 1960s, students' grades have experienced inflation, or gradeflation. Instead of the average GPA being 2.0 at most colleges (representing a C average), the average GPA is now about 2.8 (almost a B average). Prior to gradeflation a 2.8 GPA was very respectable. As with all things in a resume, use it *if* it helps to sell you. To be a selling point, your GPA should be at least 3.0.

GPA usually is dropped from your resume after you've been out of school for five years. By that time your work record should reveal much more than your GPA. It's interesting to note that most follow-up studies have revealed virtually no correlation between a high college GPA and success on the job. Many who were mediocre in school begin to shine only when they enter "the real world."

When to List Honors

If you graduated with honors or with a title like Cum Laude or Summa Cum Laude, you could include it like this:

EDUCATION

B.A.—Cum Laude, History, Beck College 1968-72.

City and State of College

The city and state in which your college is located does not need to be included in your resume. This is particularly true if your college is well known in the region in which you are conducting your job search. If you think employers might be curious, however, include the city and state.

Fraternities and Sororities

Usually your membership in a Greek organization should not be included in a resume. While mentioning the organization may score points with a member of the same or a similar organization, it can hurt you when your resume is reviewed by a "dormie." While there are no hard and fast rules, weigh the pros and cons carefully before deciding. This cautionary note does not apply to the many honorary societies such as Phi Beta Kappa.

Order of Schools

Normally schools are listed in reverse chronological order, beginning with your most recent school.

PROFESSIONAL TRAINING

It is generally best to separate Education from Training. Training mainly includes seminars and workshops, but can also include college courses taken to help you perform better in your field, but which are not part of a degree program. Seminars include those sponsored by your employer and those offered by outside consulting firms at your place of employment. Seminars and workshops also can include those you attended away from your place of employment, paid for either by yourself or your employer. Even if you have received college credit for such courses, you would normally include them under Training rather than Education. Glance at the example below and you'll see why it's a good idea to separate Training from Education.

EDUCATION

>Management by Objectives, Rainier Group (8 hours) 1983
>Terminating Employees, Human Resources Inc. (4 hours) 1982
>B.A.—Business, University of Colorado 1980
>Supervising Difficult Employees, Townsend & Assoc. (10 hours) 1977

If you hold a degree, you want the reader to spot that fact instantly. In the example above, the B.A. is hidden by the seminars. It would look better this way:

EDUCATION

>B.A.—Business, University of Colorado 1980

PROFESSIONAL TRAINING

>Management by Objectives, Rainier Group (8 hours) 1983
>Terminating Employees, Human Resources Inc. (4 hours) 1982
>Supervising Difficult Employees, Townsend & Assoc. (10 hours) 1977

Listing workshops and seminars can demonstrate growth in your field. But as valuable as seminars are, be selective. If you took a course in estate planning, but that knowledge will be of little or no value for the job you're seeking (restaurant management, say), it's better to leave it out.

Usually you should state the seminar title, the name of the organization that sponsored it, and the year you attended. If most of your seminars lasted a half day or more, it could be useful to show the number of hours spent in class. If your company sent you to seminars in different cities, it is beneficial to list those cities. It demonstrates that your company thought highly enough of you to invest in out-of-town workshops.

Some seminars have catchy titles that really don't describe their content. If ''Make The Most Of Yourself'' was really about time management, it should read ''Time Management, Simms and Associates (1980).'' Feel free to alter seminar titles so the reader will understand content. Study the following.

MANAGEMENT SEMINARS

Managing People, Harvard Business Workshop, four
days (1978)
Motivating Employees, Bob Collins & Associates, two
days (1977)
Management and Human Relations, California Institute
of Technology, 124 hours (1974)

✳

SEMINARS

Financial Management for Closely Held Businesses, 40
hours, Seattle-First National Bank (1982)
Construction Cost Improvement, 20 hours, Nevett & Associates (1981)
Scheduling, CPM, 20 hours, Nevett & Associates (1981)
Real Estate Syndication, 10 hours, NW Professionals (1980)
Construction Estimating, 30 hours, Lake Washington Vo-
Tech (1980)
Real Estate Listings, 12 hours, Tom Hopkins (1978)
Closing the Sale, 12 hours, Tom Hopkins (1978)
Goal Setting/Richer Life, 18 hours, Zig Ziglar (1978)

EMPLOYMENT

For most people Employment will be the longest section of their resume. Employment has four main purposes: (1) it reveals your career progress, (2) it describes duties and responsibilities, (3) it describes results and accomplishments, and (4) it accounts for where you've been and for whom you've worked.

Employment history should not be just a recitation of duties and responsibilities. You have a definite goal in mind: you want employers to sense your future worth to their organizations. Include whatever will create that sense of value; exclude whatever will not.

You have a definite job objective in mind, so everything in your resume should focus on your ability to master the type of job you are seeking. Duties and responsibilities are important, but avoid too much detail. Describing results and accomplishments in each job you've held will do more to reveal your capabilities than anything else. Each job description should consist of concisely described duties and at least one accomplishment. The Employment section should begin with your most recent position and move backward in reverse chronological order.

Duties and *responsibilities* are synonyms, but we'll make a slight distinction. In resumes, *duties* tend to be the things you actually did and carried out yourself, while the word *responsibilities* carries the sense of managing or supervising others carrying out tasks and duties.

JOB SKETCHES

Expect to write three drafts of each job description. Start with a Job Sketch. For the Job Sketch, think of a typical day and list the major and minor duties. Then think through the entire job and list the things you did occasionally. There might have been duties which you did regularly, but only four times a year; these can be very valuable to a person making a career change. Perhaps you've been in Shipping and Receiving for four years. Each year when the Purchasing Agent went on vacation you filled in. If your desire is now to move into purchasing, emphasize that experience over some of your shipping and receiving duties.

Next think about any projects you worked on. Briefly describe them and give the results. A project is anything that has a definite beginning and ending. Bookkeeping includes certain things that are done daily, weekly, monthly, quarterly, and yearly—book-keeping is not a project. Analyzing the present bookkeeping system and recommending and implementing changes would be a project. Some occupations consist of repetitive duties and rarely or never involve projects. People in some occupations, such as engineers, programmers, chemists, and consultants, continually move from one project to the next.

Thinking through all of these duties, responsibilities, and projects for all of your jobs will take an hour or two, but taking the time now can make the difference between a mediocre resume and an outstanding one. If you save your Job Sketch, you will never have to go through this process again, except as you add new positions.

The key to a good Job Sketch is to simply write whatever pops into your mind. Don't worry about grammar, punctuation, sentence structure, or even spelling. Just get your thoughts on paper. Go for volume. Write quickly. Don't filter out or neglect to put something down because you think it is insignificant. Remember only a small portion of your Job Sketch will end up in the resume, but you need plenty of data to work with.

Once you have thought through each job and listed your duties, responsibilities, results, accomplishments, and projects, you're ready to start writing the resume. Start by stating your objective. Your objective could be as simple as a job title or it might be a longer, more descriptive phrase such as, ``An entry-level position in marketing leading to management.'' The wording may or may not actually appear on the final resume, but now you know that everything you include in the resume should pass this test: does it demonstrate my capabilities to perform that type of work?

Begin by reviewing what you've written about your current or most recent position. What are the most important things about the job that an employer should know? Try to eliminate some of the less important duties, but don't worry if your first draft is a little too long. When you rewrite, you will be able to identify points that should be deleted, or simply described in a briefer summary.

Read the following Job Sketch. It is detailed, accurate, and very helpful. It took about forty-five minutes to write. Once this person was ready to start her resume, it practically wrote itself.

CLAIMS ADJUSTER

Daily Duties

    Put new claims in my record book.

    Prioritize—decide what needs to be done that day.

Go through files which have mail in them.

Glass breakage—call glass company and approve replacement of glass, give address, name and amount of deductible.

Accident

If our insured at fault, call claimant, learn extent of damage to car and any injuries.

Visit accident scene and draw picture, visit surrounding stores or homes to locate witnesses, get statements.

Write estimate on damage to claimant's car.

Go to body shop where insured has car, write estimate, go over estimate with shop manager, haggle about how many hours to give for straightening frame, fender, quarter panel, etc. Use crash book figures for time necessary to remove and replace parts, to paint panels and for cost of parts.

Stand up to shop owners when they say they can't repair car for your price. If you know you're right, threaten to take car to another shop. Come up with creative and cheaper ways for car to be repaired such as splicing in entire front or rear section.

Totals—if car appears to be totaled, use Blue Book to calculate value, figure in mileage, condition, and extras such as air conditioning and cruise control. If repairs over 80% of value, usually consider it a total. Negotiate if necessary with claimant or insured to determine amount to be paid. Have Midwest Auto pick up and tow car for car auction. Get bids from Midwest and award car to highest bidder. Arrange to turn over title to new owner after getting payment.

Injuries—get recorded statements from claimant and insured, usually by phone.

Visit claimant within 48 hours if accident report from insured indicates injuries. Go to hospital if necessary and explain want to make fair settlement. Try to settle on first visit for small sum and get signature on release statement. Take court reporter to hospital if necessary.

Collect all medical and hospital bills. Request diagnosis from treating physician.

Determine real extent of injury, estimate value and request enough authority from supervisor to settle.

Visit claimant and negotiate—explain why injury isn't worth as much as claimant thinks it is.

Negotiate with attorney by mail or phone. Explain any circumstances which weaken claimant's case, i.e., question of who was really at fault or extent of injury.

Respond to requests for more documentation from our attorneys if lawsuit is filed.

Auto Thefts

Get police report to make sure theft reported. Arrange for loaner car for 30 days. If car not found, arrange with insured and bank to obtain title, determine fair market value, usually using Blue Book. Go to police pounds if car recovered, inspect and photograph car. Take care of paperwork to get car released or dispose of it through auction.

Results

1979   Set record for most claims settled in one year.

1979   Out of 15 adjusters, 3rd lowest average cost per collision settlement, 2nd lowest average bodily injury settlement.

1979   Referred highest dollar volume to company-owned body shop.

This person had three years' experience as a claims adjuster and was looking for another claims position with an insurance company. The final version of the job description—eighty-six words—is given below.

CLAIMS ADJUSTER—Handled full range of Property Damage and Personal Injury claims. Wrote estimates on damage to claimant and insured vehicles, disposed of total losses and handled claims on comprehensive coverage including stolen tires and glass breakage. Investigated accidents and settled injury cases with claimants and attorneys. Had highest dollar authority in the branch—$10,000. In 1979 set record for most claims settled in one year. In 1979, out of fifteen adjusters, had third lowest average cost per collision settlement and second lowest average personal injury settlement.

Another Job Sketch has been included so you can see that there is no set way to write one.

SENIOR TECHNICIAN

A.   Test printed circuit boards, end items, and systems according to test procedures set by engineering. Troubleshoot down to component level.

B.   Interface with clinical personnel if problems occur with functionality of units, kits, etc.

C.   Interface with design and R & D engineering on fit,

form or functional flaws or problems.

D. Interface with production, test, and assembly personnel to ensure a proper production flow.

E. Work with Quality Control on functional as well as cosmetic problems. Fix if necessary or show why QC's documents are wrong.

F. Work with Material Control to ensure needed parts are in the area before they are actually needed. Expedite shipments when necessary.

G. Assist engineering in setting up pre-clinical trials for prototype products.

H. Provide work-flow information to upper management and other status reports as necessary.

I. Keep track of calibration dates on test equipment and call in vendors for calibration at proper time.

J. Cross-train into other areas to learn testing and troubleshooting of different equipment.

K. Assemble printed circuit boards and end items when there is a shortage of assemblers.

L. Check out functional test procedures for Test Engineering to ensure they are correct, practical and understandable.

M. Review printed circuit board schematics and assembly drawings and make corrections where necessary.

N. Keep and maintain a file of all new products test procedures, drawings, and parts lists.

O. Train and supervise four test technicians. Make sure they have opportunities for cross-training.

P. Rework equipment which fails testing.

In the final job description, notice how points were taken right out of the job sketch, in some cases with only minor revisions.

SENIOR TECHNICIAN—3/79 to Present. As Senior Technician for this manufacturer of CAT scanners, test printed circuit boards, end items, and systems, and troubleshoot down to component level. Rework failed equipment. Work closely with clinical personnel and design engineers to identify problems and suggest solutions. Interface with Quality Control and frequently recommend changes in QC specifications in order to speed up production.

Assist Engineering in setting up preclinical trials for prototype products. Review test procedures established by Test

Engineering to ensure tests are understandable and workable. Track use of test equipment and call in vendors for calibration as required. Review PCB schematics, assembly drawings, and parts lists and make corrections where necessary. Developed and currently maintain a file of all test procedures, drawings, parts lists, and specifications, which has significantly improved access and use of the data.

A Job Sketch serves several valuable functions. It

1. makes you recall *all* the duties and functions of the job and allows you to choose the most important ones for your resume.
2. causes you to relive some of the experiences and makes them more vivid.
3. helps you recall accomplishments and results.
4. prepares you for interviews. Employers will frequently ask questions about previous positions, and if you have not recently thought about your previous jobs, you will not respond as well as you could. Employers seek concise answers, yet they often get rambling monologs. Your job sketch will help you present those portions of your job which are most applicable to the job you are seeking.

JOB DESCRIPTIONS

Job descriptions must be concise but complete. A common problem of resumes is that the job descriptions are too short and do not adequately describe duties, experience, level of responsibility, or accomplishments. As you begin, don't be concerned about getting the resume on one page. My studies have verified that so long as it is well written and concise, a two-page resume is perfectly acceptable, and for many people, essential.

The employer should sense your positive attributes, such as diligence, efficiency, cooperation, effectiveness, and intelligence. Your duties must be adequately covered so that the employer will sense the full range of your experience. Based on the types of positions you will be seeking, you should know which duties should be given the most attention. If an employer will have no interest in a certain duty, it should either be given only a brief mention or no mention at all. If you describe your duties effectively, employers will immediately get a sense that you are ready for more responsibility. Results and accomplishments will put a very important frosting on the cake and make the employer want to meet you.

Examples will best demonstrate these points. Read the job descriptions as the person had originally written them, and then after revision. Notice what was done and how.

EMPLOYMENT

Employer	Wiggins Sportswear
Position	Marketing Coordinator
Responsibilities	Coordinate the entire clothing program
	Organizing and programming word processing, filing and Visicalc software packets
	Creating and utilizing computerized spread sheets for marketing, production, and finance projections
	Market research
	Coordinating advertising with publication
	Work with outside contractors on special projects
	Fabric and notion research/purchasing
	Calculated preliminary and final costing of garment
	Approved bills relating to the clothing program
Employer	Broadway Department Store
Position	Salesperson
Responsibilities	Sales
	Interior layout and display
	Opening and closing the department
	Handling customer complaints and problems
	Issuing merchandise transfers

Now study the revised resume of the same person and ask yourself what you know about her now that you didn't before. The revised resume is definitely longer, but it had to be to adequately describe what she did and to give an employer an understanding of her capabilities.

EMPLOYMENT

Wiggins Sportswear, San Diego, California 4/82 to present

MARKETING COORDINATOR—Coordinate the production and marketing functions for a new line of active sportswear. Came into the project when it was

33

two months behind schedule and in serious trouble. Worked with the designer and selected colors, designs and fabrics. Purchased fabric and accessories and approved for payment. Negotiated with two garment manufacturers to produce small lots, thus reducing the required unit sales to reach a break-even point. Worked out schedule arrangements with manufacturers and authorized any changes in specifications. Line was introduced on schedule with final costs one-third lower than originally projected.

Coordinated the production of the annual sales catalog. Designed order forms, verified prices, and consulted with graphics artists and printers. Had authority to make all necessary changes.

Set up the company's first computerized systems and used Visicalc and other software to provide the first accurate year-to-date sales figures and highly useful marketing, financial, and manufacturing projections.

Broadway Department Stores, San Diego, California 9/81 to 4/82

SALESPERSON—Sold women's clothing and had interior layout and display responsibilities. Selected as Employee of the Month for December in this store of approximately 190 employees. Selected on the basis of sales, favorable comments from customers, and taking on added responsibilities.

The revised version is longer than the original, but because it provides more background, you get a clearer picture of her capabilities. By mentioning that the project was behind schedule and in serious trouble, her ability to complete it on schedule and under budget makes the accomplishment especially meaningful. Her original resume contained only a brief list of duties and gave you no idea if she had been successful. In the revised resume you definitely get a sense of her potential. She was given a lot of responsibility and she handled it well. She also has a very interesting story to tell about her experiences at Wiggins, but the details must be saved for an interview.

The experience at Broadway did not receive as much space because she has no intention of returning to retail work. The experience provides valuable background, however, for her career in marketing; it is important to demonstrate that she was successful even though it was a short-term job. Simply listing her duties provides no clues about the quality of her work, and could lead an employer to believe that she did not do well. Mentioning that she was employee of the month proves that she was valuable. Mentioning the basis for the award—sales, comments from customers, and taking on responsibility—the employer immediately recognizes that she was judged outstanding in each category.

As you write your resume look for ways to get your story across and indicate that you've been successful. Even if you were fired from a job it is still possible to show that you were valuable. Do that by stressing what you did well; simply ignore your problem areas.

The next job description comes from the resume of a marriage and family counselor. One of his earlier positions was supervisor for a parks department. In the first job description you get nothing but a dull list of duties. He is a very interesting person with an excellent background, but you pick up no feeling of that from the job description.

June 1976 to May 1981　SUPERVISOR. Portland Park Department. Portland, Oregon. Overall responsibility for staff, facility, and program at a neighborhood community center; supervising, hiring, training, and recruitment; program planning, implementation, and evaluation; record keeping, budgeting, grant writing, and analyses; work with schools, local, state, and federal agencies in a variety of capacities; direct service including teaching, training, and work with adults and youth in social, educational, cultural and athletic programs; community and business presentations.

As you read the revised job description you'll sense that here is a real person. There's a personal touch that did not exist before.

Portland Park Department, Portland, Oregon 6/76 to 11/82

SUPERVISOR—Developed and promoted social, educational, cultural, and athletics programs for the community. Contracted with consultants, instructors, and coaches to provide instruction in dozens of subjects and activities at the Brewster Community Center. Interviewed and hired instructors, and conducted follow-up assessments to ensure top-quality instruction. Personally taught several courses and coached athletic teams. In three years tripled participation at the Center and took it from a $1400 deficit to $12,000 in the black.

After reading the revised job description you get the sense of a person with goals and ideals. He really cared about what he did. He got involved, he took action, and he got results. That sense comes from the action verbs like *developed* and *promoted*. You feel the action. The programs that the community really wanted didn't exist so he went out and *developed* them. Since people don't come flocking to a program just because it exists, he *promoted* them. He not only planned programs he even taught some and he coached athletic teams. He's an action-oriented person and in good physical shape besides. The ultimate result of all this effort was a tripling of participation, yet his original job description did not even mention it.

I've indicated that writing a top-quality resume takes time. From these examples you can see why. Describing oneself in positive terms is difficult for most people, yet it is necessary. Write your job descriptions and then keep editing until they approach the examples you find in this book. Everyone can do it, but it will take time and thought.

EMPLOYMENT FORMAT

The employment format you choose can make a big difference in the visual appeal and readability of your resume. I have tested formats extensively and find that one is preferred consistently:

EMPLOYMENT

Balboa's Steak House 6/78 to Present

GENERAL MANAGER, Miami, Florida, 7/80 to Present. Took over a troubled restaurant which had had six managers in two years and incurred losses each month during that time. Resolved serious morale problems, instituted an effective training program, and redesigned the menu. Increased lunch revenue 38% and dinner 29%. Losses were eliminated within two months and a consistent profit margin of 14% has been maintained.

ASSISTANT MANAGER, Ft. Lauderdale, Florida, 5/79 to 7/80. Redesigned the menu and helped introduce wine sales. Provided extensive staff training which enabled the restaurant to become number one in wine sales in the chain of twenty restaurants. Purchased all food and supplies.

36

MANAGER TRAINEE, Miami Beach, Florida, 6/78 to 5/79. Received excellent training in purchasing, accounting systems, profit and loss statements, food preparation, menu planning, food cost analysis, and food and beverage promotions.

Saga, Inc., Tallahassee, Florida 9/77 to 6/78

STUDENT MANAGER—For this college cafeteria, prepared food, scheduled part-time workers, purchased supplies, and oversaw lunch and dinner lines.

Following are sample treatments of particular work histories. One of them should conform fairly closely to your own.

Same Company, Three Positions, All in the Same City

EMPLOYMENT

Douglas Bolt Company, St. Louis, Missouri 8/68 to Present

V. P. PURCHASING, 7/79 to Present. _____

_____

DIRECTOR OF PURCHASING, 5/73 to 7/79._____

_____

MANAGER, STOCK PARTS PURCHASING, 8/68 to 5/73._____

_____

Same Company, Three Positions, Three Different Cities

EMPLOYMENT

Horizon Gear 8/70 to Present

REGIONAL SALES MANAGER, Houston, Texas 7/80 to Present.

_____

_____

DISTRICT SALES MANAGER, Atlanta, Georgia 3/75 to 7/80.

_____

SALES REPRESENTATIVE, Little Rock, Arkansas 8/70 to 3/75.

_____

One Position With Each Company

EMPLOYMENT

Shannon Electric, Garden City, Michigan 9/80 to Present

INSTALLER—_____

Preston Electric, Detroit, Michigan 5/76 to 9/80

INSTALLER—_____

_____

Work For a Subsidiary or Division of a Major Company

EMPLOYMENT

Antac, Inc., Subsidiary of A&R Industries, Buffalo, New York
5/77 to Present

It is seldom necessary to specify the parent company. If you
choose to, however, this is the easiest way to do it.

WHAT TO CALL YOUR EMPLOYMENT SECTION

*Employment, Employment Experience, Work Experience, Pro-
fessional Experience, Employment History, Work History,* and *Experience* all are good terms. Pick the one that feels right for you.

DATES

Dates should be used on nearly all resumes. If you have no
time gaps between jobs or very short gaps (two to three months),
you should use the months and years you started and left. If you
have longer gaps, simply indicate the year you started and the
year you left.
When to use month and year (example: 5/76 to 9/79):

1. No gaps in employment.
2. Short gaps only of two to three months.
3. One gap of over three months several years ago.

There is a trade-off to consider. Employers prefer to see month
and year and may wonder if you are hiding anything by omitting
months. On the other hand, if you reveal long gaps between jobs,
employers may question your perseverence and dedication. With
this in mind, decide what is best for you.

LOCATION OF JOB

Your resume should indicate the city and state you actually work in, not the location of your company's national headquarters. If you work out of your home, include your city as your location; if you live in a suburb, include either the name of the suburb or the more familiar name of the large city you live near.

CLARIFYING WHAT YOUR COMPANY DOES

If you work for General Motors, General Electric, or Boeing, there is no need to explain what the company does. If your employer is Eastside Masonry Products, it is also unnecessary to elaborate because the company name explains its type of business. If you work for SLRC Corporation, though, you may want to explain in the resume. Handle it this way:

SLRC Corporation, Montgomery, Alabama 5/78 to Present

SALES REP—For this producer of food additives, opened up a new territory and increased sales an average of 32% each year.

Or this way:

CBD, Inc., Boston, Massachusetts 1978 to Present

SALES REP—Increased sales 20% each year for CBD, the Northeast's second largest distributor of electronic components.

SPACE DEVOTED TO EACH POSITION

Principles (not laws) to keep in mind:

1. Your current or most recent position is described in the greatest detail as long as it is similar to the type of job you are seeking. Each preceding job is described in slightly less detail.

2. If the job you held three jobs ago is closest to what you're seeking, devote the most detail to it.

3. Jobs held many years ago and jobs that have nothing to do with what you want to do in the future can usually be described in one or two lines.

HOW FAR BACK?

If you are a college graduate, go back as far as your first full-time job after graduation. If you went to work right after high school, go back to your first full-time job. If you've had a lot of jobs, you can write about your four to six most recent positions and then use a Previous Employment section, which merely lists prior positions without descriptions.

Although some of your earlier jobs may not be applicable to your current occupation, employers are still curious about where you've been. For such positions simply devote one to two lines in a very straightforward description of duties or use a Previous Employment section.

If you feel certain that it would be detrimental to include all of your jobs, eliminate those in the most distant past.

PREVIOUS EMPLOYMENT

A Previous (or Prior) Employment section is particularly helpful if you are trying to shorten your resume or de-emphasize your earlier jobs.

Example (starting with the person's seventh position on a two-page resume):

Xytelin Electronics, Mountain View, California 1960 to 1962

INTERNAL AUDITOR—Discovered weaknesses in the parts inventory control procedures and recommended remedial action. Responsible for quarterly and yearly audits.

Prior Experience, 1950 to 1960: Audit Staff, CPA firm, Deputy Probation Officer, Airline Internal Auditor, Cost Clerk, Production Scheduler.

*

40

Example (starting with fifth position on a one-page resume):

Department of Social Services, Winston-Salem, North Carolina 3/70 to 4/71

> ELIGIBILITY SPECIALIST—Assisted families in obtaining all of the Medicaid benefits they were legally entitled to. Provided psychological and social support services.

Previous Experience:

> Cashier/Hostess 1/69 to 3/70; Sales Clerk 6/68 to 1/69; Long Distance Operator 7/66 to 6/68.

＊

PRIOR EMPLOYMENT

> CASHIER—Pay Less Drugs, Elgin, Illinois 5/66 to 11/67
> CASHIER—Don's Rexall, Carbondale, Illinois 4/65 to 5/66
> STOCKER—Jewel Foodstores, Peoria, Illinois 9/62 to 3/65

＊

Previous Employment

> Truck driver (1963-67); Warehouseman (1963); Machine Repairman (1962)

＊

Previous Boeing Employment

> Assistant General Foreman 1965-1967
> Flight Line Supervisor 1962-1965
> Flight Line Mechanic 1960-1962

＊

Prior positions with PACCAR 4/60 - 8/66: Material Handler, Inventory Control Planner, Assistant Inventory Control Supervisor, Material Control Supervisor

See Pages 139, 175, 198, and 201 for additional examples.

SPECIAL PROJECTS

Special Projects can be a very useful resume section for some people. I use a Special Projects section in about five percent of the resumes I write. The section can also be labeled *Accomplishments, Achievements, Projects, Noteworthy Projects, Selected Accomplishments,* or *Noteworthy Accomplishments.* Some of your projects or accomplishments may not have occurred on a job. This is especially true of the person with little or no job experience who may have been actively involved in volunteer or free-time projects. Special Projects, placed before your Employment section, also allows you to place your main accomplishments in one spot rather than spread throughout your work history. The same accomplishment may be mentioned or described under both Special Projects and Employment, but the wording should be altered. Usually descriptions in Special Projects are longer and more detailed than descriptions under Employment. This makes sense because the employer will already have read the full description but will appreciate seeing in which job it occurred. Use these examples as guides to determine if a Special Projects section will strengthen your resume.

SPECIAL PROJECTS

As President of PTA, increased parent participation by 56% over previous year. Funds raised during the school year grew from $3,000 in 1977-78 to $7,400 in 1978-79. (1978-79)

As a United Way fund raising team leader, exceeded the quota by 22%. Honored at banquet as Team Leader of the Year. (1977)

Developed a customer file which allowed the company to accurately project when customers would need to reorder products. Contacted over 100 customers and gathered data for the system. System allowed sales staff to make calls at critical times and increased sales per call by about 30%. (1972)

EMPLOYMENT

A & B Digital Electronics, Fort Wayne, Indiana 5/70 to 10/73

OFFICE MANAGER—Maintained petty cash fund, payroll records, accounts payable, and accounts receivable. Initiated computer data input and purchased office and production supplies. Worked closely with customers and acted as troubleshooter. Developed customer file system

42

which projected customers' needs and increased sales per call by 30%.

This person has been at home rearing children since 1973. She obviously is very capable and very energetic. Notice how her customer file system accomplishment was mentioned again under Employment, but in one-third as many words.

As you can see, mixing nonwork-related accomplishments with work-related accomplishments can be very effective. A project or accomplishment seldom requires over forty-five words—twenty to thirty is usually best. Do not try to describe the project in detail—concentrate on results. When writing out each accomplishment in the first draft, feel free to describe it in fifty to seventy words. Then rewrite it by concentrating on results and include just enough detail so that the reader will understand what you did. Save all other details for an interview. List the projects and accomplishments in reverse chronological order and include the year.

NOTEWORTHY ACCOMPLISHMENTS

Represented Troy, New York, at the National League of Cities Congress in San Francisco, 1978.

Planned and obtained funding for acquisition and development of land for a public park in Troy, 1978.

Wrote news articles for Troy Herald, Outdoor News, and College Forum, 1977-1980.

Chaired Regional Committee for Housing and Land Use for Northern New York, 1976-1977.

Advised Community Development and Public Affairs Committee for Troy, New York, 1976-1977.

Participated as a guest expert on a public affairs radio talk show, 1977.

Completely organized a basketball camp for disadvantaged youth in Troy, 1976.

Elected Senior Class President of Troy College, 1972.

Below is a Special Projects section used by a forty-year-old woman reentering the work force after completing an MBA and with one part-time research position in the last ten years.

SPECIAL PROJECTS

Developed highly successful parenting, exercise, and personal growth programs for the Newark YWCA, 1977-1978.

43

Developed and coordinated budgets for YWCA and Big Sisters Program, Newark, 1975-1978.

Planned and coordinated programs for the League of Women Voters, Newark, 1974-1978.

Allocated and dispensed federal monies to ten counties—CETA Advisory Board, Newark, New Jersey, 1975-1977.

Chaired "The Mayor's Conference on Aging," Newark, 1976.

The following was written by a teacher who wanted a position in private business and needed to demonstrate non-classroom abilities.

SPECIAL PROJECTS

Interned for Omaha National Bank during the summer of 1981. Received assignments working with retail credit, corporate loans, and trust departments. Developed and completed a survey to determine customer needs. (1981)

Organized record-breaking blood drives and won trophies each year from 1973 to 1981. No other schools came close to matching the high percentage of students who willingly donated blood. (1973-1981)

Developed an intern program to allow students to work in nursing homes and schools for the retarded. Dozens of students gained new skills and several now work in geriatrics. (1969-1975)

Supervised the senior class store which sold school supplies, tickets, jackets, and sweaters. The store maintained a profit each year under my management, something it had never done previously. (1968-1972)

Supervised the research and publication of the Omaha "Volunteer Directory," which helped draw new volunteers into dozens of agencies. (1971)

Sometimes other section titles such as "Honors, Awards, Publications" or "Activities" will work better than Special Projects.

HONORS, AWARDS, PUBLICATIONS

Magna Cum Laude and High Scholastic Honors, Reed College. (1970-1975)

Inspirational Person-of-the-Year Awards: Girls' Club, Senior Class. (1970)

Chairperson, Task Force on Teaching Quality. Investi-

gated teaching evaluation methods at Reed College.
Published position paper which helped initiate change
in tenure decision policies. (1976)

※

ACTIVITIES

San Diego Secretarial Council—Member of the board of
directors 1967 to 1981. Vice President 1977 to 1980. Presented seminars for entry-level secretaries and worked to
increase the professionalism of secretaries working for
the City.

Field Rep for the San Diego Credit Union. Explained to
members changes in loan policies and interest rates and
helped promote special discounts with local merchants.
(1975-1981)

※

AWARDS

Award for Leadership, Motivation, and Training—
National Restaurant Association. (1977)

Food, Wine, and Service Award for Excellence—
National Restaurant Association. (1976)

LICENSES/CERTIFICATES

Any licenses you hold that are necessary or valuable in the field you are seeking should be listed. Be selective, though. Mentioning a real estate license when you want to be a purchasing agent for a tool manufacturer would not add to your qualifications and might cause the employer to wonder whether your preferred career was selling real estate or purchasing.

LICENSES

First Class FCC Radio Telephone Operator (1974)
Commercial Instrument Pilot rating (1978), 840 hours flight time
Private Pilot (1975)

(Electronics technologist and sales rep who flies to see customers)

LICENSES

General Electrical Administrator Certificate, California (1982)
Journeyman Electrician License—California, Nevada, Arizona
Commercial—Instrument Pilots License (1980)

(Electrician who would like to do some flying for his employer)

LICENSES

Real Estate Agent, Nebraska

(Property Manager)

CERTIFICATION

1978 Standard Elementary and Secondary, Idaho. Lifetime.

(Teacher)

LICENSES

FCC, 1981

(Broadcast journalist who needs a Federal Communications Commission license to operate on the air)

LICENSES

Real Estate   Insurance   Securities

(Financial Consultant)

ASSOCIATIONS/MEMBERSHIPS/ PROFESSIONAL AFFILIATIONS

Use these categories only if they will help you. An engineer might use the following:

PROFESSIONAL AFFILIATIONS

    American Institute of Chemical Engineers
    American Chemical Society

Belonging to associations and professional organizations may mean only that you paid the annual dues, or it could mean that you are active in the organization. If you want a one-page resume and you are three lines over, affiliations can be sacrificed. The section provides interesting, but usually not crucial, information. If you are changing careers, join a professional organization to learn more about the field, meet experts in it, and demonstrate that you have more than just a passing interest in it. List any offices held. The examples below can be used as guides.

MEMBERSHIPS

    Pacific Northwest Personnel Managers Association
    American Society for Personnel Administration

✽

ASSOCIATIONS

    Homebuilders Association, member 1976 to present
        Officer 1978 to present
        Associate of the Year 1980, Minneapolis
        Associate of the Year 1981, St. Cloud
    Board of Realtors, member 1975 to present
        Chairperson, Legislative Committee 1976-78
        Chairperson, Political Affairs, and Education 1979-81

✽

AFFILIATIONS

    Electronic Representatives Association
    Pacific Northwest Ski Instructors Association—Certified
        Instructor

✽

ASSOCIATIONS

> President, Board of Directors, Southeast Community Alcohol Center (1982)
> Member of Board since 1977
> Treasurer, Northwest Nurses Society on Chemical Dependency (1981 to present)
> Member, Oregon State Council on Alcoholism (1977 to present)

✳

PROFESSIONAL ACTIVITIES AND CONFERENCES

> Member of American Water Resources Association and American Economics Association
> "Financing Energy Projects," University of Washington, 1982
> "Financial Management," Northwest Public Power Association, Portland, Oregon, 1982
> "Hydropower Financing in the Future," American Water Resources Association, Gatlinburg, Tennessee, 1980
> "Financing Coal Generating Power Plants," Pacific Northwest Power Consortium, Tacoma, Washington, 1979
> Annual Northwest Power Conference, Seattle, Washington, 1978

If you want to mention certain organizations, but you are no longer active, try this:

AFFILIATIONS

> Member, National Association of Bank Women (1977 to Present)
> Program Chairperson (1980-81)
> Member, Bank Managers International (1970 to 1980)
> Budget Committee Chairperson (1980)
> Member, Business and Professional Women (1972 to 1979)

PUBLICATIONS

A list or description of publications can be used to demonstrate expertise in a particular field. Listing publications can also demonstrate researching, interviewing, and writing abilities. If you are widely published, you'll have to be selective.

Publications include articles in newspapers, newsmagazines, trade journals, journals, school papers, anthologies, or just about anything in printed form with a circulation over fifty.

PUBLICATIONS

> Contributing Editor of <u>Retailers Northwest</u> magazine, writing articles covering children's clothing.

(Included in resume of manufacturers' representative who sells children's clothing)

✻

PUBLICATIONS

> "The Arts in Seattle," <u>The Weekly</u>, July 27, 1982
> "Marketing A Symphony," <u>The Conductor</u>, April, 1980
> "Will Bach Be Back?" <u>Symphony News</u>, November, 1979

✻

PUBLICATIONS

> "The Dismantling of Student Loans," University of Kentucky Daily, 1980
> "Tenureship Under Attack," University of Kentucky Daily, 1980
> "An Hour With G. Gordon Liddy," University of Kentucky Daily, 1980

✻

PUBLICATIONS

> "Robots and Production," Chrysler Employees Newsletter, 1979
> "Automation and Its Impact on Blue Collar Workers," paper presented at the annual Industrial Psychologists Symposium, 1977

If you are going to use a Special Projects section and have only one publication, you could include the publication with your projects. For example:

SPECIAL PROJECTS

Volunteer Probation Counselor for the City of Woodinville—1979 to Present
Authored an environmental article published in an inter-
nationally circulated magazine—1978

❋

ACHIEVEMENTS

From 1958 to 1967 sailed over 50,000 miles in sailing yachts
between Hawaii and the West Indies.
Published six articles and adventure stories in ''Cast Off''
and ''Nor Westing''.
Produced professional seminars on boat maintenance.

PERSONAL DATA

Whether you should include personal data or not is a controversial question and my studies do not provide any absolute answers. Based on one study it appears that many people prefer a resume with personal data such as birthdate, marital status, and height and weight. The problem with personal data is that it can also be used to discriminate against prospective employees. A person's age or marital status should have nothing to do with whether a person is hired or not, yet we know that discrimination persists despite federal and state legislation prohibiting it. I believe it is for this reason that in another study, personnel specialists strongly preferred resumes without personal data. Because of equal employment laws and the possibility of discrimination suits, personnel specialists have been trained to avoid anything that could cause discrimination, such as age. In other words, they don't want to know the age of a person and they don't want department heads to know the age of the person either.

Let's examine some points to help you determine if personal data should be included. First, we have established the principle that everything in your resume should be positive and beneficial to you. This is especially true with personal data. A substantially overweight person, for example, should not include height and weight. Second, if you choose not to include two or more of the items normally included in personal data, it may be better not to use the section at all, since the missing items become so obvious. Third, if many of your resumes will be reviewed by the personnel department it is best not to include personal data. As an alternative to not including a personal data section, notice how on page 57 Personal Data and Activities were combined. In such a case, simply label it Personal.

There has been a strong trend during the last fifteen years to move away from including personal data. Women took the lead by more and more frequently deciding not to reveal age, marital status, or height and weight. Stronger Equal Employment Opportunity legislation during the seventies hastened the trend. Gradually, male managers began to feel more comfortable with resumes that did not contain personal data and they stopped assuming a person was hiding something if personal data was not included.

I want you to feel comfortable if you decide against including personal data. Even if your age, marital status, health, and height and weight are all to your advantage, you may still decide not to include it. The curious employer will estimate your age by your education and employment record and today very few people care if your are married or single. I currently use personal data with less than two percent of all people.

If you use personal data, use the following information as a guide.

AGE

Age should be given by stating your birthdate. If omitted, curious employers will calculate it using the year you graduated from high school or college or by the years of employment experience you have. Do not include age if you feel you may face age discrimination. If you omit age, remember not to provide clues in other sections of the resume. You'll need to omit dates for high school or college graduation, for example.

MARITAL STATUS

Marital status would usually be included, if you are married. If you are divorced or widowed, it is best to say "single" or simply not mention your status. As in everything else, ask yourself if it is to your benefit.

BONDABLE

Include mention of this if your type of work requires bonding. Essentially, anyone who does not have a prison record is bondable. Bonding is a type of insurance employers take out on employees who handle large amounts of money. If an employee heads to Mexico with thousands of dollars, the employer collects from the bonding company.

MILITARY

If you have military experience, decide whether to include it in your Employment section or under Personal Data. If there is anything in your military experience that will help sell you, explain it briefly in a job description under Employment. If you include it under Personal Data, it could read "U. S. Navy, 1972-74," "U. S.

Navy/E-5/1972-74," or "U. S. Navy 1972-74, Honorable Discharge." I usually include military experience under Employment. If the experience is in no way related to what you are seeking, merely give it a one- or two-line description.

SECURITY CLEARANCE

Many people in the military, and civilians working on military projects, have been given security clearances, typically "Secret" or "Top Secret." After leaving the military, it quickly lapses and a new investigation is conducted before reestablishing a security clearance. By including your security clearance, however, you're really saying, "My honesty and integrity were verified by a very thorough investigation; you, too, can trust me." If you held a security clearance within the last ten years, it may be helpful to mention it.

HEALTH

Simply state "Excellent Health." If you feel your health is anything less than excellent, omit it. In other words, do not settle for "Good Health" or "Fair Health." If you have a disability that could affect your work, do not mention the disability in the resume, but be prepared to discuss it during an interview. Legally you do not need to divulge any illnesses or disabilities which will not affect your job performance. This is also true when filling out application forms and during interviews. If you have any questions in this area, consult a city or state Equal Employment Opportunity office. Personnel managers of companies will also be aware of state and federal laws and can advise you.

CITIZENSHIP

Do not include this information unless you believe an employer might question your citizenship, or if you especially want to let an employer know that you are a U. S. citizen. If you are not a U. S. citizen, you may want to state "Permanent Resident" or indicate what your status is. There is no need to specify "Naturalized U. S. Citizen;" simply say "U. S. Citizen."

HEIGHT AND WEIGHT

Men might include height and weight if they are 5'8'' or taller and if their weight is appropriate for their height. Those less than 5'8'' should seriously consider omitting height and weight. During the last ten years it has become very acceptable for women to omit height and weight entirely. Some people estimate their weight or state what it will be in two or three months.

SOCIAL SECURITY NUMBER

There is no reason to include your social security number.

Sample Personal Data Sections

Birthdate: 6/10/54　　　　　　Excellent Health
Married　　　　　　　　　　　5'10'', 165 pounds

✳

Birthdate: 5/7/48　　Excellent Health　　　5'4'', 118 pounds

✳

Single　　　　　　　　　　Excellent Health
Birthdate: 6/19/52　　　　5'9'', 155 pounds
U. S. Marines 1970-73　　Bondable

✳

Birthdate: 2/12/40　　　　　Excellent Health
Married　　　　　　　　　　U. S. Army 1958-60,
Willing to Relocate　　　　Honorable Discharge

✳

Married　　　　　　　　　U. S. Marines 1964-68,
Birthdate 1/28/44　　　　Honorable Discharge
Excellent Health　　　　　Top Secret Clearance
6'2'', 195 pounds

✳

Married　　　　Excellent Health　　　Willing to Relocate

ACTIVITIES

With each activity you select, ask yourself what impact it will have on an employer. Let's say you're an unemployed loan officer who loves to skydive. Most skydivers are viewed as high risk takers, but loan officers are noted for their conservative, low-risk approach to business. Even though you may be just as conservative on the job as your colleagues, listing skydiving as an activity could arouse just enough doubt to cause an employer not to interview you.

Give a consistent picture of yourself. Decide what image you want to convey and then select the appropriate activities. Office workers are wise to state interests that indicate a highly energetic personality. An Activities section can be a nice addition to a resume but many people prefer not to use one. View Activities as optional. An Activities section can reveal things about you, but generally they are not critical.

ACTIVITIES

Strong involvement in marathon running, skiing, and scuba diving.

＊

ACTIVITIES

Actively involved in golf, jogging, and camping.

＊

ACTIVITIES

Avid backpacker. Enjoy flying, horseback riding, and hunting.

＊

INTERESTS

Enjoy making exotic breads, creating stained glass windows, and dance exercise activities.

Sometimes it is wise to combine Personal Data with Activities, especially if you have decided to omit height, weight, and marital status. It might look like this:

PERSONAL

    Birthdate: 5/20/46
    Excellent Health
    Enjoy snow skiing, white water rafting, and racquetball

You would then label it Personal rather than Personal Data.

ACCOMPLISHMENTS

Accomplishments separate achievers from nonachievers. Duties alone cannot do this. Consider two people, each with ten years of experience and identical job titles. Applicant A has not had an original idea in three years. The drive and initiative that propelled A upward is gone. Applicant B, however, has demonstrated significant accomplishments each year and still exhibits great enthusiasm. Only accomplishments will distinguish over-the-hill applicant A from full-of-potential applicant B. Accomplishments make you seem more like a real person and will help you be remembered. Stressing accomplishments is especially important for the person making a career change.

Employers make hiring decisions based on their belief in your potential. Experience is frequently used to measure potential, but it is often a poor yardstick. If your experience is perfect for a particular job, you would certainly want to exploit that advantage, but such a match seldom occurs.

Ideally, you will list one or more significant accomplishments for each job you've held. For some jobs, however, this is not practical. Perhaps you held the job for just a short time, or didn't enjoy the job and performed below your full potential. With jobs like these, provide only very short descriptions so that the reader will concentrate on the more important jobs you held.

Describing accomplishments concisely and with impact takes practice. Every employer seeks people who can increase profits, decrease costs, increase sales, or decrease turnover. Percentages and dollar figures make accomplishments more tangible and impressive. Compare these two statements: "New personnel policies increased morale" and "New personnel policies reduced absenteeism by 27% and reduced turnover by 24%."

Your next thought is probably, "I know my idea saved time and money, but I have no idea how much." When company records can verify your figures, that's great, by all means use them. One of my clients used printed reports to verify that he increased the tons of aluminum sold in his territory by sixty-three percent in just two years. At a time when many territories decreased in tons sold, this is a very impressive statistic and says a great deal about his sales ability. During an interview he can elaborate on how he succeeded.

Arriving at a percentage or a dollar figure when you have no verifying figures requires creative thinking and sometimes creative guessing. You would not want to exaggerate the accomplishment, but you can calculate figures to the best of your knowledge. I'll give you an example.

John wanted to leave Alaska, where he had repaired heavy construction machinery. He felt he was a top-level mechanic but could think of no evidence to prove it. After talking with him a bit, I discovered he was constantly developing new tools and finding easier ways to make certain repairs. One of the tools he made helped him install a five-hundred-dollar part by aligning it perfectly in place. Without the tool the part was sometimes misaligned, and there was no way to tell until the part was clamped in; but then it was too late, the part would crack. John estimated he replaced the part twenty times per year and would have cracked two of them without the tool. About twenty other mechanics with similar duties copied his tool. On the resume we were able to state that he saved $20,000 per year with his tool. Actual savings may have ranged from $15,000 to $30,000 per year; we chose $20,000 as the most likely. If an employer asks John to verify the figure, he can explain how it was calculated. An employer would undoubtedly be satisfied with such an explanation. In an interview all you need to do is explain how you arrived at the figures and state that they're accurate, to the best of your knowledge.

Some accomplishments cannot be translated into dollars or percentages, yet are strong statements of useful accomplishments. For example: "Selected as employee of the year," or "The vice president said the marketing forecast was the best researched report he had seen in years."

In the following sample job descriptions notice that accomplishments are described very briefly. Elaborate at the interview, not in the resume. And let others praise you. Don't say, "My performance was one of the most overpowering ever witnessed on a stage." Instead, quote someone: "The Times reported, 'Alice Goodman's performance was one of the most overpowering we have ever seen on a Los Angeles stage' ".

Let's examine a job description and you'll see what I've been talking about.

Memory Academy, Dallas, Texas 5/75 to 6/77

OFFICE MANAGER/EXECUTIVE INSTRUCTOR—Office Manager of a fourteen-person office with direct responsibility for ten people. Developed detailed manuals for each position and created a smoothly functioning office. In 1976, redesigned the teaching techniques of the memory course. Instructors immediately experienced better results and received enthusiastic ratings from clients.

Imagine how you would feel about this person if the last sentence had not been included. The preceding sentences mainly described her duties, although the phrase ''and created a smoothly functioning office'' is an accomplishment. ''Redesigned the teaching techniques of the memory course'' describes a project, and the last sentence represents her key accomplishment. She did not simply rewrite the memory course, she made a significant contribution which achieved immediate results. If you eliminate her two accomplishments, only duties and one project remain. With the accomplishments, you understand her better as a person. This was not just a job to her; it's obvious she cared and invested her energy in the Memory Academy. The accomplishments let you see that she is responsible, creative, hard working, and a good supervisor and trainer. She plans, organizes, and writes well. She always looks for ways to improve an office or a program. She is comfortable speaking in front of groups and she knows how to get people to respond favorably to her. A reader will perceive all these things.

Accomplishments are loaded. One fifteen-word accomplishment can say more and have more impact than one hundred words of a job description. Look at the following samples and notice the impact of the accomplishments. Imagine what the impact would be without them.

Des Moines Trust & Saving, Des Moines, Iowa 9/80 to Present

BRANCH OPERATIONS MANAGER—Responsible for the smooth functioning of branch operations while supervising 20 employees. As Branch Operations Manager of three branches, overcame serious morale problems. Worked closely with the staffs and significantly improved morale through better training and supervision. At each branch, absenteeism, turnover, and operations charge-offs were significantly reduced. Customer service and marketing of bank services was strengthened.

✳

Central Mortgage 5/74 to Present

DIVISION MANAGER, Missoula, Montana, 9/78 to Present. Opened the Missoula office, purchased equipment and furniture, and set up all bookkeeping and office systems. Within ten months became the number-one home mortgage lender in the Missoula area and obtained 54% of the mortgage market and 68% of all construction loans. During five years averaged 48% profit on gross income, the highest in the company among 33 offices.

The need for including accomplishments is vivid in the following examples. First you will see the original version and then the revision that ultimately sold the person into a position.

SALES REPRESENTATIVE—2/78 to Present. Develop and service established accounts as well as new accounts. Set pricing structures after determining the market. Responsible for the district's western Orange County territory. Sales have increased each year.

✳

SALES REPRESENTATIVE—2/78 to Present. In the first three years moved the territory from last in the district to first. Aggressively went after new accounts and have significantly increased market share in the territory. By 1980 became the number one sales rep in total profits and have maintained the position. Profits have increased an average of 40% annually.

Is there any question which resume would result in a job interview? In the second job description, you get a sense of a salesperson who is successful, works hard, has excellent product knowledge, and knows how to get a sale. He has a very interesting story to tell describing how he accomplished what he did, but that has been reserved for an interview. For now all an employer needs to know is that he has been very successful. The job description causes an employer to want to meet him to learn if he is as good in person as he seems on paper.

Notice that the impression you have of the person is so much stronger in the second, yet it required just one more line than the first. This will often be the case. Accomplishments speak for themselves and you rarely need to go into detail regarding all the things you did to get your results. That's what interviews are for.

In the resume below a savings and loan controller describes a job but it doesn't do him justice. This was his most recent as well as his most responsible position, and therefore required more detail to indicate his potential. Although the second job description is longer, it is well written and concise. It does not contain any unnecessary words. Everything mentioned is designed to sell him and give an employer a full view of his experience.

CONTROLLER—Managed accounting department, seven-person staff; prepared financial statements and filed various reports with State and Federal agencies; assisted and advised senior management concerning regulatory accounting, and tax ramifications of decisions and policies;

61

worked with savings and loan divisions on operational and systems design; served as primary liaison with computer service bureau in Los Angeles.

✳

CONTROLLER—Managed a seven-person accounting department and significantly increased productivity by simplifying procedures, cross-training staff, and improving morale. Prepared financial statements and advised senior management of regulatory, accounting, and tax ramifications of new policies and programs under consideration. Heavily involved in the research and planning of an investment "swap" program which resulted in a $5.3 million tax refund. Successfully directed the Association's response when the refund resulted in an IRS audit.

As financial division representative, worked closely with both the savings and loan divisions to increase interdivision cooperation related to new systems design, operations, and customer service. Significantly improved communications with the Association's service bureau and implemented modifications in the general ledger system which streamlined operations and saved more than $20,000 per year.

The accomplishments are his increase in productivity, finding a unique approach for justifying a large tax credit and then defending it before the IRS, increasing cooperation among divisions in the bank, improving relations with the computer service bureau, and saving money on computer services. Because of his accomplishments an employer would certainly want to meet him.

Below are additional samples of accomplishments.

Developed a new method which increased production capacity by 10%.

Interviewed and hired new personnel. Through in-depth interviews and background checks, selected only the most promising candidates. Terminations were reduced by 30% and turnover as a whole by 23%.

Edited newsletter for professional association. Readership increased 28% in one year.

Marketed three new products in two years. These were the first new products marketed by the firm in six years.

Recommended policy changes that were adopted by the President and Board of Directors.

Produced a staffing report which indicated that a 12% cut in staff would create virtually no reduction in output. Management accepted the recommendation to reduce staff through normal attrition.

Organized a citizen task force, which successfully wrote a statewide initiative adopted with a 69% favorable vote.

Updated and reduced the list of required data from contractors for permit approvals. Cut process from forty-two days to twenty-eight. Contractors estimate their savings at $121 per home.

Enlisted help of community groups to support construction of a new plant. Community groups had previously blocked all new construction. Received favorable tax breaks from city council which saved $92,000.

As chairperson for fund raising, developed a new strategy which increased funds by 26% while reducing promotional costs.

Elected chairperson for Girl Scouts Mothers' Day Lunch. Director said it was the best organized luncheon she had seen in fifteen years.

Awarded Medal of Merit for contributions to the community.

Received praise from supervisor for consistently calming angry customers.

Received many compliments each day from satisfied customers.

Set a record of twenty straight days without an error.

Did not miss a day of work in four years.

Accomplishments and results are powerful. They sell you. Over the years I've developed a simple technique which helps identify accomplishments and results. Go over your job sketches and wherever you've listed a duty or a project, add the word *which*, and then ask yourself what the duty or project resulted in. For example, ''Wrote an office procedures manual'' becomes, ''Wrote an office procedures manual *which* decreased training time of new employees and reduced billing errors over 30%''.

Everything you've done on a job has had a result. When the result is positive *and* significant, it belongs in the resume. Train yourself to look for results. Remember, you don't need computer printouts to verify your results. Your own honest estimate is sufficient. If asked about it during an interview, just describe how you arrived at the figure and then go into more detail concerning how you accomplished it.

ASSISTED IN

In resumes I often see the phrase *assisted in*. I rarely use it because it tends to dilute the person's actual contribution. For example, Fred wrote ''Assisted in developing a quality control program which reduced rejected circuit boards 24%.'' In this case, the other person working on the program was a peer who contributed less to the success of the program than Fred. A more appropriate description would be, ''Developed a quality control program which reduced rejected circuit boards by 24%.'' During an interview Fred could explain that he was the primary, but not the sole developer of the program. Fred probably also had a supervisor who had ultimate responsibility for the success of the program, but since Fred did most of the work, he should still take credit for it.

If you don't feel comfortable taking primary responsibility for a project, you can use the phrases *instrumental in, key person in, played a key role in,* or *played an important role in*. It might read, ''Played an important role in implementing a management-by-objectives program which increased productivity 14%.''

REFERENCES

References are rarely listed on a resume, although some people like to write at the bottom, "Personal and Professional References Available Upon Request." That's fine, but it's unnecessary. Every employer knows that if references are requested, you will gladly supply them. See pages 132 and 156 for examples. List your references only if they are influential in your field.

References are nearly always required on application forms, however, so you should have a list of your references ready. You need the person's name, phone number, address, name of organization, and title. You might want to type up your list of references and make four or five copies. That way, if it seems appropriate, you can give a copy to an employer. Since employers rarely ask for references during interviews, you'll still have most of your copies left when you get your next job, but at least you'll be prepared.

Sometimes when I have a very short one-page resume, I center "References Available Upon Request" in the remaining space to give a balanced appearance. See page 132 for an example.

Prior to listing people as references, check with them to make sure they are willing to do it. Then ask them what they would feel comfortable saying about you. More than a few job seekers have been surprised to learn that an expected glowing recommendation turned out to be anything but. You can also suggest things you would like them to say about you. Most will be happy to accommodate you.

SAYING IT WITH IMPACT

Using verbs and adjectives effectively adds impact to your resume. Read this section again carefully just before you actually begin writing.

DESCRIBING RESULTS—GOING BEYOND DUTIES

The typical resume merely lists duties and does little else to sell the person. One of the best ways to sell yourself is to describe accomplishments in terms of *results*. Duties are often covered by "Responsible for ..." Results are generally covered by using the verb *developed*, such as "Developed a secretary's manual which explained hundreds of procedures and significantly reduced clerical errors." This person's duties were typing, filing, and answering phones, so to show that she stood above the rest, she demonstrated results.

The Words to Use

While *develop* is an excellent word, when used three or four times in a resume it becomes overworked. You'll need substitutes. The most common are

Created	Instituted
Designed	Introduced
Established	Set up
Implemented	

Other verbs that may be appropriate substitutes in certain circumstances would be

Built	Fabricated	Originated
Composed	Fashioned	Perfected
Constructed	Formed	Pioneered
Coordinated	Formulated	Planned
Cultivated	Generated	Prepared
Devised	Installed	Produced
Elaborated	Introduced	Refined
Enhanced	Organized	Revamped

Here are examples that will give you a feel for describing

results. In parentheses are words that could have been used instead of *develop*.

Developed (devised, prepared, produced) a creative financing/purchasing package to obtain 1900 acres of prime California farmland.

Developed (created, designed, introduced) a new concept in women's athletics and actively promoted the program. Participation by women grew from 18% in previous years to 79%.

Pioneered a mime program for gifted children age 8-12.

Developed (built, created, established, implemented, instituted) an intern program to allow students to work in nursing homes and schools for the retarded.

Developed (designed, established) training programs for new and experienced employees and supervised the new employee orientation program.

Set up apprenticeship programs for five skilled trades at the Physical Plant Department.

Developed and implemented an information and referral service for consumer complaints and human rights issues.

Developed and implemented mail and telephone solicitation programs and word processor systems.

Coordinated the company marketing effort, including advertising and promotions.

Designed and installed cash and inventory control systems for various clients.

Developed (created, designed) a unique computerized system which has dramatically increased service to customers.

For this small, 29-year-old manufacturer of toys, implemented changes in sales, marketing, and production which enabled the company to double sales and profits in a six-year period.

Developed and supervised a medical records internship program.

Created an employee orientation program which increased employee effectiveness and helped decrease turnover.

Developed (created, built) a team of highly motivated employees.

Established a sales award program which substantially reduced turnover of franchise sales staff.

Developed (instituted, introduced, designed) new operating procedures which reduced labor costs from 24% of gross revenues to 14%.

Instituted a preventive maintenance program which increased combat readiness of a unit by 10%.

ACTION WORDS

A resume should sound alive and vigorous. Using action verbs helps achieve that feeling. "I changed the filing system" lacks punch and doesn't really indicate if the system was improved. "I *reorganized* and *simplified* the filing system" sounds much better and provides more accurate information. Review the sentences below to get a feel for action words. Then quickly scan the words in the following list and check any you think you might want to use in your resume. Don't try to force them in; use them when they feel right.

Conducted long-range master planning for the Portland water supply system.

Monitored enemy radio transmissions, analyzed information, and identified enemy strategic and tactical capabilities.

Planned, staffed, and organized the intramural sports program for this 1,200-student college.

Produced daily reports for each trial and made sure documents and evidence were handled properly.

Presented seminars to entry-level secretaries and worked to increase the professionalism of secretaries in the county system.

Improved the coordination, imagination, and pantomime techniques of adults through mime and dance training.

Allocated and dispensed federal moneys to nine counties as board member of the CETA Advisory Board.

Evaluated financial health by analyzing financial statements and ratios.

Prevented the loss of numerous key accounts through effective account management and by solving long-standing problems.

Compiled extensive fisheries data from interviews with thousands of sports fishermen.

Researched and proposed a $1,000,000 project to improve warehouse storage and develop a better distribution system.

Reduced lost time due to illness 81% and reduced industrial accidents by 67%.

Negotiated a product classification change for California freight, saving $18,000 annually.

Negotiated, awarded, and administered contracts with vendors for the procurement of over 65,000 different standard parts.

Continually streamlined policies to reduce redundant procedures.

Action Verbs

Accomplished	Commanded	Determined	Fabricated
Achieved	Commended	Developed	Facilitated
Acquired	Communicated	Devised	Fashioned
Acted as	Completed	Diagnosed	Filed
Activated	Compared	Directed	Financed
Active in	Compiled	Discovered	Fixed
Adapted	Composed	Dispensed	Followed up
Addressed	Computed	Displayed	Forged (ahead)
Adjusted	Conceived	Dissected	Forecasted
Administered	Conceptualized	Distributed	Formed
Advanced	Condensed	Diverted	Formulated
Advised	Conducted	Documented	Found
Allocated	Consolidated	Drafted	Founded
Analyzed	Constructed	Dramatized	Functioned as
Approved	Conserved	Earned	Gained
Arbitrated	Consulted	Edited	Gathered
Arranged	Contacted	Eliminated	Generated
Ascertained	Contracted	Employed	Governed
Assembled	Contributed	Enacted	Graduated
Assessed	Controlled	Encouraged	Guided
Assigned	Converted	Enforced	Handled
Assimilated	Cooperated	Engineered	Headed
Assisted	Coordinated	Enhanced	Hired
Assured	Correlated	Enlisted	Identified
Attained	Corroborated	Ensured	Illustrated
Attended	Counseled	Equipped	Imagined
Augmented	Created	Established	Implemented
Balanced	Culminated in	Estimated	Improved
Bought	Cultivated	Evaluated	Improvised
Brought	Dealt	Examined	Increased
Brought about	Decided	Executed	Influenced
Built	Defined	Expanded	Informed
Calculated	Delegated	Expedited	Initiated
Clarified	Delivered	Experimented	Inspected
Classified	Demonstrated	Explained	Inspired
Coached	Designed	Expressed	Installed
Collected	Detected	Extracted	Instigated

Instilled	Ordered	Received	Shaped
Instituted	Organized	Recognized	Shifted
Instructed	Originated	Recommended	Shipped
Insured	Overcame	Reconciled	Simplified
Integrated	Oversaw	Recorded	Sold
Interfaced	Participated	Recruited	Solidified
Interpreted	Perceived	Rectified	Solved
Interviewed	Perfected	Reevaluated	Sorted
Introduced	Performed	Referred	Spearheaded
Invented	Persuaded	Refined	Spoke
Investigated	Piloted	Regulated	Staffed
Judged	Pioneered	Rehabilitated	Stimulated
Justified	Placed	Related	Streamlined
Kept	Planned	Rendered	Structured
Kindled	Played	Repaired	Substituted
Launched	Predicted	Reported	Succeeded
Led	Prepared	Represented	Summarized
Lectured	Prescribed	Reorganized	Supervised
Lifted	Presented	Researched	Supplied
Located	Prevented	Resolved	Synthesized
Logged	Printed	Responded	Systematized
Maintained	Processed	Restored	Tested
Managed	Procured	Retrieved	Trained
Marketed	Produced	Revamped	Transferred
Mastered	Programmed	Reviewed	Transformed
Mediated	Projected	Revised	Translated
Minimized	Promoted	Revitalized	Treated
Monitored	Proposed	Revived	Unified
Motivated	Protected	Saved	Updated
Negotiated	Proved	Scheduled	Upgraded
Nominated	Provided	Screened	Utilized
Observed	Publicized	Secured	Validated
Obtained	Published	Selected	Verified
Offered	Purchased	Separated	Won
Operated	Questioned	Served	Wrote
Optimized	Ramrodded	Serviced	
Orchestrated	Realized	Set up	

Verb Tenses

Describe your current job in the present tense. For all previous jobs, write in the past tense. In your current job you may need to describe an event, such as a project, which has already been completed. In that case, use the past tense to describe the project while using the present tense in the remaining portions of your current job.

Example:
STORE MANAGER—Oversee total operation of the store, supervise and schedule employees, and complete

monthly profit and loss statements. Designed a new
inventory system which has saved over $10,000.

Since the inventory system was designed over a year ago, it
must be described in the past tense.

Using Adjectives and Adverbs

Adjectives and adverbs are words that describe actions and
things. Used appropriately, they can enliven a resume and
describe more accurately what you did. Notice how they change
the tone of the sentences below.

1. Worked with industrial engineers.

   Worked closely and effectively with industrial engineers.

2. During seven years as staff pharmacist, learned the operation of the pharmacy department.

   During seven years as staff pharmacist, became thoroughly familiar with the operation of the pharmacy
   department.

3. Initiate and develop working relations with local, state,
   and federal agencies.

   Initiate and develop outstanding working relations with
   local, state, and federal agencies.

4. Establish rapport with customers.

   Quickly establish rapport with customers.

Here are more examples of how to use these words:

Dealt tactfully and effectively with difficult customers.

Outstanding record in teaching.

Comprehensive knowledge and experience in group
facilitation.

Presented technical material in objective and easily understood terms.

Able to actively involve parents in Individual Education
Plans.

Able to train experienced people and develop highly effective teams.

Consistently maintained high profit margins on all projects.

Extensively involved in staff education and development.

Significantly improved communications between nursing administration and staff.

Virtually all apartment units were completed ahead of schedule.

Continually streamlined policies and procedures to create a more reasonable work schedule.

Extremely well-organized and efficient.

Exceptionally well-trained in theatre, dance, and music.

A list of adverbs and adjectives is given below. Review the list and check the ones you feel may be useful to you. Try to include them but don't force it. Don't use a word or phrase unless it really fits your personality and strengthens your resume. After writing each draft, go back through the list to see if still another word or two might be useful.

accurate/accurately
active/actively
adept/adeptly
adroit/adroitly
advantageously
aggressive/aggressively
all-inclusive/all-inclusively
ambitious/ambitiously
appreciable/appreciably
astute/astutely
attractive/attractively
authoritative/authoritatively
avid/avidly
aware
beneficial/beneficially
broad/broadly
capable/capably
challenging
cohesive/cohesively
competent/competently
complete/completely
comprehensive/comprehensively
conclusive/conclusively
consistent/consistently
constructive/constructively
contagious
continuous/continually
contributed toward
decidedly

decisive/decisively
deep (insight)
deft/deftly
demonstrably
dependable/dependably
dextrous/dextrously
diligent/diligently
diplomatic/diplomatically
distinctive/distinctively
diverse/diversified
driving
easily
effective/effectively
effectually
efficient/efficiently
effortless/effortlessly
enthusiastically
entire/entirely
especially
exceptional/exceptionally
exciting/excitingly
exhaustive/exhaustively
experienced
expert/expertly
extensive/extensively
extremely
familiar with
familiarity with
firm/firmly

foresight
functional/functionally
handy/handily
high/highly
higest
high-level
honest/honestly
imaginative/imaginatively
immediate/immediately
impressive/impressively
incisive/incisively
in-depth
industrious/industriously
inherent/inherently
innovative/innovatively
instructive/instructively
instrumental/instrumentally
integral
intensive/intensively
intimate/intimately
leading
masterful/masterfully
meaningful/meaningfully
natural/naturally
new and improved
notable/notably
objective/objectively
open-minded
original/originally
outstanding/outstandingly
particularly
penetrating/penetratingly
perceptive/perceptively
pioneering
practical/practically
professional/professionally

proficient/proficiently
profitable/profitably
progressive/progressively
quick/quickly
rare/rarely
readily
record
relentless/relentlessly
reliability
reliable/reliably
remarkable/remarkably
responsible/responsibly
rigorous/rigorously
routine/routinely
secure/securely
sensitive/sensitively
significant/significantly
skillful/skillfully
solid/solidly
sophisticated/sophisticatedly
strategic/strategically
strong/strongly
substantial/substantially
successful/successfully
tactful/tactfully
thorough/thoroughly
uncommon/uncommonly
unique/uniquely
unusual/unusually
urgent/urgently
varied
vigorous/vigorously
virtual/virtually
vital/vitally
wide/widely

Significantly/Substantially

"Increased sales substantially through creative marketing."
"Absenteeism was reduced significantly by instituting a system of
flexible work hours." When you have no idea by what percentage
you increased or decreased something, the words *significantly* and
substantially will provide a reader with the feeling you are trying to
get across. When you use these words, you are saying that what
you did really had an impact. The word *extensive* can also be used
in similar contexts. "Produced an *extensive* revision of the company procedures manual."

73

Telegraphic Style

Resumes are best written in telegraphic style, with unnecessary words left out. The most common words to be omitted are *I*, *a*, and *the*. This frequently leads to the use of incomplete sentences, something your English teachers would never allow, but which is perfectly acceptable—even necessary—in resumes. Brevity is always appreciated. Examples illustrate the point best. In parentheses are words that have been omitted. Read the sentences out loud with, and then without, those words.

> (I have) Outstanding sales and marketing experience. (I) Built successful sales teams for electronics distributors and (I) have thorough knowledge of the industry. (I) Consistently increased the market share of products sold.

> (I am) Able to effectively handle both client contact and project coordination with other engineering disciplines.

> (I) Installed and serviced Xerox equipment and trained entry level field service representatives.

The word *I* can almost always be eliminated from a sentence. The easiest way to learn to write in this style is to write a complete sentence and then merely cross out "I," "I am," or "I have." If each *I* were not removed from resumes, most would have ten to twenty. Resumes simply read better without *I*, and employers are used to reading them that way, though it may sound funny to you at first.

I should be used if it is necessary to clarify that you personally did something. If the reader would be in doubt whether it was you personally who did the thing, then use *I*. If it is used only once or twice in a resume, *I* can be used effectively for emphasis.

Knowing what to do with *a* and *the* is a little more difficult. I tend to retain most of these because sentences usually flow better and because little space is saved by removing them.

> Promoted to Senior Field Engineer ahead of more senior staff because of full knowledge of the systems and willingness to take on added responsibilities.

> Provided product and corporate demonstrations to developers and was responsible for estimating, bidding, and negotiating contracts. Once (the) contract was secured, became Project Manager and handled (the) scheduling and inspecting.

In the first example, the sentence just wouldn't flow as well without the word *the*; in the second, *the* was strictly optional and so was omitted.

While I recommend telegraphic style, it definitely can be overdone. If in doubt about leaving a word in or taking it out, read it out loud both ways and go with the one that sounds smoother. *I,* however, should almost always be eliminated.

THE LET-IT-ALL-HANG-OUT SYNDROME

Some people feel a special need to reveal things in their resumes that might be damaging to them. Their attitude frequently is, "If they don't like it, then I don't want to work there anyway." Let's say you are seeking a position with a large private business and you're a member of Common Cause, the ACLU, Young Socialists, and the Sierra Club. You may be tempted to list them under Associations, saying to yourself, "I might as well be up front about my political and social beliefs. If they don't want to interview me for that reason, then I guess I just wouldn't fit in anyway." This sounds logical but it's not. You must remember that employers are always looking for reasons to eliminate people from consideration. Often the reasons are unconscious. Don't raise unnecessary objections; if you're like most of us, you probably have plenty of objections to overcome as it is. Keep any controversial activities to yourself. Once you're hired, your employer cares only if your job is getting done; your outside activities usually have little bearing on that. In any case, get the job offer and *then* decide if you want to take it. Unless you're applying to organizations that you know share your beliefs, eliminate references that reveal your political, social, ethnic, or religious background.

IMPORTANT VARIABLES

In this section, many important points are covered to help you make the most out of your resume.

MULTIPLE RESUMES

In order to sell you, a resume must demonstrate focus. If you are considering more than one type of job, you may need two or more resumes. Frequently I will write one resume but give it more flexibility by using more than one objective, leaving everything else the same. This is easy to do with a word processor or a memory typewriter. Having the first page completely typed twice with a different objective on each will add only about four dollars to the cost of the typing.

An example will help. Jim is a very good computer salesperson with no desire to change fields, but we used three different objectives: ''OBJECTIVE: Computer Sales;'' ''OBJECTIVE: Electronics Sales;'' and ''OBJECTIVE: Sales.'' Nothing else in the resume was changed. Computer companies got one resume, electronics companies got another, and if Jim saw something interesting outside those two industries, he sent the one that said ''Sales.''

Changing the objective is sometimes not enough. Writing a new Qualifications section for each objective will often do the trick. Far less frequently, you may need to make small changes in the Employment Section.

USING COVER LETTERS FOR FLEXIBILITY

A cover letter should accompany each resume you mail out and should be individually typed. The cover letter provides an excellent opportunity to mention points you know are important to that particular employer, but are not mentioned in the resume. See page 117 for more on cover letters.

ANSWERING WANT ADS

When a want ad provides specific job requirements, you must decide how to respond. You could (1) send your resume with a standardized cover letter, (2) send your resume with a custom-written cover letter discussing key points mentioned in the ad, or (3) completely revise your resume to hit all the important points in the ad *and* write a creative cover letter. Obviously the last approach will provide the best results, and it really won't take that much more time. The job descriptions might remain the same or have just minor changes, while the Qualifications section might require substantial changes. The entire process of rewriting might take one to two hours. If you are really interested in the position and know you could handle it, consider the time as an investment. Taking time to redo the resume will not guarantee you an interview, but it can *double* your chances.

WHAT SHOULD YOU CALL IT?

Many substitute names have been given for the word *resume* including "Qualifications Brief," "Profile," and others. I avoid the use of any such titles because everyone knows it's a resume just by glancing at it.

COLOR AND TYPE OF PAPER

The color of paper you choose can definitely make a difference in the number of interviews you get. White is always a safe color, but my studies reveal that buff or off-white paper usually provides better results. The best papers I have found so far are the 20- or 24-pound "classic laid" and "linen" finishes. Both papers have a texture that implies quality without appearing to be "too much." For management people, a light gray can be effective. Blues and greens have not tested well. Color should have a positive effect; this will nearly always mean light shades. Dark grays and browns or bright colors are not effective. Twenty-pound paper is always a safe standard. A slightly heavier paper is fine, but avoid heavy stocks.

TYPING

My studies show that sharp, clean, crisp typing is one of the most important factors in getting your resume read. Most people type their own resumes on portable typewriters, and it usually looks home-typed. Invest twenty to thirty-five dollars to have it typed professionally by a typing service (look in the Yellow Pages under Secretarial or Word Processing Service). Virtually all use models that cost over $1,000 and produce work that cannot be matched at home. A key difference is that they use one-time carbon or film ribbons instead of the multi-use nylon ribbons found on most personal-use typewriters. The difference in sharpness is amazing. Word processing gives you the advantage of being able to make changes or multiple versions more easily. Although word processors can produce a justified right margin and bold headings, I rarely use those features because they give it too fancy a look. I typically will bold the person's name, however. Studies have demonstrated that a "ragged right margin," as it is called in printing circles, is actually easier to read than justified right margins. For examples of resumes with bold headlines and justified right margins, see pages 129, 165, 170. By all means, never use a dot-matrix printer for your resume. It cheapens the appearance.

SIZE OF TYPE

Most resumes should be typed in elite (12 pitch) type. Elite is very readable and allows you to get more on a page than pica (10 pitch). If your one-page resume will not use up a full page, you may want to consider pica. A little white space is always good, but too much will make the resume seem empty. Pica can help fill up that space and make the resume more visually attractive.

TYPESETTING

Books, magazines, and newspapers are typeset. Special electronic equipment offers many sizes and styles of type, different boldnesses, italics, variable spacing, and justification of margins. Typewriters do not have variable spacing. An *i* takes just as much space as a *w* on a typewriter. Typewriters produce a justified left margin, but a perfectly straight right margin is rare.

Typesetting can give you very sharp, impressive resumes, but my studies show it is not as effective as a resume professionally typed on an electric typewriter or word processor. I will, however, often recommend that artists and graphics people demonstrate their design skills by having the resume typeset. Conversations with employers reveal that some consciously downgrade typeset resumes. In their minds, the typeset resume is a little too fancy. With the cost of typesetting a one-page resume ranging from twenty-five to forty-five dollars, it just isn't worth it. For examples of typeset resumes, see pages 140, 142, 143.

PHOTOGRAPHS

Photographs are rarely submitted with resumes, although they are desirable for models, flight attendants, actors, actresses, performers, and television personalities. Many organizations are leery of receiving photographs with resumes because it increases the likelihood of charges of age and race discrimination. Employers are nearly unanimous in preferring not to receive photographs.

CONFIDENTIALITY

Employers who receive your resume probably will not inform your current employer that you're job hunting, but it does occasionally happen. Several options are available if you are concerned about confidentiality.

1. Write "Confidential" at the top of your resume.
2. At the bottom of the resume type and underline, "Please do not contact employer at this time."
3. Replace the name of your present employer (and possibly your next-to-last employer) with a description such as, "A major manufacturer of automotive parts," "A Fortune 500 Corporation," or "A National Retail Chain."
4. Utilize an executive recruiter (headhunter). A recruiter will sell you to an employer over the phone without revealing your name and will send your resume only if the employer is particularly interested.

SALARY

Salary history and salary requirements nearly always should be omitted from a resume to avoid giving anyone a cause for eliminating you. You currently may be earning $26,000, but for a really great opportunity you might settle for $22,000. A company willing to pay a maximum of $24,000 probably would not contact you for an interview. If your current income is below what others with similar experience are making, the employer may assume you're not capable of handling the responsibilities of the job. Want ads frequently ask for desired income or income history. Your cover letter is the place to provide that information if you choose to reveal it. It is perfectly acceptable to simply ignore the request for salary history since your income is a very personal matter. Seldom will your resume be thrown out merely because you omitted your salary history. Since some risk is involved by not following instructions, only you can decide what is in your best interest.

RELOCATION

If you are seeking a position with a national company, you'd better be prepared to relocate. Since many people are unwilling to relocate, a statement under Personal saying ''Willing to Relocate'' will make you stand out in a positive way.

REASON FOR LEAVING

Everyone has a reason for leaving a job, but the resume is rarely the place for stating it. Invariably an attempt to explain the reason will simply raise more questions than it answers. Save the explanation for an interview where the issue can be handled much more effectively.

ABBREVIATIONS

Avoid abbreviations; they can often cause problems if a reader is not familiar with them. Some exceptions: ''B.A.,'' ''M.A.,'' and ''Ph.D.'' are preferred over spelling them out.

Rule of thumb: if you are certain that *everyone*, from the personnel clerk who may screen the resume to the person with power to hire you, will understand it, then consider the use of an abbreviation. Words are more visually attractive, however, when spelled out. This is especially true of states. In your address and Employment section, avoid "WA," "CA", "VT," "MD" and the like—spell them out. Washington, D.C. would be an exception.

LETTERS OF RECOMMENDATION

Letters of recommendation can be useful when used properly. In the past, most experts, including myself, recommended against using letters of recommendation with resumes. In the course of my research on effective resumes, I studied secretarial resumes. I received many resumes with letters of recommendation included. I decided to find out if such letters were actually beneficial. In many cases the resume with a letter of recommendation was strongly preferred.

Based on my interpretation of the findings, I will offer some basic guidelines. By all means do not feel you must use a letter of recommendation. Use a letter only if it speaks glowingly and convincingly about you. Anything less and the letter will appear to be only a formality. The typical letter merely confirms the dates of employment, and the type of work performed. It may close with a statement such as, "I can strongly recommend that John would be a real asset to any organization he would choose to join." Actually this is a pretty good recommendation, but it is not strong enough to be included with the resume. For inclusion, the letter should speak highly of your technical ability as well as your personality and character. The letter should seem personal, as though coming from a person who really likes you and hates to see you go, since you had become so valuable to the organization. Office workers and people with less than five years experience seem to benefit most from letters of recommendation. Managers and other more experienced people should let their accomplishments speak for them. When you leave a job or are terminated, it is usually a good idea to ask for a letter of recommendation. The letter will help you to know what may be said about you if potential employers check you out. It is perfectly fair even to suggest some of the points you would like covered. Your supervisor, however, will write only what he or she feels comfortable with, and it will not necessarily be to your liking. If it's not a well-written letter, or it does not speak as glowingly about you as you would like, don't be bothered. A very strong letter of recommendation can be helpful, but it will not make or break your job search.

Annual reviews by supervisors can also be used in place of letters of recommendation. Military personnel in particular should save their reviews.

WRITING IT!

Before you actually start writing your resume, you should complete a job sketch for each position you will describe in your resume (see page 28). The job sketch is important because it will get you thinking about each job and cause you to actually relive some of your experiences, especially your accomplishments. Jot down thoughts as they come to your mind, without any concern for whether the thought is polished and suitable for inclusion in your resume.

GETTING STARTED

After reviewing your job sketches, you're ready to start. Use a pencil and feel free to erase. If you compose well at a typewriter, by all means use one, but double space so you can edit between the lines. I always begin by writing the name, address and phone number at the top and writing in the Objective. I then write in ''Qualifications'' and skip enough space to complete it after I've written the rest of the resume. Since Qualifications is often the most difficult section to write, I leave it until last. I then complete Education and the Training section if there is one.

At that point I have spent only about three minutes writing, but psychologically I am totally into the resume. Three minutes earlier I was looking for an excuse to postpone the writing, but now I'm *into* it. So I tackle Employment next, the section which nearly always requires the most time and thought. As you prepare for writing the Qualifications section, review the resume and determine what points should be covered. Use Qualifications to introduce yourself to the reader and to give an overview of why you are qualified for your stated objective. To do this ask yourself, ''Why would I be good at this occupation?'' Or if you already have experience ask yourself, ''What makes me successful in this field?'' Remember, in Qualifications it is permissible to repeat or paraphrase points made elsewhere in the resume. If you have strong work experience, you will probably want a short Qualifications section. If you are seeking to break into a new field, Qualifications is usually the best vehicle for bringing in related experiences and selling an employer on your potential.

While relatively short, the Qualifications section is nearly always the most difficult to write. Because it can strengthen the overall effectiveness of the resume, it deserves a great deal of attention and effort. One hour spent writing and editing Qualifications is not too much.

Begin by listing some of the strengths and assets that you want employers to pick up about you. For a Quality Control Manager a Qualifications sketch might look like this:

1.   Ten years in quality control. Familiar with all techniques that have been developed for the electronics industry.

2.   Saved money and reduced rejects for three different companies.

3.   I work well with other department heads, particularly production, and coordinate and cooperate well with them rather than work against them.

4.   I've developed creative programs which really work.

5.   I like my work and enjoy a challenge.

6.   I'm always looking for a better method, technique, or system and am open to new ideas from others.

7.   I'm an excellent supervisor. I train my staff well, I listen to them, I maintain high morale, and productivity is always high.

8.   I'm hardworking, loyal, reliable, creative, and efficient.

Check through your resume next to see if the points made in your Qualifications sketch are already adequately covered or implied. Of course, just because a certain point is well made in the resume does not mean it should not be mentioned in Qualifications. Remember, this section is a summary of your strengths and experience as well as an opportunity to sell yourself in a way that cannot be done in other sections of a resume.The final version of the Quality Control Manager's Qualifications section might read like this:

QUALIFICATIONS

Strong experience in quality control gained during ten years in supervision and management. For three electronics manufacturers implemented new quality control programs which decreased rejects at each plant by at least 23%.

Develop excellent relations with all department heads and always work well with production personnel.

Excellent supervisor. Consistently increase productivity of quality assurance personnel, and through effective staff training increase their technical capabilities.

If you review the eight points the person originally wanted to cover, you'll notice that everything is included here either explicitly or implicitly (points 5 and 8 were covered implicitly). By reading the Qualifications section in the context of the entire resume, you would certainly pick up that he enjoys a challenge and that he is hard-working, loyal, reliable, creative, and efficient.

In writing Qualifications sections there is a tendency to use the words *excellent* and *strong*, such as "Strong experience in quality control ..." and "Excellent supervisor." Both are excellent words, but try not to overuse them. I've searched the thesaurus and just haven't found many good substitutes. Sometimes I'll use the word *good*, but usually that just isn't strong enough. I sometimes use the words *outstanding*, or *superior*, but they can be a little too strong, so use them carefully and selectively.

Over the years I've noticed other phrases I use to help make a point. If you use "Excellent experience" in one paragraph, you could use "Broad experience," "Broad background," or "Excellent background," in the next. Don't be bothered if you use the word excellent three times, but you'll want to find substitutes to avoid using it excessively. *Excellent* seems to be an excellent word because it is not as humble as *good*, nor does it run the risk of seeming boastful, as *outstanding* sometimes does.

Frequently I start a Qualifications paragraph with a short statement, such as "Excellent management experience." In general, just make a positive statement and then back it up. In this case the follow-up might be "Consistently obtain high productivity from employees." Or "Consistently implement new techniques and procedures which increase productivity and lower costs." Another effective backup statement would be, "Proven ability to turn around projects which are behind schedule and over budget." Get used to thinking that whatever general statement you make should be explained or reinforced with details. Look at the resumes on pages 128, 135, and 166 and notice how percentages or other statistics have been included in Qualifications. This can be very effective but is not always necessary or possible, particularly if you are making a broad statement about your entire career. Notice how the various backup statements look when paired with the original short statement.

Excellent management experience. Consistently obtain high productivity from employees.

Excellent management experience. Consistently implement

85

new techniques and procedures which increase productivity and lower costs.

Excellent management experience. Proven ability to turn around projects which are behind schedule and over budget.

Opening with a short statement provides impact. It hits the reader and makes her want some evidence, which you will have provided in your very next sentence. Of course, you need to be able to verify anything you say, such as "Consistently obtain high productivity from employees," either in other sections of your resume or in a personal interview.

To write really effective Qualifications statements you'll need to study several examples, and I do mean *study*. Analyze them, notice what makes them effective. When you're through writing, compare what you have to some of the examples. If you're not pleased, set the resume aside for a day and return to it from a fresh perspective. Let others see it and get feedback from them. Don't use the Qualifications section as filler. Include only those facts which you really think will sell you.

Some people just can't come up with a good Qualifications section. If you fall into that category, do try to improve it, but you also need to finish the resume and get it out to the right people. In such a case I would recommend that you wrap it up with a short summary of fifteen to twenty-five words. In qualifications, don't try to make any hard-hitting statements. Here's an example.

OBJECTIVE: Programmer/Analyst

QUALIFICATIONS

Excellent background in data processing gained during eight years in programming and systems analysis.

Even though this Qualifications section lacks punch, it serves a purpose. As soon as an employer sees an objective, he immediately asks himself what makes this person qualified. By seeing the word *QUALIFICATIONS* followed by a statement, the employer instantly assumes the person *is* qualified and goes on to seek evidence in the Education and Experience sections.

In a sense I'm giving you a way out if you have difficulty with your Qualifications, but use this approach only after you've spent at least two hours working solely on Qualifications. Once you've used your resume for a while, try working on Qualifications again. You'll probably have some new thoughts, and it may come together for you after all.

DON'T HESITATE

You should write your first draft relatively quickly without worrying about perfection. Concentrate on getting your thoughts on paper; you can polish the phrasing later. Once you write a phrase, read it out loud to get a feel for how it sounds. When reading most people subvocalize; while they may not move their lips, their mind is actually saying each word almost audibly. In other words, the way a phrase sounds to you when you say it out loud is the same way it sounds when read by an employer. By the time I finish a resume I have read every phrase aloud four to ten times. While I don't worry about perfection on the first draft, I will rewrite some phrases and add or delete words as I go along.

Frequently I will finish the first draft of a resume late in the afternoon. I may know that I'm not at all satisfied but I do know that all the main thoughts and descriptions are there. I will simply set it aside until the next morning. When I pick it up the next day, my thoughts are fresh and I'm able to look at it objectively. Improvements often come spontaneously.

Read over the resume and ask yourself if all the important points have been made. Frequently you'll think of a point that could be covered in Employment or an important idea or concept you want to get across in Qualifications. Make those changes on the original draft. Go through the draft sentence by sentence and phrase by phrase, constantly rereading them out loud. Simply cross out extraneous phrases. Ask yourself if you can make the same point with fewer words. Use action words whenever possible. Having done this, you have completed your first draft.

SPIT AND POLISH

Next rewrite or type the draft with your new improvements. You will probably find that further improvements will occur to you as you go along. Once the second draft has been written, again set it aside for at least half a day.

When you pick it up again, take care as you go through the resume; this may be your last draft. Step back and look at it. Are there any phrases or words you have used more than twice? If so, look for alternatives. Are all of your sentences very long or all very short? A mixture of short, medium, and long sentences reads best. Too many short sentences makes the resume seem choppy and abrupt. Lots of long sentences cause a reader to forget the main point. As you read your resume out loud, it should flow.

Look for any troublesome phrases. This could be a phrase that sounds awkward or which could cause a misunderstanding. Your desire is to have employers read your resume completely and thoroughly. You don't want them to stop at any point and wonder what you mean. Just one awkwardly written, hard-to-understand sentence can reduce your perceived value by ten percent. Don't let it happen.

Of course you know exactly what you mean by everything you've written, so poorly written sentences may be hard for you to spot. Have others read your resume and ask if any sentences tripped them up. In writing this book, I did the same thing. If my wife, Lois, did not understand a section or found it confusing, I changed it. Also ask for their overall impression.

Avoid big words. The mark of a good writer is the ability to say exactly what is meant by using everyday words. If you do choose a seldom-used word, make sure you have used it precisely. Trying to impress someone with your vocabulary and then using words incorrectly is a turn-off, to say the least.

Spelling must be perfect. It is worth one quick scan through your resume, dictionary in hand, looking up words you "know" are correct. You may be surprised to find that you have been misspelling a word for years.

Type the final draft and review it one last time for phrasing, spelling, and punctuation. The secretarial service will use this draft for the final typing. Presenting a typed draft will help them space the resume exactly as you want it and will reduce your expense.

THE KEY

Now for my final advice on writing a resume. Once you have your job sketches completed, simply start *writing*. The biggest problem most people face is getting started. People seem to feel that when they write, the words must come out perfectly. This rarely happens, even for the most gifted writer. *Just start writing*. Don't stop even if you're not pleased. Write a paragraph, then if you're totally dissatisfied with it, throw it away. Your next attempt will be better. At least you will have started.

Even best-selling authors must write and rewrite. Still their publishers will find a number of ways to polish and strengthen their manuscripts. By all means, try to find people who can edit your writing. You don't have to accept all their suggestions, but you will very likely find many ideas helpful. Remember, the resume is yours, so you must make the final decisions.

PROFESSIONAL EDITING

Writing a top-quality resume is one of the most difficult parts of an effective job search. As I prepare clients for their job search I advise them on resume writing and then assist them by editing their completed resume. With the help of *Resume Power* most write a very fine resume which would get excellent results. If I edit what they've come up with, effectiveness is often increased twenty to fifty percent.

By following the advice of *Resume Power* and by spending six to ten hours writing and editing, you should produce a top-quality resume. If you feel that professional editing could strengthen it, however, Career Management Resources would like to help. The cost of the editing service is $35.00. We will review your resume and look for ways to improve the layout and the writing. If you have specific questions about a portion of the resume we will make recommendations. Perhaps you're not sure if you should include your height and weight, or an organization you belong to. Give us your thoughts—pros and cons—and we'll tell you what we think and why.

What You Need To Do

1. Send us your double-spaced, typed final draft. It's okay if you've made a few final corrections on it. Send your resume only when you believe it is the best you can possibly do.
2. Include your job sketches. They must be as complete as possible and legible. Typed job sketches are not necessary although certainly desirable. Be sure your sketches have included all possible results and accomplishments.
3. List any questions you have. Perhaps you're wondering if you should include personal data, a seminars section, a particular job duty. A person may have dozens of questions regarding a resume.
4. Answer completely the questionnaire on page 92.
5. Enclose a check or money order for $35.00 made payable to Career Management Resources.

What We Will Do

1. Within forty-eight hours of receipt of your material we will have your resume heading your way by first-class mail.
2. We will review your job sketches and resume. First we'll look at any possible ways to improve the layout and eye appeal of the resume. Next we will review each portion of the resume sentence by sentence. We might, for example, recommend an objective with more punch or a way to combine two sentences. Occasionally we will completely rewrite a sentence or paragraph—but always based on information you have supplied to us. If we feel a sentence or a piece of information is unnecessary, we will cross it out and briefly explain why.
3. If necessary we will call you so we can gain a better understanding of a particular job or experience.
4. We will return your draft with our suggestions; we keep a photocopy for our records.

Notice in the examples below how each job description or qualifications statement was strengthened through editing.

<u>REGIONAL MANAGER</u> - 7 '84-Present. *give the reader an idea of the type of company it is* ^For this equipment manufacturer,^ Responsible for total operation of the Midwest Regional Office providing sales and service to customers through local field representatives. Supervise eleven salesmen and twelve office personnel with responsibility for ~~interviewing,~~ *(not necessary, assumed to be part of hiring)* hiring, and training all regional personnel. Travel extensively working closely with field representatives to promote sales to end users, dealers, and original equipment manufacturers. *(This is assumed and is not a powerful or a needed phrase)* ~~Supply information to Corporate as requested and~~ Represent the company at ~~various~~ *(A number is better than various)* 4-6 trade shows *annually*. Improved office efficiency and morale by opening lines of communication between management and staff. Increased sales *—%* and reduce*d* expenses *—%* by realigning sales territories and job responsibilities~~x~~, *as well as by ... (adding another point will strengthen it)* *(Since you've been in the territory just over a year, and sales have increased, you should do some research to come up with an exact figure of the increases.)*

90

Qualifications statements are especially difficult to write. It is in this area that editing is often most useful.

ORIGINAL VERSION

Eight years of professional accounting experience. A Certified Public Accountant. Excellent manager of people and projects for productivity and efficiency.

EDITED VERSION

Strong accounting and financial management background gained during eight years of professional accounting experience. A Certified Public Accountant. Excellent manager of people and projects, with the ability to increase productivity and efficiency.

ORIGINAL VERSION

Twelve years in sales, middle, and upper level management. Possess a strong personality dynamics to create self-motivation in others. Extremely well organized and efficient. Excellent written and verbal communications skills.

EDITED VERSION

Twelve years in sales, middle, and upper level management. Consistently able to increase revenue and productivity and decrease operating costs. Develop highly motivated staffs. Excellent written and verbal communications skills.

Name_____

Street Address_____

City, State, ZIP_____

Home Phone: (_____)_____

        Best times to reach me:_____

Work Phone: (_____)_____

        Can we talk freely if we reach you at work?

        Yes____ No____

        Best times to reach me:_____

☐ I've enclosed my check or money order in the amount of $35.00.

☐ I've enclosed my job sketches.

Send to:

Career Management Resources
1750 - 112th N.E. C-247
Bellevue, Washington 98004

JOB SKETCHES MUST BE INCLUDED

     Your job sketches are critical for us as we edit your resume. They provide more complete information about your background and enable us to decide whether information should be added or deleted. By having the more complete information of a job sketch, we can better understand the points you are trying to make in your job descriptions. See pages 27-32 for a complete explanation of job sketches. Writing good job sketches will also enable you to write a better resume, faster.

RESUME FORMATS

Review the following seven resumes for ideas on formatting your resume. All are very good and should give you excellent results. Notice all of the variations. You may want to develop a format using a combination of the ideas. Explanations of the key changes in each resume are given below.

RESUMES 1, 2, and 3

Resume #1 is my preferred format and I use it for over ninety percent of the resumes I write. Resumes #2 and #3 are only slight variations and both are very acceptable. The use of lines across the page as in #2 can be very effective. For an attractive alternative to the name and address centered at the top of the page, I like format #3.

1. Standard format, preferred for most resumes.
2. Names and companies capitalized. Job titles are not capitalized. Roberta Jennings is not capitalized.
3. All headlines are underlined. Name and address of Roberta have been laid out in a different style.

RESUMES 4 and 5

The employment section format here can be very good for people who have never had more than one position with a company. Roberta, however, had two positions with Air Florida, but you could easily miss that fact with this format. It looks like she changes companies more frequently than she really does. With that one reservation, this can be a very attractive style. I prefer the job title capitalized at the left side for most people, unless I am trying to de-emphasize job titles.

4. Format of job title, dates, company, and city is different from the first three formats.
5. Job titles are moved from the left to the right side and are not capitalized.

RESUMES 6 and 7

The major difference in this set is the use of the left margin for headlines and dates of employment. This is a fairly common format and can be very effective. It tends to emphasize dates. If you have any sizeable gaps in employment, you will want to use a different format or else show your employment in years rather than months and years.

6. Names of companies are capitalized and underlined.
7. Name and address have been moved over to the left margin. Names of companies are not capitalized but are underlined. Job titles are capitalized.

ROBERTA JENNINGS
1121 Peach Drive
Atlanta, Georgia 30601
(404) 574-8769

OBJECTIVE: Airline Management

QUALIFICATIONS

Excellent Management and Supervisory capabilities. Highly respected by subordinates and able to obtain high performance levels from employees. Created one of the best on-time performance records in the airline industry.

EDUCATION

B.A. - Business, University of Southern California (1969-1973)

EMPLOYMENT

Air Florida 2/77 to Present

CUSTOMER SERVICE/RAMP SERVICE SUPERVISOR, Miami, Florida; Atlanta, Georgia, 6/80 to Present. Opened the Atlanta airport facility for Air Florida and created one of its most efficient and effective operations. Supervised and trained thirty Customer Service Agents and Ramp personnel. Responsible for all day-to-day operations decisions and handled all crises related to crashes, passenger deaths and illnesses, bomb threats, hijackings, and weather delays.

Established one of the top records in the industry by successfully loading planes and preparing them for departure in twenty minutes or less, 97% of the time. Effective planning and scheduling permitted up to four planes to be serviced simultaneously. Reduced lost time due to illness by 68% and industrial accidents by 71%.

CUSTOMER SERVICE AGENT, Miami, Florida 2/77 to 6/80. Functioned as Ticket Sales Agent, Boarding Agent, and Customer Service Representative. Provided the type of service and concern for customers which made Air Florida one of the fastest growing airlines in the U. S. Became adept at solving problems and satisfying customers' complaints. Consistently maintained monthly sales in the top 10%.

Alaska Airlines, San Francisco, California 1/76 to 2/77

CUSTOMER SERVICE AGENT - Worked closely with customers to provide the best connecting flights and make each flight an enjoyable experience.

The Spoke and Wheel, Long Beach, California 6/73 to 1/76

ASSISTANT MANAGER - Sold Peugeot and other fine bikes and purchased bikes, parts, and supplies. Managed the retail side of the business. Sales increased 42% in 1975.

Roberta Jennings
1121 Peach Drive
Atlanta, Georgia 30601
(404) 574-8769

OBJECTIVE: Airline Management

QUALIFICATIONS

Excellent Management and Supervisory capabilities. Highly respected by subordinates and able to obtain high performance levels from employees. Created one of the best on-time performance records in the airline industry.

EDUCATION

B.A. - Business, University of Southern California (1969-1973)

EMPLOYMENT

AIR FLORIDA 2/77 to Present

Customer Service/Ramp Service Supervisor, Miami, Florida; Atlanta, Georgia, 6/80 to Present. Opened the Atlanta airport facility for Air Florida and created one of its most efficient and effective operations. Supervised and trained thirty Customer Service Agents and Ramp personnel. Responsible for all day-to-day operations decisions and handled all crises related to crashes, passenger deaths and illnesses, bomb threats, hijackings, and weather delays. Established one of the top records in the industry by successfully loading planes and preparing them for departure in twenty minutes or less, 97% of the time. Effective planning and scheduling permitted up to four planes to be serviced simultaneously. Reduced lost time due to illness by 68% and industrial accidents by 71%.

Customer Service Agent, Miami, Florida 2/77 to 6/80. Functioned as Ticket Sales Agent, Boarding Agent, and Customer Service Representative. Provided the type of service and concern for customers which made Air Florida one of the fastest growing airlines in the U. S. Became adept at solving problems and satisfying customers' complaints. Consistently maintained monthly sales in the top 10%.

ALASKA AIRLINES, San Francisco, California 1/76 to 2/77

Customer Service Agent - Worked closely with customers to provide the best connecting flights and make each flight an enjoyable experience.

THE SPOKE AND WHEEL, Long Beach, California 6/73 to 1/76

Assistant Manager - Sold Peugeot and other fine bikes and purchased bikes, parts, and supplies. Managed the retail side of the business. Sales increased 42% in 1975.

96

_____ ROBERTA JENNINGS _____

1121 Peach Drive   Atlanta, Georgia 30601   (404) 574-8769

OBJECTIVE: Airline Management

QUALIFICATIONS

Excellent Management and Supervisory capabilities. Highly respected by subordinates and able to obtain high performance levels from employees. Created one of the best on-time performance records in the airline industry.

EDUCATION

B.A.-Business, University of Southern California (1969-1973)

EMPLOYMENT

Air Florida 2/77 to Present

CUSTOMER SERVICE/RAMP SERVICE SUPERVISOR, Miami, Florida; Atlanta, Georgia, 6/80 to Present. Opened the Atlanta airport facility for Air Florida and created one of its most efficient and effective operations. Supervised and trained thirty Customer Service Agents and Ramp personnel. Responsible for all day-to-day operations decisions and handled all crises related to crashes, passenger deaths and illnesses, bomb threats, hijackings, and weather delays.

Established one of the top records in the industry by successfully loading planes and preparing them for departure in twenty minutes or less, 97% of the time. Effective planning and scheduling permitted up to four planes to be serviced simultaneously. Reduced lost time due to illness by 68% and industrial accidents by 71%.

CUSTOMER SERVICE AGENT, Miami, Florida 2/77 to 6/80. Functioned as Ticket Sales Agent, Boarding Agent, and Customer Service Representative. Provided the type of service and concern for customers which made Air Florida one of the fastest growing airlines in the U. S. Became adept at solving problems and satisfying customers' complaints. Consistently maintained monthly sales in the top 10%.

Alaska Airlines, San Francisco, California 1/76 to 2/77

CUSTOMER SERVICE AGENT - Worked closely with customers to provide the best connecting flights and make each flight an enjoyable experience.

The Spoke and Wheel, Long Beach, California 6/73 to 1/76

ASSISTANT MANAGER - Sold Peugeot and other fine bikes and purchased bikes, parts, and supplies. Managed the retail side of the business. Sales increased 42% in 1975.

ROBERTA JENNINGS
1121 Peach Drive
Atlanta, Georgia 30601
(404) 574-8769

OBJECTIVE: Airline Management

QUALIFICATIONS

Excellent Management and Supervisory capabilities. Highly respected by subordinates and able to obtain high performance levels from employees. Created one of the best on-time performance records in the airline industry.

EDUCATION

B.A. - Business, University of Southern California (1969-1973)

EMPLOYMENT

CUSTOMER SERVICE/RAMP SERVICE SUPERVISOR   Air Florida
6/80 to Present   Atlanta, Georgia

Opened the Atlanta airport facility for Air Florida and created one of its most efficient and effective operations. Supervised and trained thirty Customer Service Agents and Ramp personnel. Responsible for all day-to-day operations decisions and handled all crises related to crashes, passenger deaths and illnesses, bomb threats, hijackings, and weather delays.

Established one of the top records in the industry by successfully loading planes and preparing them for departure in twenty minutes or less, 97% of the time. Effective planning and scheduling permitted up to four planes to be serviced simultaneously. Reduced lost time due to illness by 68% and industrial accidents by 71%.

CUSTOMER SERVICE AGENT   Air Florida
2/77 to 6/80   Miami, Florida

Functioned as Ticket Sales Agent, Boarding Agent, and Customer Service Representative. Provided the type of service and concern for customers which made Air Florida one of the fastest growing airlines in the U. S. Became adept at solving problems and satisfying customers' complaints. Consistently maintained monthly sales in the top 10%.

CUSTOMER SERVICE AGENT   Alaska Airlines
1/76 to 2/77   San Francisco, California

Worked closely with customers to provide the best connecting flights and make each flight an enjoyable experience.

ASSISTANT MANAGER   The Spoke and Wheel
6/73 to 1/76   Long Beach, California

Sold Peugeot and other fine bikes and purchased bikes, parts, and supplies. Managed the retail side of the business. Sales increased 42% in 1975.

ROBERTA JENNINGS
1121 Peach Drive
Atlanta, Georgia 30601
(404) 574-8769

OBJECTIVE: Airline Management

QUALIFICATIONS

Excellent Management and Supervisory capabilities. Highly respected by subordinates and able to obtain high performance levels from employees. Created one of the best on-time performance records in the airline industry.

EDUCATION

B.A. - Business, University of Southern California (1969-1973)

EMPLOYMENT

Air Florida	Customer/Ramp Service Supervisor
Atlanta, Georgia	6/80 to Present

Opened the Atlanta airport facility for Air Florida and created one of its most efficient and effective operations. Supervised and trained thirty Customer Service Agents and Ramp personnel. Responsible for all day-to-day operations decisions and handled all crises related to crashes, passenger deaths and illnesses, bomb threats, hijackings, and weather delays.

Established one of the top records in the industry by successfully loading planes and preparing them for departure in twenty minutes or less, 97% of the time. Effective planning and scheduling permitted up to four planes to be serviced simultaneously. Reduced lost time due to illness by 68% and industrial accidents by 71%.

Air Florida	Customer Service Agent
Miami, Florida	2/77 to 6/80

Functioned as Ticket Sales Agent, Boarding Agent, and Customer Service Representative. Provided the type of service and concern for customers which made Air Florida one of the fastest growing airlines in the U. S. Became adept at solving problems and satisfying customers' complaints. Consistently maintained monthly sales in the top 10%.

Alaska Airlines	Customer Service Agent
San Francisco, California	1/76 to 2/77

Worked closely with customers to provide the best connecting flights and make each flight an enjoyable experience.

The Spoke and Wheel	Assistant Manager
Long Beach, California	6/73 to 1/76

Sold Peugeot and other fine bikes and purchased bikes, parts, and supplies. Managed the retail side of the business. Sales increased 42% in 1975.

ROBERTA JENNINGS

1121 Peach Drive   Atlanta, Georgia 30601   (404) 574-8769

OBJECTIVE   Airline Management

QUALIFICATIONS   Excellent Management and Supervisory capabilities. Highly respected by subordi-
                     nates and able to obtain high performance levels from employees. Created one of
                     the best on-time performance records in the airline industry.

EDUCATION   B.A. - Business, University of Southern California (1969-1973)

EMPLOYMENT

                     AIR FLORIDA

6/80-Present   Customer Service/Ramp Service Supervisor, Atlanta, Georgia; Miami, Florida

                     Opened the Atlanta airport facility for Air Florida and created one of its most
                     efficient and effective operations. Supervised and trained thirty Customer
                     Service Agents and Ramp personnel. Responsible for all day-to-day operations
                     decisions and handled all crises related to crashes, passenger deaths and illnesses,
                     bomb threats, hijackings, and weather delays.

                     Established one of the top records in the industry by successfully loading planes
                     and preparing them for departure in twenty minutes or less, 97% of the time.
                     Effective planning and scheduling permitted up to four planes to be serviced
                     simultaneously. Reduced lost time due to illness by 68% and industrial accidents
                     by 71%.

2/77-6/80   Customer Service Agent, Miami, Florida

                     Functioned as Ticket Sales Agent, Boarding Agent, and Customer Service Repre-
                     sentative. Provided the type of service and concern for customers which made
                     Air Florida one of the fastest growing airlines in the U. S. Became adept at
                     solving problems and satisfying customers' complaints. Consistently maintained
                     monthly sales in the top 10%.

                     ALASKA AIRLINES

1/76-2/77   Customer Service Agent, San Francisco, California

                     Worked closely with customers to provide the best connecting flights and make
                     each flight an enjoyable experience.

                     THE SPOKE AND WHEEL

6/73-1/76   Assistant Manager, Long Beach, California

                     Sold Peugeot and other fine bikes and purchased bikes, parts, and supplies.
                     Managed the retail side of the business. Sales increased 42% in 1975.

ROBERTA JENNINGS
1121 Peach Drive
Atlanta, Georgia 30601
(404) 574-8769

OBJECTIVE	Airline Management
QUALIFICATIONS	Excellent Management and Supervisory capabilities. Highly respected by subordinates and able to obtain high performance levels from employees. Created one of the best on-time performance records in the airline industry.
EDUCATION	B.A. - Business, University of Southern California (1969-1973)

EMPLOYMENT

Air Florida

6/80-Present CUSTOMER SERVICE/RAMP SERVICE SUPERVISOR, Atlanta, Georgia; Miami, Florida

Opened the Atlanta airport facility for Air Florida and created one of its most efficient and effective operations. Supervised and trained thirty Customer Service Agents and Ramp personnel. Responsible for all day-to-day operations decisions and handled all crises related to crashes, passenger deaths and illnesses, bomb threats, hijackings, and weather delays.

Established one of the top records in the industry by successfully loading planes and preparing them for departure in twenty minutes or less, 97% of the time. Effective planning and scheduling permitted up to four planes to be serviced simultaneously. Reduced lost time due to illness by 68% and industrial accidents by 71%.

2/77-6/80 CUSTOMER SERVICE AGENT, Miami, Florida

Functioned as Ticket Sales Agent, Boarding Agent, and Customer Service Representative. Provided the type of service and concern for customers which made Air Florida one of the fastest growing airlines in the U. S. Became adept at solving problems and satisfying customers' complaints. Consistently maintained monthly sales in the top 10%.

Alaska Airlines

1/76-2/77 CUSTOMER SERVICE AGENT, San Francisco, California

Worked closely with customers to provide the best connecting flights and make each flight an enjoyable experience.

The Spoke and Wheel

6/73-1/76 ASSISTANT MANAGER, Long Beach, California

Sold Peugeot and other fine bikes and purchased bikes, parts, and supplies. Managed the retail side of the business. Sales increased 42% in 1975.

HOW TO USE A RESUME

I wonder sometimes if perhaps the world is kept afloat on a sea of resumes. Nearly a billion are mailed out annually—few result in interviews. The only study I have located determined that employers were granting, on an average, one interview for every 245 resumes received, less than one-half of one percent.* Not very good odds.

Why such a low success rate? Let's consider some factors that reduce effectiveness.

1. *Shotgun Approach.* Some people send out over five hundred resumes and don't receive a single interview offer. They have simply developed or purchased a list of employers and addressed their cover letters (usually printed, almost never individually typed), "Dear Personnel Manager," "Dear Sales Manager," "Dear Mr. President," or "To Whom It May Concern." People sending out over one hundred resumes rarely take the time to discover who the person is with the power to hire them.
2. *Lack of Focus.* People really aren't sure what they're looking for, and their resumes show it.
3. *Poor-Quality Resumes.* The resume looks messy, is filled with typographical errors and misspellings, is poorly written, and doesn't really say anything about the individual. Written hastily, or an old resume slightly updated, it usually describes only duties with no hints of accomplishments.
4. *Career Changing.* Career changers have the lowest success rate when mailing resumes. On the other hand, they are often the most satisfied with the results they do achieve when they utilize the systematic job search methods recommended in this book.

Resumes traditionally have been used in three main ways: to respond to want ads, to give to employment agency counselors, and to mail out shotgun fashion to up to three hundred employers. There is a time and place for each of these strategies, but understanding and caution should be applied.

---

*Deutsch, Shea & Evans, Inc. quoted on page 63 in Electronic Design 16

WANT ADS

I recommend reading the want ads. In cities with two or more newspapers, one paper usually predominates and gets ninety-five percent of all jobs advertised. Of course, some employers will advertise in more than one paper, but generally speaking only about five percent of the jobs will be advertised in the secondary paper and *not* in the primary one. In addition, ninety-six percent of all jobs advertised will appear in the Sunday paper. For the sake of time, read only the primary paper, and read only the Sunday edition. Scan it from A to Z. Some very interesting jobs can be listed with job titles you would never expect.

Circle a job if it interests you and if you meet at least half the qualifications. Frequently the perfect candidate does not show up and employers must then compromise.

If a want ad is vague, mail out your standard resume and hope for the best. If the ad is fairly explicit concerning the desired qualifications and experience, you must decide whether to mail your standard resume with a custom cover letter or whether you will take the additional time to tailor your resume to the position. If you feel strongly enough about a position, and your standard resume does not adequately cover some key points, it is worth redoing the resume. It can double your chance of getting an interview.

Blind ads are rarely productive, but may be worth trying. Most are legitimate, placed by companies that for one reason or another want to maintain anonymity. A blind ad is a help-wanted ad in which the name of the employer has been omitted, and all you are given is a box number in care of the newspaper. If you are concerned about the ad being placed by your own company, use a pseudonym and change the names of your last three employers. Or you can send a marketing letter (see page 113). On the envelope you can also state, ''Do not forward this resume if the Employer is A.J. Dunn & Sons.''

In addition to your local paper, other good sources of want ads are the *Wall Street Journal* (Tuesdays and Wednesdays contain the most ads) and the *National Business Employment Weekly*, which carries most of the ads from all four regional editions of the *Wall Street Journal*. Both are found in most libraries. The *National Business Employment Weekly* can be found at some newsstands and costs $2.50 a copy. You can also subscribe— $15.00 for six weeks.

What kind of competition should you expect? An ad for a good position can draw up to five hundred applicants (fifty to one hundred is most typical), and rarely will more than eight people be interviewed. Your results will depend on how closely the job matches your qualifications and how much time you spend tailoring your letter and resume. If you emphasize accomplishments and potential, you will certainly get a better response than average. About twenty percent of all managers, sales workers, professionals, and clerical workers who answer ads get their jobs through a help-wanted ad.*

UNSOLICITED RESUMES

Resumes are frequently sent to employers unsolicited in hopes that a position may be available at the time the resume is received. Resume campaigns typically result in less than one interview for every hundred resumes sent out. If you use the strategy I'm about to discuss, you should get ten to fifteen interviews for every hundred resumes you mail.

Obviously you must start with an absolutely top-notch resume. Then develop a list of fifty to two hundred employers of the right size, in the right industry, and in the right geographical area. See Employer Research on page 245 to locate the best resources for obtaining names of employers. Determine the department in which you would most likely work. Making about twenty calls an hour, call each organization and ask the receptionist for the name of the appropriate executive or department head. Be sure to get the correct spelling and title. Then and only then are you ready to send out resumes. Address each cover letter and resume to the specific person who would have power to hire you. This alone will almost double your interviews than if you merely addressed it "Dear Mr. President," "Dear Marketing Manager," or "Dear Personnel Manager." If you simply cannot identify to whom your resume should go, address it to the president *by name*. The resume may still wind up in personnel, but it is just as likely that it will be delivered to the most appropriate person.

Decide whether you will follow up with a phone call to each person or simply wait for interview offers. Calling and asking for an appointment will usually result in appointments twenty to forty percent of the time, while waiting for interview offers (assuming you

---

*Department of Labor, Bureau of Labor Statistics Bulletin 1886 (1975)

have a top-quality resume and sent it to a specific person) should result in a ten- to fifteen-percent success rate. Of course your actual percentage will be determined by the quality of your resume, the amount of experience you have in the field you are seeking, the impressiveness of your accomplishments and results, the job market, and the care with which you select potential employers.

The decision to call or wait is important because it will affect the wording in your cover letter. If you will be calling for an appointment, you simply state in the letter, "I will call you next week to set up a brief appointment." This statement will cause the reader to pay more attention to the resume, to be prepared for your call, and it likely will be kept close at hand rather than filed or discarded. With the waiting approach, you can end your letter with something like, "I look forward to hearing from you soon."

A surprising finding, first described by Carl Boll in *Executive Jobs Unlimited*, is that resumes sent to the same organizations, six or more weeks after the first batch, will usually obtain results equal to the first mailing. In other words, if one hundred resumes netted you eight interviews, the second batch of one hundred should provide another eight. Give serious consideration to a second mailing.

RECEIVING CALLS

Make it easy for an employer to contact you. If you are rarely home and there will be no one else to answer your phone, consider a telephone answering machine or an answering service. Answering machines can be purchased for between $80 and $200. An answering service will take messages for you just as a secretary would. If you use an answering service, include it like this.

BETTY BABCOCK
2452 - 165th N.E.
Redmond, Washington 98052
(206) 883-0629 or 883-5907

The second number would usually be the answering service. I prefer not to identify the second number as an answering service or a message phone. Employers generally arrange interviews by phone. If they fail to reach you after three or four tries, they may simply give up. With a top-quality resume, you'll make employers want to meet you, but don't press your luck—make it easy for them to reach you. An alternative would be to include the number of a friend or relative who is usually home.

THE FUNCTIONAL RESUME

The functional resume offers some people the best way to get their story across to employers. If your strengths can readily be put into categories, then you should seriously consider using a functional resume.

A pure functional resume includes only functions with job titles; dates and names of employers are omitted. I almost never recommend a pure functional resume because it usually raises more questions than it answers. When dates and employers are omitted, hiring authorities tend to wonder if the applicant is hiding anything, such as a long gap in employment. If you have strong reasons for not revealing details of your employment, however, consider a functional resume, or a marketing letter.

Notice in Suzanne's resume on the next page, employment was included but job descriptions were not. This is common in functional resumes. In Suzanne's resume only the duties as Personnel Manager and Assistant Personnel Manager were relevant to the position she was seeking. In a chronological resume, however, she could never have devoted as much space to all her areas of experience in the Employment section as she did in Qualifications. A functional resume was her only logical choice.

Read the sample functional resumes to get a feel for their construction and what makes them effective. Although the backgrounds of the people will differ from yours, you should be able to determine whether your experience is better suited to the functional format or the more chronological format illustrated and discussed throughout the book.

When I review functional resumes, I often wonder "When and where did this experience occur?" My eyes dart up and down the page for the answers. I become frustrated because the applicant is making me work too hard. My standard format has all of the advantages of the functional resume *and* the chronological resume with virtually none of their individual drawbacks. I do, however, write a functional resume for about five percent of my clients.

SUZANNE HALL
18852 52nd S.E.
Bothell, Washington 98011
(206) 481-2756

OBJECTIVE: Personnel

QUALIFICATIONS

Personnel Management - Five years experience in Personnel with three years as Personnel Manager of a store with 230 employees. Supervised and trained a staff of four. Significantly increased morale among store personnel and successfully fought off a unionizing effort.

Recruiting, Interviewing, Hiring - Very effective interviewer. Screened and hired all sales, supervisory, clerical and support personnel. Over 80% of all people hired remained with the store at least one year. Turnover was reduced 22% by careful screening and by implementing other improvements throughout the store.

EEO - Performed periodic surveys and ensured all quotas were met as required.

Wage and Salary Administration - Identified unfair wage differentials between recent hires and those with longer service. Pay rates were improved and nearly eliminated turnover among more experienced staff.

Promotions - Worked closely with supervisors to determine those ready for promotions. Wrote all final recommendations for promotions.

Terminations - Arbitrated in all firing situations and participated in all firing interviews. Conducted all exit interviews and identified causes for termination. By taking quick action, several terminations were actually averted.

Manpower Planning - Predicted staffing needs for Christmas and major sales and hired necessary personnel.

Career Counseling - Provided extensive career path counseling to store employees.

Training and Development - Developed and conducted a sixteen-hour training program emphasizing customer service and job training. Turnover and customer complaints were reduced substantially after the program was increased from eight to sixteen hours. Supervised additional training during the probationary period.

EMPLOYMENT

Briggins Department Stores, Bothell, Washington (1970 to Present)
Personnel Manager (1980 to Present)
Assistant Personnel Manager (1980)
Schedule Coordinator (1978 to 1980)
Credit Manager (1977 to 1978)
Credit Adjustment Processor (1971 to 1977)
Sales Associate (1970 to 1971)

EDUCATION

Attended Bellevue Community College (35 credits)

PAUL SHUPBACH
2917 S. E. 112th
Pittsburgh, Pennsylvania 15203
(412) 579-0002

QUALIFICATIONS

Technical Expertise - Hands-on person. Capable of operating and troubleshooting
virtually any piece of equipment. Understand the day-to-day problems faced by
machine operators in the metal working industry and can use engineering knowledge
and plain horse sense to solve those problems.

Engineering - Degrees in Industrial Engineering and Industrial Management.

Proposals, Contracts and Negotiations - Have written and developed dozens of
proposals and negotiated over forty contracts. Heavily experienced in all types of
contracts, including DCAS, ASPR and DAR. Consistently negotiate the most
favorable terms for Cost Plus, Cost Sharing, Cost Plus Incentive Fixed, and R&D
Contracts.

Cost Management, Cost Analysis, Cost Control - Over fifteen years of Cost
Management experience with all types of products and components, including
processing equipment, engines, fiberglass and sheet metal parts. Able to establish
Program Financial Controls to pinpoint manufacturing problems and prevent cost
overruns. Expert in Value Engineering.

Cost Estimating - Experience covers all facets of manufacturing including machined
parts, sheet metal, plastics, fiberglass, and software. Highly experienced in all
methods of estimating including Parametric Estimating.

Supervision - Supervised sixty technical staff and skilled craftsmen. Always develop
smooth-functioning operations.

EDP - Work closely with programmers and systems analysts to develop all necessary
data for management decision making.

Vendor Selection - Inspect and analyze vendor facilities, equipment, capabilities and
quality. Recommendations to use a vendor have virtually always been adopted.

Sales Engineer - Marketed fabrication services in the metal working industry to
Industrial, OEM, Aerospace and Electronic accounts. Worked effectively with
architects, engineers and production supervisors to determine the most appropriate
products and the required specifications.

EDUCATION

B.A. Industrial Management, University of Pennsylvania (1964)
B.S. Industrial Engineering, University of Pittsburgh (1960)

EMPLOYMENT HISTORY

Shupbach Consulting, Pittsburgh, Pennsylvania 1975 to Present

INDUSTRIAL ENGINEERING CONSULTANT - Work on assignments ranging in length
from six months to one and a half years, primarily in the areas of Bidding, Estimating,
Selecting Vendors, Cost Management and Manufacturing Planning. Enabled one
manufacturer to obtain their first ever contract with U. S. Steel. Production expanded
from $13,000 per month to $130,000 per month with no increase in personnel.
Researched and adapted a new technology which allowed the firm to underbid all
competitors.

Dixon Wheel, Pittsburgh, Pennsylvania 1972 to 1975

COST MANAGEMENT SPECIALIST - Estimated, analyzed and monitored the costs of purchased goods and services.

Pennsylvania Division of Purchasing, Scranton, Pennsylvania 1966 to 1972

SPECIFICATION ANALYST - Developed quality standards and specifications for many raw, semi-processed and processed materials. Established practical test procedures to determine quality and compliance with specifications. The capabilities and sophistication of the Division were substantially increased through these efforts.

DAVID GOLDMAN
2430 Stoneway North
Little Rock, Arkansas 72202
(501) 254-3242

OBJECTIVE: Project Management

QUALIFICATIONS

Supervising. Took over a district with high turnover and low morale and created one of the top teams in the company. Work closely with individuals to enable both company and personal needs to be satisfied.

Negotiating. Negotiate contracts that are fair, workable and satisfactory to customer and manufacturer. Work hard to get the best for both.

Coordinating/Planning. Installations have always been completed on schedule. Maintain close contact with customers, manufacturing and field engineering to deal with all problems as they arise. Able to get commitments and favors from those not directly responsible to me.

Computers. Excellent training and broad work experience installing and maintaining computer systems.

EMPLOYMENT

Data Systems, 1969 to Present

SENIOR PROJECT MANAGER, Little Rock, Arkansas, 1978 to Present. Negotiate contracts, schedule deliveries and troubleshoot all phases of computer installations; work closely with customers to determine their needs, then gain contractual commitments from manufacturing and field engineering to install systems by specific dates. Monitor factory schedules and software support schedules to ensure delivery schedules are met. Despite many difficulties, all deliveries and installations have been completed on schedule.

DISTRICT MANAGER, FIELD ENGINEERING, Los Angeles, California, 1975 to 1978. Supervised and scheduled the work of eighteen field engineers installing and maintaining computer systems. Took over a district with high turnover, low morale, and a poor reputation for customer service. Within one year turnover was reduced from 30% to 4% annually. Response time was reduced from six hours to two hours. Functioned as Project Manager for the installation of a branch on-line system for Security Western Bank (600 branches). All installations were completed on time.

FIELD ENGINEER, Washington, D. C., 1969 to 1975. Installed and maintained systems for banks, hotels and airlines. Customers were kept very satisfied because of extremely low downtimes.

U. S. Air Force, 1965 to 1968

COMPUTER TECH - Maintained and serviced on-board aircraft computer systems. Supervised a five-man team.

EDUCATION

Field Engineering, Data Systems Manufacturing School - 6 months, 1969-1970
Computer Repair, Computer Learning Institute - 6 months, 1969
Electrical Engineering, Old Dominion University - 1 year, 1968-1969
Computer Tech School, U. S. Air Force - 9 months, 1965

IS A FUNCTIONAL RESUME FOR YOU?

You may be wondering if you should use a functional format. Most people shouldn't. A functional resume may be right for you if you agree with both of the following statements.

1. I don't think the Qualifications/Chronological Employment format is suitable to my background.
2. My background can easily be listed under categories such as Management, Supervision, Coordinating, Troubleshooter, Motivator, or Training.

If you think a functional resume may be good for you, go ahead and write one. At the very least it will be an excellent exercise and will help you clarify your strengths. After completing your resume, test it out on friends or business associates. Ask them if it does you justice and if it was easy to read. If you get positive feedback, you made the right decision. If the feedback is not positive, write a chronological resume and look for ways to use some of the material you worked so hard on. Some things will fit in the Qualifications Section while others will fit in Employment.

MARKETING LETTERS

Being different often brings positive results. Marketing letters are successful for that reason—they're different. Refreshingly different. The marketing letter presents your strongest experiences and accomplishments to entice the reader. Dates and names of employers are seldom mentioned. The marketing letter acts as a substitute for a resume with cover letter. In contrast to resumes, marketing letters are more personal in nature and more like business correspondence in appearance, consequently they are rarely screened out by secretaries.

Less than five percent of all job seekers use marketing letters, yet nothing I know of can lead to more appointments and job interviews. By sending only the marketing letter, your resume is held in reserve for later use. The key to success is addressing it to a specific person and informing that person that a phone call will follow. Your goal is to meet as many people with the power to hire as possible, regardless of whether any openings exist at the moment. This is accomplished by requesting just ten minutes of their time. For more on this strategy, see "The Systematic Job Search" beginning on page 209.

The use of marketing letters has revolutionized the way my clients find jobs. In the past I had clients cold call potential employers to ask for brief appointments. They understood the importance of the calls, knew they would work, and had practiced what they would say. However, some failed to make their calls, and those who did call, often procrastinated. Now they make their calls with much less hesitation, and the calls get easier with practice. Knowing that the person is expecting your call and is already convinced that you are a high quality person, makes a real difference psychologically. Using the marketing letter should get you in to see people with the power to hire, between forty and eighty-five percent of the time. Those needing to speak to presidents of companies should expect to make appointments ten to twenty percent of the time. Notice the impact of the following marketing letter and you'll begin to see why they get results.

1121 65th S.W.
Red Rock, California   92006
(916) 456-9874

January 28, 1988

John Campbell
Executive Vice President
Diversified Products Inc.
2187 N.E. 15th
Redding, California

Dear Mr. Campbell:

When I joined my current employer five years ago as Production Superintendent, quality control was rejecting 10% of all printed circuit
boards. Today that figure is 2% and falling.

You may be interested in a person with my broad experience in solving
production problems. Here are some other things I've done:

   Reduced absenteeism 42% and turnover 31%. With less turnover we
   invested more in training, with a corresponding increase in quality
   and productivity. While rejections have dropped from 10% to less
   than 2%, productivity has increased 22% per employee.

   Introduced an idea program with incentives. Implemented suggestions grew from four in 1984 to 65 in 1987. Bonuses cost $15,000
   in 1987 while documented savings amounted to $197,000.

   Implemented an inventory control system. Increased production 34%
   with only a 9% increase in inventory. Delays due to unavailable
   parts dropped from 186 in 1983 to 21 in 1986.

   Instituted a company-wide safety program. Lost time due to accidents was reduced 21% during the first six months. Reductions in
   insurance premiums have saved over $87,000 annually since 1985.

I graduated from the University of Wisconsin in 1968 with a degree in
business. Since then I have experienced rapid promotions during 19
years in manufacturing.

I'll call you next week to arrange a time when we might meet for
fifteen or twenty minutes.

Sincerely,

John Gaddly

   This marketing letter is especially strong because each
accomplishment has been quantified. Marketing letters always
have more impact when results are quantified, and most people

can easily come up with at least four good solid accomplishments. You can sense that an employer would want to meet such a person even if no position currently existed.

To demonstrate the flexibility of marketing letters, the next example uses more of a narrative format and is less quantifiable, yet it also has a strong impact on the reader.

11918 NE 143rd Place
Kirkland, Washington   98034
(206) 821-3830

February 14, 1988

Peter Phillips
Sahalee Development Corp.
2119 Fourth Avenue
Seattle, Washington   98124

Dear Mr. Phillips,

In anticipation of the next development upsurge, You may be looking for a person with a broad background in land development and marketing. I have saved projects from failure, reduced development costs, and increased project marketability.

Recently, at the developer's request, I was retained to save a mobile home project that had been rejected during preliminary hearings. By creating a new marketing strategy, employing a more imaginative design, and representing the client throughout the remainder of the public hearings process, I was able to negotiate the project's approval.

As part of a team of consultants for a 1900-acre/$680 million new town development, I prevented costly delays by reducing agency review time and ensuring project approval with appropriate planning and design concepts. This saved the developer hundreds of thousands of dollars in additional consultant fees and penalty payments for an extension of the land-purchase option.

I have nine years' combined experience in civil engineering, land planning, and urban design. I graduated from the University of Washingon with a B.A. in Urban Planning.

I will call you next week to arrange a time when we might meet briefly to discuss my background and your future needs.

Sincerely,

Roger Cricky

1298 N. Rosewood Ave.
Portland, Oregon 97221
(503) 682-9874

March 8, 1988

Don Harris
Vice President, Sales and Marketing
MicroCad
4309 Sepulveda Blvd. North
Los Angeles, California

Dear Mr. Harris,

I am currently looking at sales management positions with medium-sized high tech manufacturers in the Southern California area. During the last fifteen years I have worked for Datacomp and Syngestics and am currently district sales manager for a major manufacturer of computer and tele-processing equipment.

I was given a mandate three years ago to strengthen the Pacific Northwest district. During that time we have increased sales an average of 35% annually, the highest rate in company. I'm known as a motivator. I work closely with my saff to develop marketing strategies and I give them the independence they need to be effective. In 1987 we led the six districts in the region in gaining new accounts, with eighty-four.

I've been successful in both sales and sales management. As a senior account manager for six years with Datacomp, I took my territory from a ranking of 19th nationally to 7th and exceeded quota each year. I got my start in the industry with Syngestics. As a field marketing support rep for two years, my district achieved its sales quota each year. Then as area supervisor for three years, I supervised six field marketing support engineers. The staff was rated number one in the region for providing technical support, two years in a row.

With a history of success behind me, I believe I can contribute to the further growth of MicroCad. I am strong in marketing, sales training, staff recruiting, and staff development. I will call you next week to learn about your future plans.

Sincerely,

Paul Sanderson

Writing an effective marketing letter requires that you first have a results oriented resume. Once the resume is complete, the marketing letter almost writes itself. In fact, the results statements used in the marketing letter can come almost word for word from the resume.

The primary portion of any marketing letter is a description of your results and experience. To write a strong marketing letter, review your resume and think through how you want to summarize your background. If you have four to six key projects or results that can be quantified, simply describe them, as was done in the first sample marketing letter. If your background does not lend itself so easily to that approach, the more narrative form will work best for you. Although names of companies are usually not mentioned, if you choose to, that's fine. Even dates or time periods can be mentioned, but are usually not necessary.

Remember, this is not a resume. The reader is not expecting to know everything about you. Your goal is to have impact. Cause the person to recognize your value and to remember you when you call. Write like you would in a letter. Let it flow. Take a look at your qualifications statement. Perhaps it can be included almost as is. If you are going to emphasize results, they can be used almost word for word, although you'll probably want to make minor changes. Lead-ins for your results could be worded:

> You may be interested in my labor negotiating experience. Some of my additional accomplishments are:

✻

> My six years in customer relations could be valuable to you. This experience includes:

✻

> If your advertising department needs a person with strong experience, you may be interested in what I've done:

If you choose to describe past jobs, as in the third example, phrases can again be lifted from the resume. Since this is a marketing letter, you may choose to describe only the last three jobs, even if in the resume five were described. Don't be concerned if your resume and marketing letter have similar phrases in them; no one will notice.

Each marketing letter should be individually typed and addressed to the person with the power to hire. By supplying a word processing service with ten or more names at a time, you should be able to keep your costs down to about two dollars for each letter and envelope. There will be an initial inputting charge for the letter, but after that you'll essentially just be paying for printing time.

COVER LETTERS

Cover letters accompany resumes sent through the mail. The cover letter personalizes your resume and gives it greater flexibility. If your resume does not contain an objective, the cover letter is the place to express it. When answering a want ad, specify the exact job title in the cover letter. When a want ad explicitly requests certain types of experience which you have, but which is not adequately covered in the resume, use your cover letter to fill in the details. The alternative would be to rewrite your resume slightly to include the necessary details. Rewriting the resume will usually provide better results but is also more time consuming.

My advice is to not rely too heavily on the cover letter. Cover letters can easily become separated from the resume. If personnel gets the resume, the cover letter may no longer be attached by the time it reaches the person with the power to hire you. In addition, hiring authorities are more impressed with a resume which seems custom-designed for the job.

With these reservations in mind, let's look at the ingredients of an effective cover letter. Cover letters generally consist of two to four short paragraphs, and seldom total more than twenty lines. The first paragraph should open with a strong statement about you that arouses interest and curiosity. Devote a middle paragraph to an accomplishment that will further arouse interest. The accomplishment can come from your resume but should be slightly reworded. When I write cover letters, nine times out of ten I'll pick the strongest accomplishment from the resume and include it in the cover letter.

> I can save money for your firm by utilizing my experience in cost control. At Standard Products I reduced paper usage by twenty-four percent and photocopying costs by thirty percent.

☀

> I can help increase the impact of your agency. While at Family Services I wrote a proposal which was funded for $22,000. This allowed us to significantly increase the quantity and quality of our services.

Appeal to the employer's self-interest by indicating that you are a problem solver and that hiring you will lead to increased production, greater efficiency, better planning, less waste, higher profits, more satisfied customers.

In using the Systematic Job Search method (pages 209 – 244), you will want to meet the person with power to hire, even if no openings currently exist. Indicate in your cover letter that you will be calling to arrange a meeting. Avoid using the word *interview*. Use instead, "I'll call next week to arrange a brief meeting," or "I will call next week to arrange a time when we can meet." The word *interview* is always associated with formal hiring procedures; what you would like is a relaxed meeting in which you both learn more about each other.

Cover letters should be individually typed. Consider how insulting it would be to receive a printed cover letter which starts, "My research reveals that your company is one of the real leaders in the field." The fact that the letter is printed indicates that as many as one hundred companies are "leaders" in the industry. Remember, one of the purposes of the cover letter is to *personalize* your resume. Printed or photocopied resumes have been acceptable for years, but no employer wants to receive a printed cover letter.

Even if you develop a standard cover letter to be sent to one hundred or more companies, you still can make it personal. Write the cover letter so you can insert the name of the company somewhere in the body of the letter. With today's word processors and memory typewriters, this is easy and relatively inexpensive. A secretarial service should be able to type your letters and address your envelopes for about two dollars each, and each one will look perfect.

If you know the company by reputation or your research has revealed some interesting information, don't hesitate to include it in the cover letter.

One of your competitors told me Alpa has the best quality control of any winch manufacturer in the country. The quality control system I established at Braddigan Gear also became recognized as tops in the industry.

✳

Your recent acquisition of Marley & Sons indicates to me that you could use someone with my international marketing background.

✳

John McNamara at IBM believes you are one of the top management consulting firms in the country.

The recent article in Inc. Magazine about your rapid expansion was of great interest to me.

Review the sample cover letters, then simply start writing.

April 20, 1988

Mr. John Travis, Director
Home Energy Department
N. W. Center for Energy Efficiency
323 Sixth Avenue
Seattle, Washington 98021

Dear Mr. Travis:

Your recent efforts to promote energy conservation is of great interest to me. My experience as Energy Consultant for Seattle City Light would make me an excellent candidate for several positions in your organization.

While at City Light I have inspected and provided energy savings estimates on over five hundred homes. Eighty percent of the homeowners have acted on one or more of my suggestions and have averaged over seventeen percent in energy savings.

I will call you next week to arrange a brief meeting.

Sincerely,

Brad Tolliver

＊

March 11, 1988

Leslie Acosta
Regional Sales Manager
Peoples Pharmaceuticals
5825 146th Avenue S.E.
Bellevue, Washington 98006

Dear Ms. Acosta:

I was attracted to Peoples Pharmaceuticals when I read your annual report. My medical background and my human relations skills make me an excellent candidate for a sales/marketing position in your organization.

While at Danton Instruments, I was a key person involved in the writing and organization of new product manuals. My oral presentations to the sales force were always valuable and well received. District sales managers and the sales representatives themselves consistently expressed appreciation for the sales aids and information given to them. In addition, a large part of my time was spent working closely with our customers, successfully troubleshooting problems, answering questions and informing them of new products or instrument applications that might better serve their needs.

I will look forward to hearing from you soon.

Sincerely,

Sandra Gulliver

June 30, 1987

Bob Pruitt
Superintendent of Construction
Handler & Case Construction Company
1127 - 15th N.E.
Houston, Texas

Dear Mr. Pruitt:

During twenty years of construction experience, most of it in project management, I've created a record of success I'm proud of. Often working in extremely difficult circumstances, I have always completed projects on schedule and within the budget.

My experience with fast track projects and my proven ability to save money through value engineering should make me valuable on any projects you may have at this time or in the near future.

As General Superintendent of Structures on the huge $1.3 billion Ramon Air Base in Israel, my abilities were at times stretched to the limit—training inexperienced workers to become craftsmen, working in heat that nine months out of the year exceeded 100 degrees, constructing facilities for 4,000 employees and completing a five-year project in three years.

I will be calling you in a few days to learn more about your projects and to tell you more about my background.

Sincerely,

Layne Sencen

P.S. I'd be very interested in any foreign projects you may have. I proved very effective in training Portuguese and Israeli workers, and I developed excellent relations with Israeli inspectors, engineers and vendors. I pick up languages quickly, and this has been a real asset.

August 30, 1987

Paul Meyers
National Sales Manager
San Sebastian Winery
San Sebastian, California 95476

Dear Paul:

At the Blue Panda Restaurants I was always a producer. I believed, and still believe in their corporate concepts. Just as strongly I believe in San Sebastian and its family concept and would very much like to be a part of your organization. I am committed to remaining in the Northwest and am confident I could substantially increase your wine sales in this region.

I know the wine business. I personally trained all my waiters and waitresses in the art of selling wine. At all my restaurants wine sales experienced dramatic increases. I have a personality well suited to wine sales and would like to talk to you further to discuss opportunities.

✳

Your ad for a Western Region Dealer Representative was of great interest to me. I am very impressed with the Mitsubishi Company and the cars it produces. I would very much like to be a part of Mitsubishi, particularly in the area of Service.

I know what is required to make Service and Parts Departments run smoothly and profitably. Just knowing isn't enough, however. I also have the ability to develop close working relations with the dealership owners and the parts and service managers. They're willing to try my suggestions and invariably they work. I believe my results speak for themselves. In Hawaii I worked closely with six VW dealerships. Most were poorly managed and barely making money. The service departments were all losing money. Within a year their appearances were tremendously improved, mechanics and service managers had received additional training, and quality control and inventory control systems had been established. Parts sales jumped, and sales of new cars rose from sixty per month to over four hundred per month.

I was raised in the automotive business, and that is where I am still committed. My experience in Hawaii is just one example of what I have been able to do with dealerships. Please feel free to contact me so I can tell you more about my background.

✳

As a Project Manager and Construction Manager for Danson Construction, I have overseen both large and small projects. As an architect I can design projects or work with an architect to come

121

up with the best and most cost effective design. I have hired contractors and have been very successful in making sure the projects were completed on time and were of high quality.

My degree in Architecture, along with four years experience in designing, cost estimating and managing construction projects, plus nearly one year of drafting, make me an ideal candidate for your Facilities Engineer position. I am a person of high energy, which has enabled me to watch the many details of a construction project and make sure everything was completed correctly. That same energy and hard work will prove most helpful as I oversee projects at your many facilities along the East Coast.

✳

During my sixteen years in the dental industry, I have become very familiar with the Wilson Gold Refinery Company. Without a doubt the quality of your products is among the best.

Since 1978 I have sold gold and dental products for K. L. Dental covering Washington, Oregon, Idaho, Montana and Alaska. My gold sales have averaged over 200,000 pennyweights per year. Throughout this territory I have established a reputation for integrity and service. My technical knowledge in the dental field is unsurpassed.

I have recently left K. L. Dental and would be very interested in talking to you about covering the Western States. My customers are very loyal to me personally. In the first year with Wilson I undoubtedly can sell 90,000 pennyweights and increase that to 120,000 by the second year.

I will call you next week so we can arrange a time and place where we can get together.

✳

Since age eleven, I have wanted to work as a flight attendant. Restaurant work provides an excellent background since the duties and responsibilities are so similar.

I moved up into restaurant management so quickly because I proved I could handle the responsibility. I mix very well with customers and their guests and make each one feel important. This has increased the number of steady customers at each restaurant I have worked.

I am also a problem solver. At Leo's I helped reduce operating costs significantly. At J. K. Jake's I reduced turnover by working more closely with the staff. At Wooden Lake and Ashki's I helped lay the groundwork so they could be successful from the day they opened.

I am very much looking forward to interviewing for a flight attendant position.

✻

I have had a very exciting nine years in hotel sales, six of those years as Director of Sales. During that time I have developed highly successful techniques for attracting association and corporate business.

I would enjoy very much the opportunity to describe in more detail why those techniques have worked so well, and why I would function effectively as your next Sales Manager.

✻

Can you use a production manager with the ability to . . .

Increase productivity 14 percent per employee through the introduction of quality circles?

Decrease absenteeism 19 percent?

Decrease lost time due to industrial accidents 26 percent through a low-cost but highly effective safety program?

Reduce rejected parts 21 percent?

During four years with Alliance Screw my staff and I achieved these documented results. Because of the exciting changes you have introduced at Benson Industries since becoming president, I would very much like to be a part of your management team.

On the assumption that you may soon need abilities of this type, I will call in a few days to learn when we might get together to discuss opportunities.

RESUME SAMPLES

Over seventy sample resumes have been included to be used as guides. Find several resumes which come close to your background and study them. Notice what makes them effective. The people seem like real, living people, a quality rarely found in resumes.

Note: Most of the resumes included are all on one page. Many were originally two pages but were shortened by removing a job or two or by eliminating Personal Data. Determine for yourself whether your resume should be on one or two pages.

Special Groups

ADVICE FOR SPECIAL GROUPS

Some people have special issues or problems to deal with in writing a resume. Specific advice along with sample resumes have been provided for graduating college students, women returning to the workforce, those over fifty, people who use portfolios, military personnel, computer programmers, salespeople, and career changers.

GRADUATING COLLEGE STUDENTS

Don't be depressed because you don't have ten years' experience. You'll probably be competing with other college graduates who are in exactly the same situation—lots of low-paid summer and part-time jobs. Don't look down on those jobs, however, since they can reveal many positive attributes. Make the most of any related experience you have. Bookkeeping is valuable for an accounting major. It's not the same as accounting, but it is excellent, practical experience and is recognized as such by employers. A forestry major would emphasize any work with a timber company even if it was menial summer work.

As a recent or soon-to-be graduate, you have four things to sell: your education, your personality and character, related work experience, and work experience in general. Since you probably have little or no related work experience, the majority of space on your resumes will be devoted to revealing your personality and character. Employers need to sense the type of employee you will be. College graduates typically remain with their first employers a very short time, so it's fair for employers to try to find those who will stay longer and who will also learn quickly and become an asset to the organization.

So look for ways to reveal your personal qualities. Citing offices held in high school and college reveals leadership and responsibility. Lettering in sports indicates learning the value of teamwork and cooperation. Excellent grades indicate discipline and intellectual capacity. Participation in debate and theater can reveal speaking ability, quick thinking, and willingness to take risks. Participating in school committees and organizations reveals responsibility, willingness to put out a little extra, and loyalty.

The Qualifications section of a resume is an excellent place to describe some of the qualities you want an employer to know about.

OBJECTIVE: Mathematics/Statistics

QUALIFICATIONS

Excellent training in math and statistics.

Have always maintained excellent relations with my immediate superior. Always a valued employee. Very loyal, cooperative and easy to work with.

Work well under pressure, learn quickly, hard working.

You may have noticed that none of these statements was backed up with facts. The student who wrote this statement picked qualities which she knows to be true about herself; she is more than ready to give details or examples during an interview. Pick the qualities you mention carefully. Be sure they are accurate—don't pick them just because they sound good. You may get an interview as a result, but you'll never get the job unless the "you" in person matches the "you" on paper.

Students who earn fifty percent or more of their total college and living expenses should consider stating it in the resume.

Holding offices in college is nearly always beneficial, but be careful about fraternity and sorority offices. Before you make a decision, remember that while most people hold neutral feelings about Greek organizations, there are more people who hold strong feelings against than for them. It may not be worth the risk. As an alternative you might state "President of living group."

Class projects are often worth mentioning under Special Projects or under Education. Maybe you were in a group of business students who developed a complete marketing plan for a small company or a group of industrial engineering students who solved an actual manufacturing problem.

You will notice that most of the sample resumes for recent college graduates have included coursework. This was done to show the options available. You must decide if including courses would be beneficial to you. If you think you want to include courses but don't want to use much space, Paul Husted's example on page 131 would be useful. Seeing your coursework will be appreciated by some employers because it gives them a better sense of your training. Those employers who are not interested in your coursework will simply skip over it.

JOHN ETTER

Current Address
426 Harris Hall
Burlington, Vermont 05401
(802) 795-2631

Permanent Address
1227 Pineway N.W.
Ascutney, Vermont 05030
(802) 683-2796

OBJECTIVE: Entry Level Training Position

QUALIFICATIONS

Excellent program development skills. Developed new intramural programs and increased participation by women 220%.

Strong research and writing ability.

Speak well before the public. Won numerous debate tournaments and placed fifth in the 1982 national tournament.

Cooperate well with supervisors; reliable and responsible; work hard and complete projects on schedule.

EDUCATION

B.A. - History, University of Vermont, will graduate June 1983 (3.6 GPA)
Business Courses: History of 20th Century Business, Macroeconomics, Micro-economics

PUBLICATIONS

"Effects of the Abolition Movement in Burlington, Vermont 1826 to 1866" Vermont Historical Society Quarterly, January 1983 edition.

AWARDS

"Outstanding History Senior" selected by the History Faculty (1983)
Fifth place, national debate tournament, extemporaneous speaking (1982)

EMPLOYMENT

University of Vermont, Burlington, Vermont 9/81 to Present

DIRECTOR OF INTRAMURAL SPORTS - Planned, staffed and organized the intramural sports program. Working with a tight budget, assessed equipment needs, received bids from sporting goods suppliers, and purchased sports equipment. Supervised two assistants and recruited and supervised many volunteers. Developed a new concept in women's athletics and actively promoted the program. Participation by women grew from 20% in previous years to 76%. Maintained the high participation rate in the men's program and organized a successful basketball refereeing clinic.

Summer Employment:

RECORDS CLERK, Stephenson Steel, Ascutney, Vermont 6/82 to 9/82
MAIL SORTER, U.S. Postal Service, Ascutney, Vermont 6/81 to 9/81
LABORER, Isaacson Contracting, Ascutney, Vermont 6/80 to 9/80
FARM WORKER, John Tyler, Ascutney, Vermont 6/79 to 9/79

POLLY GLADSON
275 S. Pine Blvd.
Henniker, New Hampshire
(603) 971-2653

OBJECTIVE

Entry level accounting position within a certified public accounting firm.

QUALIFICATIONS

Excellent college training and on-the-job experience. Have worked closely with a CPA firm and helped prepare taxes. Prepared documents for an IRS audit. Have practical business experience handling all bookkeeping functions at a busy restaurant.

EDUCATION

B.A. - Accounting, New England College, 3.21 GPA (June, 1983)

EXPERIENCE

Gulliver's Restaurant, Henniker, New Hampshire (1/77 to Present, full time)

Waitress (2/82 to Present). Able to read and understand customers and determine how they want to be served. Highly professional. Provide outstanding service and consistently receive the highest tips among the restaurant staff.

Bookkeeper (4/78 to 2/82). Responsible for accounts receivable, reconciling charge slips, payroll, balancing five registers, recovering on bad checks, reconciling petty cash and inventorying bar supplies monthly. Tracked daily receipts and found proof of theft by two managers. Monitored costs by preparing monthly reports comparing gross sales to labor costs for each department.

Worked closely with accountant and prepared figures as requested. Each year helped auditor track and reconcile all financial transactions. A 1981 IRS audit stated the books were very complete and accurate. Highly respected and trusted - had full access to safe and every part of restaurant. Missed only five days of work in five years.

Podium Hostess (1/77 to 4/78). Redesigned the reservation system which significantly improved service to customers. Developed excellent relations with customers and helped create a loyal clientele. Trained seating hostesses in all facets of the job.

Village Inn, Henniker, New Hampshire (6/76 to 1/77, full time)

Hostess/Waitress - Greeted and seated customers, opened and closed the restaurant and prepared the registers each day.

ACTIVITIES

Member, American Society of Women Accountants
Active in jazz dancing and dog obedience training.

STEVE JONES
1459 134th Place N.E.
Bellevue, Washington 98024
(206) 455-1276

OBJECTIVE: Management Training Position

QUALIFICATIONS

Strong education and experience in business. Valued as a hard worker and for sound judgment. Effective in stressful situations. Friendly, personable, and easy to work with. Gain confidence of people quickly.

EDUCATION

B.S. - Economics, University of Puget Sound (1983-1987)

Coursework included: Accounting, Managerial Accounting, Business Statistics, Business Calculus, Management, Business Law, Money and Banking, Labor Market Issues, International Corporations, Macroeconomics, Microeconomics, Labor Economics, Econometrics, Collective Bargaining, BASIC.

SPECIAL PROJECTS

Planned and organized the UPS 1987 Spring Parents Weekend and set a new record for attendance. Arranged programs and activities, obtained speakers, made hotel arrangements, ordered food, and headed up a four person committee. Increased attendance 20% over the previous year. Evaluations by parents indicated it was the best organized program since its inception in 1977.

Published the first Parents Association Newsletter sent to 5,000 parents of UPS students. The first two editions were well received and the newsletter has become an official school publication published three times each year.

Awards Coordinator (1986 and 1987) for the Spring Awards Luncheon. Obtained nominations from faculty and administrators for worthy students, formed selection committees, and selected presenters. Due to more effective publicity than in the past, increased attendance 31%.

SUMMER EMPLOYMENT

Green Oaks Apartments, Renton, Washington 5/87-9/87

ASSISTANT RESIDENT MANAGER - Supervised three full-time employees and had responsibility for leasing and maintaining a complex with 160 units made up of apartments, duplexes, and single family homes. Collected rent, purchased supplies, patrolled the premises, and responded to emergencies on a twenty-four hour per day basis. Supervised a $9000 renovation project made necessary by the poor upkeep of the previous management company. Renovation resulted in the quick renting of sixteen of the twenty vacant units.

Smith & Company, Inc., Seattle, Washington 6/86 - 9/86

ASSISTANT PROPERTY MANAGER - Coordinated weekly with the resident managers at four apartment complexes with a total of one thousand units. Inspected the properties, collected rent from past due renters, and purchased supplies.

PAUL HUSTE
18706 - 192nd Avenue NE
Woodinville, Washington 98072
(206) 778-2512

OBJECTIVE: Forest Engineer

QUALIFICATIONS

Excellent training and experience in Forest Engineering. On-the-job experience with unit layouts, designing and construction staking of roads, selecting landings and road locations, running skyline profiles, surveying property lines, and supervising P-Line surveys.

Experienced with Theodolite, Electronic Distance Measuring Device, Transit, Level, Hand and Staff Compass, Clinometer, Relaskope, Chainsaws and interpreting aerial photos.

Received strong recommendation from each employer.

EDUCATION

B.S. - Forest Engineering, University of Washington GPA 3.5 (Graduate June 1983)
A.A. - Forest Technology, Everett Community College (1979)

Coursework in Statics, Soil Mechanics, Engineering Drafting, Computer Programming, Road Engineering, Hydraulics, Engineering Mechanics, Construction, Logging Plan and Design, Engineering Economics, Plane Surveying, Topographic and Route Surveying, and Aerial Photogrammetry and Mapping.

SPECIAL PROJECT

With 15 Forest Engineering students developed a complete logging plan for a section of state land. Wrote and designed preliminary plan, did reconnaissance, performed P-Line surveys, designed roads, did construction staking and laid out units. Developed a complete cost analysis covering road construction, logging, and hauling costs.

FORESTRY EXPERIENCE

Northern Pacific Timber Co., Tacoma, Washington 6/82 to 9/82

LOGGING ENGINEER - Completed road and cutting unit reconnaissance to determine locations of roads, landings, and unit boundaries. Developed trial grade lines and laid out roads in the field. Established center lines and right of way boundaries, and in difficult terrain developed paper plans and did construction staking. Did property line surveying and corner locations using staff compass and theodolite. Placed roads and units on map after traversing.

U. S. Forest Service, Skykomish, Washington

PRESALE FOREST TECHNICIAN 5/81 to 9/81. Through reconnaissance laid out units and selected locations for landings. Ran skyline profiles on cliffs and other trouble spots to ensure logging operations were feasible. Performed traversing functions after units were laid out. Units were logged by helicopter and by cable operations. Assisted in slash and burn activities.

PRESALE FOREST TECHNICIAN 6/80 to 9/80. Involved in cutting unit reconnaissance and layout, unit traversing, running skyline profiles, marking timber for thinnings, and slashburning.

131

TENSLEY WARNER
1526 28th SE
Morgantown, West Virginia 26505
(304) 271-9872

OBJECTIVE: Technical Writer

QUALIFICATIONS

Strong technical background developed through coursework leading to a Bachelor's Degree in Zoology.

Work well independently and as part of a team.

Excellent writing skills. Able to write clearly and concisely. Consistently earned A's on writing assignments.

Able to gather information from many sources and tie it all together. In numerous reports and essays successfully synthesized large amounts of data and created very readable documents.

EDUCATION

B.A. Zoology, West Virginia University (1979-1983)

Writing (25 hours) Bioscientific Vocabulary, Publication Editing, Magazine Layout, Expository Writing, English - 3.50 G.P.A.

Sciences (98 hours) Biology, Chemistry, Physics, Anthropology, Fisheries, Environmental Sciences - 3.30 G.P.A.

Mathematics (13 hours) Calculus, Computer Programming, Statistics - 3.10 G.P.A.

WORK EXPERIENCE

Janitor, Landor Company, 1978 to Present (Full- and part-time)
Laborer, Bowdish Construction, Summer 1977

PERSONAL DATA

Birthdate: 6/20/58   Excellent Health   5'11", 158 pounds

References Available Upon Request

132

JOANNA PIERCE
3619 15th SW
Lincoln, Nebraska 68124
(402) 564-8217

OBJECTIVE: Ultrasound Design Engineer

QUALIFICATIONS

Strong interest in ultrasound engineering. B.S. in Electrical Engineering to be
completed in June, 1983. Studied ultrasound technology and have hands-on experience
with ultrasound equipment.

Always a highly valued employee. Work quickly and efficiently and work well with
superiors and coworkers. As a Medical Laboratory Technician maintained excellent
relations with doctors and patients.

EDUCATION

Electrical Engineering, University of Nebraska, B.S. to be completed June, 1983
Certificate - Medical Laboratory Technician, Brakken Community College (1975)

COURSEWORK

Engineering - Technical Report Writing, FORTRAN, Engineering Graphics, Engineering
Problem Solving, Engineering Physics, Engineering Dynamics, Statics, Advanced
Calculus, Digital Electronic and Computer Logic, Solid State Electronic Physics,
Electrical Circuits, Semiconductor Circuits, Electrostatics and Magnetism. Spring
1983 - Semiconductor Circuit Design, Electrical Engineering Laboratory, Digital
Systems Design.

Ultrasound/Radiography - Ultrasound Physics, Ultrasound Mechanics and Diagnostics,
Human Anatomy and Physiology, Radiography.

EMPLOYMENT

Gall-BioAssay Medical Laboratory, Lincoln, Nebraska 6/75 to 9/79

MEDICAL LABORATORY TECHNICIAN - Performed manual clinical blood chemistry
analysis. Drew blood and tested serum blood cholesterol, uric acid, triglycerides, total
lipids and others. Frequently complimented for ability to work well with patients and
doctors. Very fast, efficient and accurate with tests.

MEMBERSHIPS

IEEE - member since 1982. Read two bimonthly journals, Bio-Medical Engineering and
Sonics and Ultrasonics.

133

WOMEN RETURNING TO THE WORKFORCE

Typically you are thirty-five to fifty, worked for a few years before and/or right after getting married, and haven't held a full-time position for perhaps ten years or more. You're probably not feeling very confident, and you probably feel there is nothing of substance to put in your resume. You couldn't be more wrong. You *undoubtedly* have some valuable experiences to put on a resume.

Volunteer Activities

Volunteer activities are jobs you didn't get paid to do. They can be as mundane as licking stamps or as interesting and challenging as organizing a blood donor drive, or handling public relations for a small nonprofit organization. If you consistently spent ten or more hours weekly on a volunteer position, treat it as a job with a job title and a job description, with results included. In the resume there is no need to state the number of hours spent weekly. If an employer is curious you can explain in the interview.

If more of your volunteer activities were of short duration, you could treat them as projects (see Special Projects page 42). Concentrate on results, but also describe duties.

Make the most out of each activity. If you held an office, say so. If you obtained excellent results, describe them. *Don't be modest.*

Focus

How good a position you get depends on your resume and how well focused you are. There is probably no need to return to school for a degree, but you may need to study your preferred field on your own or take a few classes at your local community college. Study enough to know the terms, history, and trends in your field. The person with little recent paid work experience usually needs special assistance. Look for organizations which help women re-entering the job market. If you are divorced or widowed you may qualify for a "displaced homemakers" program. Such programs can really help women get through an emotionally trying period and help them make the transition back into the workforce. In addition to developing job-finding skills, you'll receive valuable support from the counselor and the members of the group.

If your area has no such organization, find someone you can work with who is also going through a job search. Encourage each other. Studies show that working with someone typically cuts the job search time by twenty-five percent or more.

SHARRON COSGRAVE
526 South State Street
Wilmington, Delaware 19803
(302) 543-9161

OBJECTIVE: Administrative Assistant to Director of Nonprofit Agency

QUALIFICATIONS

Strong experience in developing effective new programs, motivating and coordinating large numbers of volunteers, and making office systems more efficient.

Excellent fundraiser. Have written three successful grant proposals, one of which was funded for $20,000. Through PTA fundraising activities increased revenue 36% above the previous record.

EDUCATION

University of Delaware, Liberal Arts 96 credits, 1962 to 1964

PROJECTS/ACTIVITIES

PTA President, Robert Frost Elementary, 1982 to Present. Increased attendance at monthly meetings from 51 to an average of 107. Worked with principal and teachers to develop six new volunteer programs for parents. Participation in one or more of the fifteen programs and functions increased from 26% of parents to 58%. Because of active parent involvement, vandalism at the school decreased to almost zero.

Fundraising Chairperson, Robert Frost PTA 1981 to 1982. Coordinated the efforts of over 200 children and 95 adults in six fundraising activities. Raised funds at a level 36% above the previous record.

Board Member, Wilmington Crisis Clinic, 1977 to Present. Analyze and approve annual budgets, interview and select new directors, and study proposed program changes. President of the board 1980 and 1981. Wrote grant proposal which obtained $20,000 from HEW.

President, Wilmington Chapter, MADD (Mothers Against Drunk Drivers) 1980 to Present. Organized the local chapter and tripled dues-paying membership each year. Testified as an expert witness before the Delaware Legislature. Coordinated state-wide lobbying efforts and helped pass legislation which significantly strengthened laws against drunk driving.

Train and sell thoroughbred horses. Actively training eight to ten horses at a time. Travel throughout the East Coast to inspect and buy thoroughbred colts. Consistently obtain one thousand dollars profit on each horse. Actively involved since 1972.

EMPLOYMENT

McClinton, Brandeis & Nelson, Wilmington, Delaware 7/64 to 9/66

OFFICE MANAGER - Handled bookkeeping, payroll, bank statements, accounts payable and accounts receivable. Purchased office equipment and supplies. Greeted clients, answered phones, scheduled court reporters for depositions, and developed an improved appointment and court scheduling system for eight attorneys.

JANICE STEVENS
4060 W. Warwick
Chicago, Illinois 60626
(312) 476-2917

OBJECTIVE: Assistant Store Manager of small retail shop

QUALIFICATIONS

Excellent retail experience. Work very effectively with customers - able to identify needs, tactfully answer questions, sell products and services, and solve problems.

EDUCATION

Northeastern Illinois University, Psychology, 20 credits 1979 to 1982
Bates Community College, Liberal Arts, 42 credits 1966 to 1968

WORKSHOPS

Window Dressing, Retail Merchants Association, 12 class hours (1983)
Retail Bookkeeping, Retail Merchants Association, 24 class hours (1983)
Buying for the 80's, Retail Merchants Association, 14 class hours (1982)
Retail Selling/Know Your Customer, Retail Merchants Association, 20 class hours
   (1982)

EMPLOYMENT

Debbie's Designs, Chicago, Illinois 2/83 to 4/83

STORE MANAGER - During extended vacation of store owner, functioned as Store Manager. Consulted with customers in the selection and coordination of furniture, fabrics, carpeting, wallpaper, draperies, and gift items. Purchased and priced all items and developed attractive displays.

Illinois Arts & Crafts Association, Chicago, Illinois 9/74 to 8/79

GALLERY ASSISTANT - Assisted customers in the purchase of art objects, explained the processes used by each artist, and trained and supervised other volunteers. Handled numerous details for the annual arts and crafts fair, including registering artists, assisting jurors, judging art work, and overseeing sales and bookkeeping.

THOSE OVER 50

The greatest concern of people over fifty years of age is usually age discrimination. Of course, we know that federal law prohibits discrimination on the basis of age, but we also know that it persists in both overt and subtle ways. You must decide whether you will reveal your age, since employers by law cannot ask your age or birthdate. Your resume should contain only information you choose to reveal to an employer. An insurance executive, age fifty-nine, decided it was in his best interest not to include age. We took off his birthdate from Personal Data, changed "U. S. Navy 1942-1947" to "U. S. Navy, Honorable Discharge," and eliminated his first two positions after college, which accounted for six years of work experience. Deceptive? Not at all. It is the law of the land not to discriminate on the basis of age.

On the other hand, make the most of your experience and maturity. Some people unnecessarily worry that youth always has the edge. In your resume, during interviews, and during all verbal communications, reveal yourself to be an energetic and youthful person, but one who has the maturity and sound judgment that comes only with age and experience. If you have planned your career carefully, you will probably be at a level where only those with similar age, experience, and results will even be considered as qualified. If that is not your case, then simply recognize that your age is another barrier that must be overcome. Everyone has handicaps, but the only really handicapped people are those who dwell on them.

TRENTON McGRATH
2215 Broadway North
Minneapolis, Minnesota 55402
(612) 785-2761

OBJECTIVE: Sales/Marketing Management

QUALIFICATIONS

Complete knowledge of Mortgage Lending/Mortgage Finance/Secondary Markets.

Recognized as an outstanding trainer and motivator of sales staffs. Substantially increased market share in each position held.

Broad marketing experience. Developed and marketed new products and services which have consistently been accepted in the financial community.

Develop effective internal controls and always operate within budget.

EMPLOYMENT

Diversified Mortgage Insurance Company, Minneapolis, Minnesota 1/74 to Present

REGIONAL VICE PRESIDENT 1/81 to Present, St. Louis, Houston. Moved into a troubled sixteen-state zone and increased market share 61% from 3.2% to 5.2%. Aggressively marketed new services and became active with the Bond Business, Pension Funds, Swaps, and assisting lenders with Portfolio Sales. Increased market share in Texas 220% by strongly marketing mortgage insurance and secondary trading. Traveled extensively and worked closely with four district sales managers and twenty sales people.

SENIOR VICE PRESIDENT, SALES AND MARKETING 12/79 to 1/81, Minneapolis. Developed and implemented a reorganization of the national sales force, moving from 12 divisions to 4 zones. Reorganization has been credited with strengthening DMI's national market share. Took part in the development of the Mortgage Finance Unit which has successfully moved DMI into new markets. Developed strategies for participation in Mortgage Revenue Bonds, Pass Through Certificates, Pension Funds Issues, Builder Buy-downs and Pay-through Bonds.

VICE PRESIDENT, NORTHWEST DIVISION MANAGER 9/77 to 12/79, Portland. Covering nine western states, trained and supervised a staff of nine account executives, three underwriters and two secondary market managers. Increased market share in the territory by 88%. Traveled extensively throughout the territory and made calls on CEOs.

PRODUCT MANAGER 1/74 to 9/77, Minneapolis, Minnesota. Developed and implemented marketing plans for specialized insurance products for mortgage lending financial institutions - Error/Omission Coverage, Special Hazard Coverage, and Directors/Officers/Employees Liability Coverage. Responsible for national marketing of the products. Sales volume for these products increased sevenfold in six months.

American Insurance Company, Atlanta, Georgia 6/70 to 1/74

DIRECTOR OF FIELD OPERATIONS 6/72 to 1/74, Atlanta. Had total responsibility for sales production of six regional and twenty-one state managers. Introduced new mortgage life and disability insurance programs and created a highly effective sales training program.

REGIONAL MANAGER 5/71 to 6/72, St. Louis. Supervised operations of four state managers and personally generated new business in metropolitan St. Louis.

STATE MANAGER 6/70 to 5/71, Oakland. Developed new business and supervised sales personnel within the State of California.

Niagara Home Life Assurance Company, Palo Alto, California 8/64 to 6/70

ASSISTANT VICE PRESIDENT - Negotiated exclusive contracts with S&Ls for the sale of Niagara Home Life's Mortgage Life Plan and Disability Plan. Designed and implemented a specialized Insured Savings Plan for Savings and Loan depositors which had an excellent effect on insurance sales. Recruited and trained sales agents.

Prior Employment

SALES AGENT/TRAINER, Home Owners Security, Inc. 2/62 to 8/64
SALES AGENT/TRAINER, Home Security Associates 2/61 to 2/62

RENALDO GUEVARA
3516 Alhambra Blvd.
Albuquerque, New Mexico 87109
(505) 876-2917

OBJECTIVE: Lithography Management/Production

QUALIFICATIONS

Expertise in all phases of color work, including Stripping, Color Separation, Camera Screening, Dot Etching and operating a scanner.

Strong production management background. Provide excellent training for employees and always maintain very low turnover. Developed reputation for turning out extremely high quality work.

At Color Printers and Shenson purchased equipment which significantly reduced production costs. Thoroughly researched available products and selected equipment which would be compatible with future expansion.

EMPLOYMENT

Shenson Colorgraphics, Albuquerque, New Mexico 6/76 to 5/83

PLANT SUPERINTENDENT 11/79 to 5/83. Managed all plant production—supervised six lithographers, scheduled work, and kept it flowing at peak efficiency. Duties included stripping, camera separation, camera screening, dot etching, and scanner operation. Researched, tested and purchased new equipment which significantly reduced production costs and increased quality. Maintained and repaired all equipment.

PRODUCTION 6/76 to 11/79. Proofmaker, Camera Operator, Scanner Operator, Stripper and Dot Etcher. Maintained and repaired all equipment.

Color Printers, Phoenix, Arizona 4/56 to 6/76

FOREMAN, PREP DEPARTMENT 6/69 to 5/76. Supervised four employees and did production work, including stripping, camera work, proofing and platemaking. Scheduled jobs, approved all finished work and estimated costs. Purchased new equipment and personally maintained and repaired all equipment in the shop.

FOREMAN, PREP AND PRESS DEPARTMENTS 4/56 to 6/69. Supervised seven employees, scheduled and inspected jobs and maintained tight schedules. Serviced and repaired equipment.

This resume was set in Zapf Book Light Roman and Helvetica Bold Italic.

140

PEOPLE WITH PORTFOLIOS

Architects, drafters, artists, designers, photographers, models, writers, and others all use portfolios to help sell themselves. They often mistakenly place too little emphasis on a top-quality resume, assuming the portfolio alone will sell them.

As important as your portfolio is, don't shortchange yourself. There are lots of talented people out there with outstanding portfolios. Taking the time to develop an effective resume will make an important difference to your job hunting success. Your resume can reveal qualities and background that won't come across in your portfolio. A portfolio can express your technical or creative ability, but a resume reveals where you've been and how you developed your ability. In fact, without an effective resume you often won't get the opportunity to show that fantastic portfolio you so painstakingly put together.

Artistic people are stereotyped as temperamental. In your resume do everything possible to demonstrate that you are flexible and easy to work with.

Consider reproducing two or three samples of your work on 8½" x 11" paper and making them an attachment to your resume. Reviewing the samples a week or two later will help the employer remember both you and your portfolio better. Writers should attach clippings or short pieces for a similar effect.

Graphic artists and designers should feel free to come up with creative formats for their resumes. This is one of the few groups of people who will benefit from having a resume typeset since it is an opportunity to show their ability.

BOBBIE BLANE
1127 Mariposa Drive
Santa Barbara, California 93110
(805) 651-2720

OBJECTIVE: Graphics/Illustration Artist

QUALIFICATIONS

Develop excellent relations with clients and have satisfied even the most demanding. Specialty is personality portraiture used in advertising.

Excellent graphics and illustration training and experience. Skilled in design, layout, paste-up, lettering, story boards, and the use of darkrooms and stat cameras. Knowledgeable of printing procedures and experienced in preparing work for printing.

EDUCATION

Bachelor of Fine Arts, Illustration, Seymour Art Center (1981)

EMPLOYMENT

Freelance Work 1977 to Present

Painted and sold over forty-five portraits and scenes using water color, graphite, pen and ink, egg tempura, and oil (1976 to Present).

Provided graphics and illustration for numerous projects: notebook cover, Advancetec (1983); brochure cover, Barr & Associates (1983); map and tour guide, Santa Barbara Museum of Natural History (1982); catalog and advertising design, Briton Engineering (1981); work order design, Armor Advertising (1981); logo and menu design, Silk Oyster Restaurant (1981); logo, business card design, Donner Electronics, Inc. (1981).

Johnathan Edwards Galleries, Santa Barbara, California 6/82 to Present

ART DEALER — Assist customers in purchasing art works for both personal viewing and as investments. Help customers in understanding the artist and the art piece. In a short time, have developed an excellent reputation for knowledge, helpfulness, and tact. Already seeing many repeat customers.

Redecorate the gallery as new works are shown and touch up damaged pieces. Commissioned through the gallery to do portraits. Currently showing several personal works of children and scenes including "Cool Mist," "High Noon," "Children in the Sun."

This resume was set in Clarendon Light Roman and Benguiat Gothic Bold and Medium.

CRAIG ANDERSON
131 124th SE
Inglewood, California 90301
(213) 597-2513

OBJECTIVE:

Mechanical Design position where my abilities and experience can be challenged and expanded in professional growth.

QUALIFICATIONS:

Eight years of design, drafting, and field experience includes: plumbing, fire protection, HVAC and piping systems for industrial, commercial, residential, governmental, and institutional facilities. Field surveying and preparation of contract shop drawings. Checking of plans and field coordination during construction of mechanical systems.

EDUCATION:

A.A.—Plumbing Design, Santana Community College (1976)

EXPERIENCE:

Sanders Engineering, Los Angeles, California—5/81 to 1/84

PLUMBING DESIGNER—Design and preparation of contract drawings and details for the Mechanical Department. Major projects include: Hospital remodel and addition, Austin Memorial Hospital, Austin, California. Concept drawings: 400-bed hospital medical center, Lackland Air Force Base. Complete design: Petersburg General Hospital, Petersburg, Alaska; NOAA Research Laboratory, San Diego, California; 30-floor office building, Los Angeles, California; laundry, warehouse and nursing home care facility, Los Angeles, California.

Holmes & Narver, Inc.—Orange, California—2/79 to 5/81

PLUMBING DESIGNER—Designed and prepared contract drawings and details for the Building Mechanical Systems Department. Major projects included: desalinization, sewage and diesel-fuel oil power plants, a computer facility plumbing system, including compressed air and vacuum piping, and a $600,000,000 brewery facility expansion.

Stensrud Mechanical Contractors, Boston, Massachusetts—7/76 to 2/79

DETAIL DRAFTSMAN—One of five detail draftsmen in firm which worked closely with field engineers and contractors for commercial building projects. Experience included: plumbing layout, field coordinating. Much of responsibility was working at project sites.

This resume was set in Video Medium and Quadrata Bold Roman.

MILITARY PERSONNEL

To write a successful resume, the person with six to thirty years in the military needs to have confidence that the abilities he or she possesses are marketable. Without that assurance the resume will probably come out bland and next to useless. Feel good about yourself. Regardless of your function in the military, you developed skills which are valuable in the civilian job market. Those responsible for getting you to re-enlist have probably painted a pretty bleak picture of the difficulties of finding a civilian job. If you plan well, analyze your strengths, and are clear on what you want to do in civilian life, you should have no more difficulties than anyone else.

Use Your Strengths

If you have been involved in any phase of electronics, data processing or mechanics, or other technical fields, you are highly marketable. The U.S. Government has invested thousands of dollars of training in you, and there are employers who desperately want that expertise and experience.

Many ex-pilots have gone to work for airlines and defense contractors, but don't feel limited. As an officer you were assigned various command positions. Describe them properly, and you can sell yourself into a midmanagement or executive position. Whatever your background, sell your experience.

Things to Avoid

Avoid militarese or military lingo. Let a civilian read your resume to determine if your descriptions are understandable.

Don't talk about commanding or supervising huge numbers of people; this frightens civilians, whose normal reference is only to those reporting directly to them, usually three to fifteen people. In other words, the president of General Motors would never say he supervised the work of one million workers.

Avoid phrases like "Responsible for overseeing a $95 million budget." In the military overseeing large budgets is common, but in the private sector, only presidents of the largest companies could make such statements.

The same principle would apply if you were a pilot or ship's captain: "Responsible for a $21 million piece of equipment" (pilot) or, "Had total responsibility for operating and maintaining a $260 million piece of equipment" (captain of a destroyer). The statements may sound impressive, but they are actually counterproductive.

As a military person you have undoubtedly saved your evaluations and letters of commendation. Selected short quotations within the resume can often be used to make positive statements about yourself. Praise coming from an objective third party, especially from a superior, will carry more weight than if you made the same statement about yourself. Rarely should anyone include more than one or two quotations, so choose them wisely.

See page 151 for an example of a retired military person who used extensive quotes from evaluations as an addendum to his resume.

PETE SANDERS
237 Durham Way
Durham, California 95938
(213) 628-9714

OBJECTIVE: Safety Administrator

QUALIFICATIONS

Developed a comprehensive safety program which resulted in six years without a serious accident to any of the 800 personnel.

Proven ability to set up effective, low cost industrial safety programs which rely heavily on instilling a safety consciousness in all employees.

Totally familiar with OSHA regulations and compliance procedures and have worked closely with OSHA inspectors.

Certified to administer all forms of emergency medical aid.

WORK EXPERIENCE

Durham Fire Department, Durham, California 9/80 to Present

VOLUNTEER FIREFIGHTER - Recently elected president of Fire District #25, Volunteer Association. Fight fires, provide emergency medical aid including CPR and defibrillation, inspect local businesses for fire hazards, assist county arson investigators, and train volunteer firefighters. Currently developing videotaped safety training films.

U. S. Army 3/60 to 5/83

SAFETY OFFICER - 1971 to 1983

While Safety Officer at Ft. Bradley for ten years, was responsible for the safety of 800 air field personnel ranging from mechanics, machine operators, and vehicle operators to supervisors and management staff. Developed a comprehensive safety program which set a Ft. Bradley record for safety. Awarded a six-year safety award for 72 consecutive months without a major accident (over $500 property damage or loss of life).

Directly supervised three safety technicians and coordinated the efforts of twenty officers responsible for safety in their immediate areas. Held monthly safety seminars to promote and enhance safety awareness within each specialized group.

Made daily and weekly inspections of offices, maintenance facilities, and mechanical, paint, electrical, and machine shops, to ensure compliance with safety regulations and performed on-the-spot corrections for minor infractions. Identified potentially hazardous practices and recommended changes. Handled personnel grievances related to safety in the workplace.

Formulated and administered safety policies and procedures to ensure compliance with federal and state safety acts. Worked closely with OSHA inspectors and developed excellent knowledge of OSHA regulations. Instrumental in starting an effective noise protection program which included annual hearing tests. Very involved with identifying hazardous materials. Wrote, filmed, and edited videotaped safety training films for the base fire department.

AIRFIELD SAFETY OFFICER/PILOT, Ft. Bradley, California 1978 to 1983
AIRFIELD SAFETY OFFICER/PILOT, Munsun-ni, Korea 1977 to 1978
AIRFIELD SAFETY OFFICER/PILOT, Ft. Bradley, California 1972 to 1977
PILOT/SAFETY OFFICER, Da Nang, Vietnam 1971 to 1972
PILOT, Chu Lai, Vietnam, 1967 to 1969
PILOT, Ft. Benning, Georgia 1966 to 1967
ARMOR CREWMAN, 1960 to 1965

ASSOCIATIONS

Federal Occupational Safety and Health Council, active member 1973 to Present

EDUCATION

Business - University of Texas, 85 credits (1969-1971)

SAFETY EDUCATION

Accident Prevention, U. S. Army Agency for Aviation Safety, 640 class hours (1975). Emphasis on improving safety of mechanics, refuelers, and other ground support personnel.

U. S. Air Force Crash Investigators School, 320 class hours (1975)

Aviation Safety Officers Course, University of Southern California Safety Center, 960 class hours (1974). Course covered metal fatigue, reconstructing accidents, investigative procedures, evidence acquisition, analysis of causation factors, methods of accident prevention, and gaining employee cooperation.

Accident Prevention Management, 40-hour correspondence course, U. S. Army Agency for Aviation Safety (1973)

SAFETY SEMINARS

Defibrillation Tech Course, Wayne County Emergency Medical Services (EMS), 40 class hours (1982)
Defensive Driving Instructor Training, State of California Fire Service Training Program (FSTP), 60 class hours (1982)
Defensive Driving, FSTP, 40 class hours total (1980, 1981, 1982)
Emergency Vehicle Accident Prevention, FSTP, 32 hours (1982)
Electrical Hazards, FSTP, 16 class hours total (1980, 1981, 1982)
Hazardous Material, FSTP, 24 class hours total (1980, 1981, 1982)
Arson Investigation, FSTP, 24 class hours total (1980, 1981, 1982)
Liquid Petroleum Gas Fires, FSTP, 10 class hours total (1981, 1982)
Teaching Firefighting Techniques, FSTP, 32 class hours (1980)
Emergency Medical Technician Course, Los Angeles Community College and Wayne County EMS, 160 class hours total (1977, 1981, 1983)
Electrical Emergencies, FSTP, 20 class hours total (1980, 1981)
Safety Program Management, U. S. Army Agency for Aviation Safety, 30 class hours (1977)

RICK TOLSON
PreComUnit USS Antrim FFG-20
1102 S W Massachusetts Avenue
Seattle, Washington 98134

QUALIFICATIONS

During nine years of Naval Communications experience I have developed a strong ability to troubleshoot electronic systems. My specialty is recognizing system or circuit deterioration, isolating the fault and restoring the system or circuit to normal operation through corrective procedures or by an alternate route. I construct, operate and maintain all types of communication systems.

AREAS OF EXPERTISE

Constructing Communications Systems
Satellite Systems, High Speed Data Systems, Voice Systems, Teletype Systems, Continuous Wave.

Maintaining Communications Systems
Perform quality control and performance monitoring on audio and DC circuits.

Electronic Communications Equipment
Transmitters, transceivers, receivers, modems, multiplexers, demultiplexers, cryptogear, microwave, couplers, antennas, high level black patch panels, high and low level red patch panels, and numerous types of test equipment.

EDUCATION

Graduated Pisgah High School, Pisgah, Iowa (1970)
Navy Schools - Technical Control, Satellite Communications, Management, Communications Supervision, Maintenance and Material Management, High Frequency Transmitters, Antenna Maintenance.

WORK HISTORY

Tech Controller, 1st class Radioman   U S Navy
May 1972 to February 1982

Assignments have included Naval Communications Stations, Naval Telecommunications Centers and three Navy ships. During the past six years have supervised numerous groups of men and trained them to use sophisticated Naval communications equipment. While involved with the construction of an FFG-7 class ship, I developed an extensive set of lesson plans to explain the construction of the circuits and also diagrammed all of the wiring and block schematics for this new class of ship. These two projects will save hundreds of training hours. Participated in the quality control tests of the USS Antrim.

PERSONAL DATA

Birthdate   7/10/52   Security Clearance: Top Secret
Excellent Health   5'10"   185 lbs.

PAUL HANDLE
3715 Pearl Ave. N.
Everett, Washington 98206
(206) 954-3721

OBJECTIVE: Electrical, Electronic, Mechanical Maintenance

QUALIFICATIONS

Consistently rated superior in both technical expertise and supervisory ability.
Constantly looking for and discovering simpler and more effective methods of making
repairs and reducing downtime of equipment.

EDUCATION

Graduated - Sheppton High School, Sheppton, Pennsylvania (1954)

EMPLOYMENT

The Boeing Company, Seattle, Washington 12/80 to 9/82

NUMERICAL CONTROL ELECTRONIC TECHNICIAN 6/81 to 9/82. Performed
electronic, electrical, and mechanical maintenance and repair of microcomputers,
microprocessors, and numerically controlled production machinery. Received a Boeing
award for streamlining machine utilization data collection, which provided data more
useful to management and saved over 156 personnel hours annually.

MECHANIC TECHNICIAN 12/80 to 6/81. Maintained and repaired mechanical systems
on automated industrial machines including riveting machines, milling machines, and
high speed wire coding machines. Maintained a record of extremely low downtime on
equipment valued at up to $900 per hour. Won a Boeing award for designing an
inexpensive component for a wire marking machine which reduced machine downtime
and saved $18,000 annually.

US Navy, 10/54 to 12/80

ELECTRONICS INSTRUCTOR 2/74 to 12/80. Provided comprehensive instruction to
maintenance technicians and pilots covering aircraft electrical and electronic systems.
Courses ranged from basic electricity and electronics to advanced solid state theory
and repair. Taught thirteen separate courses averaging eighty classroom hours each.
Course Manager for five of the thirteen courses. Took very difficult courses and made
them more practical and easier to understand. Wrote numerous manuals and lesson
guides which simplified previous courses. Students consistently outscored the students
of other instructors.

SENIOR SUPERVISOR 7/64 to 2/74. Typically supervised two shift supervisors and up
to thirty-five technicians. Developed work schedules for personnel, scheduled maintenance and provided overall management of a large maintenance shop. Trained new
technicians and personally performed many repairs on state of the art aircraft
electrical systems, automatic flight control systems, and navigational systems.
Completed a 160-hour program in Human Problems and took on added duties as a drug
abuse and personal problems counselor.

Took over one command position where maintenance procedures and record keeping
were totally outdated, creating serious maintenance problems. Reorganized the
reporting and maintenance procedures and streamlined the operation. In thirty-six
months the unit moved from poor to excellent in battle readiness.

ELECTRONIC MAINTENANCE SUPERVISOR 6/58 to 7/64. Supervised up to twenty technicians in the repair of electrical and electronic aircraft systems.

AVIATION ELECTRICIAN 10/54 to 6/58. Maintenance and service technician on aircraft electrical and navigational systems.

TRAINING - Boeing, 1981-1982

Numerical control mechanical maintenance, hydraulic and servo drive systems (160 hours)
Numerical control electrical/electronic maintenance with eight different micro-processors (530 hours)
Disk drive memory storage (32 hours)
Electric drive systems (32 hours)
Silicon rectifier control systems (16 hours)

TRAINING - Navy Schools (completed over 150 courses with a total of 3,900 classroom hours)

Advanced Electronics Courses (1959 - 1979) high tech theoretical and application of:
Polyphase power and control systems (400 hours)
Advanced magnetic devices (240 hours)
Analog, solid-state and T.T.L. devices (960 hours)
Advanced syncro/analog/solid state control and indicating systems (640 hours)
Hybrid solid-state inertial navigation systems (360 hours)
High resolution hydraulic/electronic T.T.L. control systems (160 hours)
Component/miniature component repair, including P.C.B (160 hours)

Aviation Electrician Course, 1954 (320 hours)

Instructor Training, 1974 (120 hours)

Management Training
Human problems and individual and group counseling, 1970 (120 hours)
Maintenance and material management, 1962 (160 hours)
Management and supervision, 1961 (160 hours)
Management and supervision, 1956 (120 hours)

ACTIVITIES

Enjoy fishing, camping, backpacking, and volleyball. Custom build remote control airplanes and miniature trains.

PORTIONS OF SEMIANNUAL EVALUATIONS

Handle's broad qualifications and maintenance know how on A6A electrical systems have enabled him to become a particularly valuable instructor. He is always striving to make difficult courses easier for the students to comprehend by ensuring that proper mainte-nance procedures are included in his lessons. His willingness to work at any task, no matter how large or small, has contributed materially to the mission of NAMTD. His conduct sets an example worthy of emulation by other Petty Officers. He has amply demonstrated a fair and unbiased attitude, readily accepting each and every man as an individual. Handle is industrious, thorough and accurate in this work and extremely conscientious in all duties and endeavors. He is alert and stable, displaying a creative mind. He shows great ability to develop effective procedural methods and to prepare excellently written and easily understood lesson guides. He secures the attention and respect of his students whom he guides and directs with understanding and tact. He is frequently called upon by other rate groups of this detachment to help solve technical problems in the writing of lesson guides. He attacks these problems with a cheerful and aggressive nature, seeing any problems through to a successful conclusion. Success in his work is shown by the students' final grades and their comment sheets.

December, 1978

Handle is intelligent, exceptionally quick to learn, with the ability to grasp pertinent details rapidly. Given broad guidelines, he accomplishes assigned tasks in an enthusiastic and exemplary manner. Handle is a conscientious and concerned instructor who demon-strates a sincere feeling of responsibility towards his students and works very hard to insure they receive maximum benefit from his instruction. He is equally at ease before a group of juniors or seniors. He is very effective in conveying his thoughts clearly and fluently, both in casual conversation or when presenting a formal lesson. During this reporting period, he has been assigned the task of writing the avionics portion of AZF under the individualized instruction format. He willingly assisted other instructors with this new format and readily assumed the responsibility of insuring that uniformity was met by all rate groups. He spent many hours researching instructions. Acting as liaison between rate groups, he arranged and conducted meetings to achieve this goal.

January 1977

Handle has been extremely instrumental in the training of the less experienced men assigned to the branch. He can be counted on to do any assigned task correctly, effi-ciently and safely.

January 1976

Petty Officer Handle is a dedicated, knowledgeable First Class Electrician, who strives to ensure work is completed safely and that the proper maintenance procedures are utilized. He keeps his superiors informed of all potential trouble areas and draws on his vast experience to propose viable solutions. He leads with an easy-going, unobtrusive manner, never interfering with the personal initiative of those he supervises. He plans the work load efficiently and utilizes a smooth rapport with the men to carry out the work.

June, 1974

Petty Officer Handle has demonstrated a high proficiency in his field and is very adept at putting his knowledge and experience to good use. He has an ability to quietly evaluate difficult situations and to arrive at practical solutions while working under trying conditions. He is a very thoughtful and sincere person who has the ability to communicate with the younger men and to define some of their problems.

December, 1972

PROGRAMMERS/ANALYSTS

Data processing is a unique field and requires a special type of resume. DP managers are very concerned about experience. Since the average programmer stays only eighteen months with an organization, managers usually look for someone who can step right in and do the job, based on past experience with both the computer and language used in that organization. This is a source of great frustration for programmers because many feel that in two to three weeks they can master any new system—all they need is an opportunity to prove it. Your task is to make the most out of the experience you have and demonstrate your adaptibility.

The DP resume is actually fairly simple to write because it consists of several distinct sections that practically write themselves. Start with Areas of Experience. Typically, it will consist of Languages, Systems, Special Programs, Computers, Conversions, and Applications. Applications can be further divided into New Applications and Maintenance. It should be easy, almost like filling in the blanks.

Notice *how* the projects are described. Provide just enough information to give an employer a feel for what you did, then concentrate on results. This section is very important and will probably require three drafts. Start by listing the projects you feel would be most impressive. Since employers usually use resumes as a basis for interviews, be sure to choose projects that you would want to explain and describe in more detail in an interview. If you've been a programmer for three years or less, you may want to include nearly every project you've worked on.

For the first draft of your Projects section, don't worry about length, just get your thoughts down on paper. In the second draft look for unnecessary words or phrases. The employer does not require a complete understanding of all the details, just enough information to indicate the degree of complexity and what was required to complete the project. Finish the project by describing the result. Your third draft will simply be a finer tuning of the second.

By concentrating on Areas of Experience and Projects, your job descriptions will probably be quite short.

KEN WANDER
119 Tri-Cities Way
Richland, Washington 99352
(509) 454-4413

QUALIFICATIONS:

More than nineteen years experience in analyzing and solving complex problems involving electronic data processing and engineering.

Consistent track record of systems analysis and programming applications that are maintained easily and run quickly.

Demonstrated ability to apply sound knowledge of data processing concepts to diverse applications.

Use structured approach in programming.

EDUCATION:

B.S. - Mechanical Engineering, Ohio State University (1967)

AREAS OF EXPERIENCE:

Languages: COBOL, RPG II, FORTRAN, QUIKJOB, BAL, Macro Assembler, APL, OS and DOS JCL, ADASCRIPT, GE Command Language.

Special Programs: CRJE, SPF, PANVALET, ICCF, OS and DOS Utilities, S/3 Utilities, POWER, ASAP, HASP, JES, ADABAS.

Computers: IBM 360/30,40,50; IBM 370/135,145,158; IBM 3031,4331; IBM 1130/1800; IBM System/3,7,32.

New Applications: Program Inventory Reporting; Budget Updating and Reporting; Auto Engine Emission Analysis; Contact Resistance Analysis; Cash Flow Reporting; Data Decoding/Translating Systems; Automated Record Updating Systems; Records Management System Updating; Payroll Accounting; Mailing Label System Program Generator.

Maintenance: Billing, Inventory Control, Accounts Receivable, and Sales Analysis; Purchase History Reporting; Bill-of-Material Updating and Reporting; Finished Goods Processing and Reporting; Mortgage Loan Reporting.

FUNCTIONAL EXPERIENCE:

Business Applications:

Developed in six weeks a versatile system of RPG II programs for budget revising and reporting to reduce Daytex corporate budget preparation time from twelve to one man-week.

Developed a translator in RPG II to convert S/7 prepared order entry data to fixed format for S/3 processing.

Installed Billing, Inventory Control, Accounts Receivable, and Sales Analysis Systems.

FUNCTIONAL EXPERIENCE (continued):

Information Management Applications:

Developed in three weeks a series of COBOL programs to inventory COBOL application programs directly from compressed records in DOS source library.

Developed for WPPSS an ADABAS utility replacement which dynamcially formats records plus cuts record-add run time from three hours to less than thirty minutes.

Enhanced and simplified complex reporting system accessing ADABAS files via dynamically callable modules.

Automated record updating using QUIKJOB for 80% of Iowa registered voters from state drivers license tapes and telephone company directory listing tapes.

Developed an ALC program generator which reduced time to fill special mailing label requests from three days to less than thirty minutes.

Financial Applications:

Developed complex, request-driven cash flow reporting application at WPPSS using COBOL report writer.

Maintained ALC programs for mortgage loan applications at FIS.

Manufacturing Applications:

Responsible for enhancing and final testing of Olympic Stain Corp. Inventory Control System.

Installed several plastic injection molding control packages on S/7.

CHRONOLOGICAL EXPERIENCE:

1975 - Present (Self-employed Consultant)	Programmer/analyst responsible for new applications and program maintenance in Dayton, OH; Davenport, IA; Richland, WA.
1971 - 1975 (IBM Corp.)	Systems engineer. Responsible for filling SE Services Contracts with large, small and sensor-based computer installations; marketing and technical support for customer installations.
1967 - 1971 (IBM Corp.)	Mechanical engineer. Various APL analysis applications for test equipment design. Line engineering responsibilties.

ANNE PROWDY
125 S. Meridian
Kent, Washington 98031
(206) 521-7255

QUALIFICATIONS

Excellent background in D. P. Consulting, Project Management, Systems Analysis, and Programming.

Work effectively with users and upper management to define and solve problems and design user-friendly systems.

Learn new computer systems and languages quickly.

Strong academic background and work experience in Accounting, Finance, and Management Information Systems.

EDUCATION

B.A. - Business/Management Information Systems, University of Hawaii at Manoa, 1979

DATA PROCESSING EXPERIENCE

Languages - COBOL, JCL, MVS/TSO CLIST, VM/CMS EXEC, PL/I, BASIC, IMS

Special Languages - ISPF, SPF, SPF/Dialog Management Services, GDDM, PGF, OS/VS2 MVS Utilities, Easytrieve

Project Management Applications - PMS IV, VISION, E-Z-PERT Project Graphics, ARTEMIS

Computers - IBM 3081, IBM 3033, IBM 3270 Information Display System, IBM Series I, HP 1000, HP 3000, PRIME 550, VERSATEC

EMPLOYMENT

Boeing Computer Services, Kent, Washington 6/80 to Present

SYSTEMS ANALYST/PROJECT MANAGEMENT CONSULTANT/PROGRAMMER 7/81 to Present

Designed and currently developing a user-friendly, menu-driven front end to existing project management software package with project graphics interface. Development work is done using SPF/DMS. Project known as Automated Scheduling and Planning System (ASAP).

Frequently provide demonstrations and seminars to upper management covering project management and Data Processing topics. Demonstrated the ASAP System to corporate executives.

System Analyst in support of project management activities for the Boeing Computer Services' (BCS) contract with the Pacific Missile Test Center in California. Utilized PSM IV to reduce cost overruns during development of the Trident program. As a result of the success of the PMS IV System, BCS in California has gained additional contracts.

System Analyst on the Liquid Metal Fast Breeder Reactor Project for Boeing Engineering and Construction. Tracked the work of seven contractors to enhance the interface between Boeing and the contractors. Received letter of commendation from the Deputy Project Director.

BCS Program Manager for two PRIME 550 sites. Contact person with clients, vendors, and Boeing departments of Finance, Procurement, and Technology.

PROGRAMMER ANALYST, Business System Group 6/80 to 7/81

Converted a masterfile from a 7080 variable length record to a sequential file. Changed, tested and, documented the existing programs to be able to read and write the new file format. Optimized programs to run 50 to 75% faster and cost 50 to 60% less than the original. Completed the project ahead of a very difficult deadline.

Redesigned existing special reports for Boeing Marine Systems Production Control Records. Original system had resulted in erroneous reports for a full year. Met with users, gathered new specifications, and created new report modules. The system began delivering error-free reports immediately.

Production Control Analyst to maintain Boeing Marine Systems Business applications. Responsible for Parts Inventory Control, Manufacturing, and Material.

Wrote, tested, and maintained production JCL.

Developed custom reporting modules for management personnel based on special needs. Created 1-2 hour quick turnaround reports using utilities and existing software.

Analyst for Boeing Marine Systems' Industrial Relations on-line reporting system, which measures attrition rate, tracks personnel changes, and analyzes personnel performance.

Installed an on-line statistical/reporting application for the Equal Employment Opportunity division of Boeing Marine Systems.

REFERENCES: Personal and professional references available upon request.

CHARLES FORTIER
6214 Steelway North
Allentown, Pennsylvania 18101
(215) 192-7215

QUALIFICATIONS

Strong background in project development gained during twelve years in data processing including: analysis, specifications, design, documentation, programming, testing, training and troubleshooting.

Effectively work with users to obtain an excellent grasp of the problems they want the computer to solve.

Able to relate large numbers of details and exceptions into an integrated design.

Demonstrated ability to estimate the scope of a project, determine the time requirements and complete the project on schedule.

Learn new computer systems and languages very quickly.

Develop excellent user and technical documentation to make the system more useful.

AREAS OF EXPERIENCE

Languages: COBOL, BASIC, RPG II, FORTH, ALGOL, FORTRAN, PL/I, Assembly (several), SNOBOL, PHOCAL

Computers: IBM 5110, IBM System 34, IBM 360/65, Univac 1108, Univac 70/46, Burroughs 2500/3500/2700, Burroughs B-300, L-series, Delta 8016A Micro, Varian V-72/620-F, PDP-8, CA 90/4, Phillips P-330

Special Programs: CSC Infonet

New Applications: Magazine Subscription Accounting, Newspaper Circulation Accounting, Property Management, Job Cost Accounting, Production Management, Production Scheduling, Source Program Manager, IBM 3270 Emulator, Character Recognition Education Package, Raw Materials, Inventory

Maintenance: Payroll, Accounts Payable, Accounts Receivable, Sales Analysis, Financial Management, Raw Materials, Mailing List

Conversions: Medical Billing B-300 Assembler to B-3500 COBOL; Raw Materials and Inventory from IBM 1401 to Burroughs B-2500 COBOL; Over 300 COBOL programs converted from cards to B-2500 on-line library system; Magazine subscription list from batch tape system to on-line disk

EDUCATION

BSE   Computer Engineering, Case Western Reserve University (1967-1971)
Completion of all coursework toward MSEE Computer and Information Science University of Pennsylvania (1971-1975)

157

SELECTED ACCOMPLISHMENTS

Developed a highly reliable on-line magazine subscription accounting system which provides demographic data on subscribers and can provide over one hundred reports and screens to management. The system has required very few enhancements or corrections and is easily learned and used by clerical staff.

Quickly developed a mastery of PHOCAL and created a highly useful turn-key Job Cost Accounting and Production Management System with Payroll interface. Production bottlenecks can now be identified months in advance. System has been operational for nearly three years and has required almost no enhancement or corrections.

Contributed innovative techniques during the development of an on-line modular programming system that allows sophisticated audit trails to be made.

EMPLOYMENT HISTORY

Datapro, Allentown, Pennsylvania 1979 to Present

CONSULTING PROGRAMMER/ANALYST - Responsibilities include analyzing needs, specifying requirements, coordinating and programming projects including: File Restructure, Data Management extensions, Subscription Accounting and Circulation Accounting. Managed final phases (quality assurance) of Data Base Backup/Restore Utility.

Independent 1975 to 1979

SOFTWARE DESIGNER - Developed applications and tools: Production Scheduling, Job Costing, Property Management, COBOL On-line Interactive Library System. Worked with users to define needs and specifications.

Online Data Systems Corp., Cornwells Heights, Pennsylvania 1975

PROJECT LEADER - Programmed a micro (Delta 80-16A) to cluster terminals to emulate IBM 3270 terminal. As project leader supervised three team members.

OCR Systems, Inc., Bensalem, Pennsylvania 1972 to 1974

PROGRAMMER/ANALYST - Used DAS Assembler on Varian minicomputers and developed on-line user interface and reports to document teaching the computer to recognize different print fonts. Rewrote interrupt handlers for document and page reader systems. Trained and managed six junior programmers.

RANDALL BERNARD
1118 Crestview Court
Montclair, New Jersey 07042
(201) 744-8214

JOB OBJECTIVE: Senior Analyst/Project Lead

QUALIFICATIONS

Ten years in Data Processing with four years as Project Manager and Senior Analyst.

Outstanding record of satisfying clients while bringing projects in on schedule and within budget.

EDUCATION

Certificate - Sinclair Computer Institute, Newark, New Jersey (1972) COBOL, RPG, Coursework in Accounting and Systems Design

EMPLOYMENT

Dataform, Inc., Newark, New Jersey 8/79 to Present

SENIOR SYSTEMS CONSULTANT - Responsible for all facets of installation and implementation of financial systems, with emphasis on Systems Analysis and Project Management. Duties include scoping, scheduling, budgeting, status reporting and directing client analysts and programmers. Extensive user interface with clerks to senior management. Established outstanding record for completing projects on schedule and within budget and for leaving clients extremely satisfied with their system. Selected projects include:

Orange County, California, Project Manager/Lead Analyst, 3/82 to Present. Developed proposal and made sales presentations to the County. Installed a complete Financial Management System involving conversion from batch to online and from IBM equipment to Hewlett Packard.

Phoenix School District, Project Consultant/Lead Analyst, 4 months. Co-authored conceptual design document used in the selection of a new Payroll/Personnel System.

Long Beach School District, Project Manager/Lead Analyst, 8 months. Modified an Accounts Payable System previously developed for the City of Newark, New Jersey.

Union County, New Jersey, Project Manager/Lead Analyst, 3 months. Installed a Cost Accounting Module in the previously installed financial system.

Phoenix School District, Project Manager/Lead Analyst, 6 months. Designed and implemented a Position Control System.

City of Denver, Colorado, System Analyst, 4 months. Installed a Financial Management System and converted software from an IBM mainframe to a Honeywell.

Datex, Philadelphia, Pennsylvania 6/74 to 8/79

ACCOUNT MANAGER/PROJECT LEADER - Responsible for all data processing
management for three newspaper publishers. Supervised programmer/
analyst staff and scheduled and coordinated operations.

Pittson Manufacturing, Philidelphia, Pennsylvania 8/72 to 6/74

PROGRAMMER - Wrote programs for payroll and personnel applications.

AREAS OF EXPERIENCE

Hardware - IBM 370/145/158; IBM 360/30/40; Honeywell 2040, Honeywell dual
6400; Univac 9080 and 9200; Burroughs dual 4700, 1860, 2800.

Software - COBOL, IBM Assembler, RPG, IBM DOS, IBM OS, CICS, HASP, GRASP,
GCOS, Honeywell OS 2000.

Applications - Payroll/Personnel, General Ledger, Accounts Receivable,
Accounts Payable, Bill of Material, Purchasing, Material Release, Position
Control, Governmental Financial Management, Fixed Assets.

ACTIVITIES

Enjoy hunting, fishing, camping and hiking.

SALESPEOPLE

Salespeople usually hate to write, and that fact is generally quite evident in their resumes. Most are poorly written, poorly designed, and reveal very little of substance. Taking just four to five hours of your valuable time to write a quality resume could net you an extra $100,000 in your lifetime earnings.

The sales resume is usually one of the easiest to write because it is so results-oriented. Sales resumes rarely require extensive details about duties because sales managers really care only about the bottom line—how well did you do? Don't tell a sales manager how hard you worked or how many telephone calls you made or how many sales calls you went on. Did you sell? That's all that counts.

There are a number of ways to show results: sales awards, your ranking within your sales organization, improving the position of your territory compared to other territories in the company, increasing sales, increasing profits on sales, or increasing market share. Use whatever is most appropriate. If you know your market share or can estimate it pretty closely, use that figure. Market share is good because it provides an excellent method of comparison. During an economic boom with high inflation, the gross sales of even a mediocre salesperson will increase five to eight percent annually. To increase market share, however, means you have taken business away from competitors and increased your share of the pie. It means you're doing something right. Employers won't know if you've done it on the basis of your great personality, your outstanding closing techniques, your strong product knowledge, your hard work, or your excellent time management, but it won't matter. Sales managers care only about results.

Showing increases in market share is great, but most companies simply don't know what those figures are. Use whatever figures will work best for you. During the last recession even many outstanding salespeople were not able to say that they increased sales. In some industries just holding steady was the mark of a great salesperson. To show yourself in the best light you might use a combination. Let's say from 1970 to 1973 you sold office machines. Those were recession years in some parts of the country. You took over an established territory and only increased gross sales fourteen percent in three years, slightly less than inflation. You obviously won't brag about your sales increases. Out of a sales staff of eighteen, you were second in sales, since no one else sold well either. That would be the result you would use. In 1974 and 1975 you sold photocopiers. You were in the right place at the right time and sales really took off and increased twenty percent each year for an actual increase of forty-four percent over two years. Assuming you didn't know your market share, nor how you did compared to the rest of the sales staff, you would certainly want to use the sales increases. In 1976 through 1978 you decided to sell cars. You did well and each year won an award from the manufacturer. You were also Salesperson of the Month eight times during your thirty-four months with the dealership. You were competing with twelve other salespeople. For that job you would mention the awards and the number of times you were Salesperson of the Month. In 1979 you went to work for a tractor manufacturer which paid a research firm to determine the market share in each territory. Between 1979 and the end of 1982 the market share in your territory increased from fifteen to twenty percent, a thirty-three percent increase in market share. In 1983 you joined a heavy equipment distributor and moved the territory from seventh to second. Sales were flat due to the recession. The resume might look something like this.

B & N Machinery, Tempe, Arizona 1/83 to Present

MARKETING REPRESENTATIVE—Developed and implemented marketing strategies to increase heavy equipment sales to the construction industry in Arizona. Took the territory from seventh (out of eight) in the company to second during the first six months.

John Deere, Phoenix, Arizona 10/78 to 12/82

DISTRICT REPRESENTATIVE—Assisted twenty-six dealers in Arizona and New Mexico with marketing of John Deere products. Set up five new dealers and developed their sales, parts and service departments. Moved seven dealers from near bankruptcy to very strong financial positions. Market share in the territory grew thirty-three percent.

Gerald Lincoln Mercury, Phoenix, Arizona 1/76 to10/78

SALESMAN—Each year won the Professional Sales Counselor award for sales excellence. With a sales force of twelve, was salesperson of the month eight times in thirty-four months.

Canon Corporation, Trenton, New Jersey 11/73 to 12/75

SALES REPRESENTATIVE—For the fifth largest selling photocopier manufacturer in the U.S., sold a full line of photocopiers to end users. In two years territorial sales increased forty-four percent.

Olivetti Corporation, Trenton, New Jersey 1/70 to 11/73

SALES REPRESENTATIVE—Sold typewriters, calculators and dictating equipment to office equipment stores throughout metropolitan Trenton. Worked closely with store managers

and sales staffs and provided excellent training in selling
Olivetti products. Ranked second in sales in 1973 with a
regional sales force of eighteen.

Review all of the sales resumes to get ideas for the best way
to sell yourself. Also review pages 58 to 63, which cover
accomplishments.

If you haven't been doing so up to this time, begin collecting
and saving all the sales data you can. Whenever you start a new
position, get data on what the territory was doing prior to your taking over. In the absence of cold, hard figures, rely on your memory
and your knowledge of the territory. Estimate and guesstimate
when you must, but do come up with some figures which you feel
are accurate, and be sure you can explain how they were
derived.

PAUL KIRSTEN
525 Bates S.W.
Beaverton, Oregon 97006
(503) 962-0013

OBJECTIVE: Sales Representative

QUALIFICATIONS

Excellent Sales track record.

Thorough knowledge of manufacturing processes and procedures. Experienced in Expediting, Production Scheduling, Purchasing, Inventory Control, Traffic, Warehousing, Shipping/Receiving and Office Management.

EDUCATION

B.S. - History, University of Oregon (1970 - 1974)

EMPLOYMENT

Prescal & Hemsted Wire Rope Company, Beaverton, Oregon 10/75 to 9/83

Sales Representative (4/78 to 9/83). Sold wire rope through 18 distributors and through direct sales to OEM accounts, covering Oregon, Washington and Alaska. In 1980 increased sales from $652,000 to $1,404,000 and maintained that level despite the logging industry depression. Trained all inside sales staff.

Inside Sales/Office Manager (10/75 to 4/78). Handled all inside sales, purchasing, inventory control and traffic. Supervised the warehouse and shipping/receiving operations. Reorganized the office and production procedures, which increased efficiency and on-time deliveries and significantly decreased complaints. Heavily involved in a switch from a manual to a computerized inventory control and billing system. Sales increases between 1975 and 1978 were substantially attributed to the new level of professionalism at the order desk.

Peterson Manufacturing Company, Coos Bay, Oregon 2/73 to 10/75

Sales Representative (9/74 to 10/75). Sold replacement parts for the barkers and chippers manufactured by Peterson, covering Oregon, Washington, Idaho and Montana. Sales and profits of replacement parts increased substantially.

Inside Sales (3/74 to 9/74). Called on customers of Peterson products and sold replacement parts. Worked closely with purchasers of new machines to ensure an adequate inventory of the parts most likely to need replacing. When replacing 10- to 25-year-old parts, worked with engineering to determine if newer parts could be adapted or required new castings.

Expediter (2/73 to 3/74). Responsible for expediting, scheduling, and inventory control in the manufacturing of custom-made wood barkers and chippers. Significantly increased total production and on-time deliveries.

GAIL SHUMWAY
2928 Sunset Blvd.
Phoenix, Arizona 85004
(602) 755-2428

QUALIFICATIONS

As Division Manager and Area Marketing Manager, consistently increased market share by effectively identifying new markets, recruiting and developing successful sales teams and obtaining quantifiable results through Management By Objectives.

Strong experience in all phases of Management, Marketing, Sales and Engineering.

Proven ability to market and sell high technology products.

EDUCATION

MBA - Marketing, University of Colorado (1977)
BS   - Electrical Engineering, California State Polytechnic University (1973)

EMPLOYMENT HISTORY

Dyatech Inc. 11/76 to 1/82

DIVISION MANAGER - Phoenix Division 7/79 to 1/82

Responsible for the total operation and profits for this distributor of electronic components and systems, with sales to industrial users, original equipment manufacturers and federal and state agencies. Supervised 45 employees. Introduced an effective MBO program into an organization with low morale and loose controls. As a result, market share increased from 10% to 14%, while employee turnover was reduced by 50%.

DIVISION MANAGER - Denver Division 11/76 to 7/79

Managed the 32-employee Denver Division covering Colorado, Wyoming, Utah and Montana and doubled sales. Created and implemented a new concept in technical marketing and increased market share from 14% to 18%.

Insofen Corporation 5/75 to 10/76

FIELD ENGINEER - Denver, Colorado

Covering Colorado and Utah, sold high technology semiconductor products to major manufacturers of electronic equipment. Worked closely with engineers to get proprietary devices designed into new products. Increased sales from $40,000 to $180,000 per month.

Xytex Corporation 7/73 to 5/75

ENGINEER - Boulder, Colorado

Designed power systems and interfaces for data processing peripheral equipment.

WARREN DRISCOL
927 Honeycut Drive
Atlanta, Georgia 30032
(404) 527-6819

OBJECTIVE: Sales/Marketing Management

QUALIFICATIONS

Strong Sales and Marketing background. Increased territorial market share 45-400% in each position held.

EDUCATION

B.S. - Forest Engineering, University of Georgia (1963)

EMPLOYMENT

Ubasco Machinery Company, Atlanta, Georgia 8/80 to Present

FOREST PRODUCTS SALES MANAGER - As Ubasco's first Forest Products Sales Manager, responsible for selling to key accounts and for training the sales staff in methods of increasing sales of earth moving equipment to forestry related companies. Perform extensive market research to target sales and identify sales potential. In 1982 increased unit sales 62% and increased gross profit from 14% to 18%.

John Deere Tractor Company 7/63 to 8/80

FOREST PRODUCTS SALES REPRESENTATIVE, Atlanta, Georgia 8/75 to 8/80. Developed and implemented marketing strategies to increase sales to the forest industry through 24 Southeastern John Deere dealers. Worked closely with the dealers and trained their sales people to sell earth moving equipment to the forest industry. Created a special training program which covered sales techniques and forestry applications of John Deere equipment. Unit sales increased 148% and market share was increased from 4% to 27% between 1975 and 1979.

DISTRICT REPRESENTATIVE, Bangkok, Thailand 11/72 to 8/75. Responsible for increasing sales and service levels among all dealers in India, Sri Lanka, Bangladesh, Thailand, Taiwan, South Korea and the Philippines. Identified new market areas, developed marketing strategies for dealers and trained sales forces in effective sales techniques. Increased John Deere's market share from 14% to 21%.

SALES REPRESENTATIVE, Singapore 8/69 to 11/72. Worked with dealers in the Philippines, Malaysia, Indonesia and Singapore. Enabled a new Indonesian dealer to land a single order of $10 million from a multi-national customer which had always bought from one U. S. dealer. Increased market share from 13% to 35% in two years.

PRODUCT/MARKET REP, Hong Kong 2/66 to 8/69. Conducted market studies and consulted with dealers on applications and modifications of John Deere equipment. On own time developed an extensive market study on the uses of wheel loaders in Asia. Concluded a huge untapped market existed for wheel loaders to replace track-driven loaders. Visited dealers throughout Asia and made sales calls with them. Businesses immediately switched to wheel loaders. Sales of wheel loaders increased an average of 76% each year between 1968 and 1973 and captured over 60% of that market.

MARKET REP, Spokane, Washington 7/63 to 2/66. Acted as machinery application consultant to dealers. Studied mill and mining operations and made recommendations for the most appropriate John Deere equipment.

PRISCILLA BEACHMAN
2820 232nd Place SE
Renton, Washington 98055
(206) 765-2321

OBJECTIVE: Marketing and Sales

QUALIFICATIONS

Proven ability to market products and services and substantially increase sales.

Quickly promoted by Modern Circulation because of high sales and increased circulation. Opened up magazine sales in chains that had never before sold magazines. Cultivated good relations with those buyers and demonstrated how a carefully monitored magazine sales program could increase profits.

Developed new marketing techniques and tools which are now used throughout the industry.

Create very strong working relations with wholesalers.

Excellent reputation and high credibility with buyers from all grocery and drug chains in Washington, Oregon, British Columbia, and Alberta.

EDUCATION

Riverside Community College, Business, 72 credits (1965-67)

EMPLOYMENT

Modern Circulation 6/74 to 5/83

MARKETING AND PROMOTION MANAGER, Renton, Washington 9/78 to 5/83. For the largest circulation company in the U. S., responsible for increasing the circulation of 750 magazines within Washington, Oregon, British Columbia and Alberta. Supervised seven District Managers with a total volume of 40 million dollars. Worked closely with buyers from chain stores to obtain rack space for publications and to help increase the chain's profits through magazine sales. Developed a marketing strategy for Pay Less Drugs and introduced a magazine sales checkout program into 148 stores on the West Coast. Handled publicity and special promotions for various magazines and promoted magazines through national and regional trade shows. Rated second in productivity among fifteen Marketing Managers in 1981.

DISTRICT SALES MANAGER, Portland, Oregon 3/77 to 9/78. Worked directly with five magazine wholesalers and dozens of retail accounts to increase circulation of publications. Solved serious problems with one major wholesaler and enabled it to move from 14th largest on the West Coast to 6th. Increased the Modern line 30% on 6 million dollars of annual sales.

SALES REPRESENTATIVE, Seattle, Washington 6/74 to 3/77. Significantly increased magazine sales to independent retailers and was quickly promoted to District Sales Manager to work with larger accounts.

Colgate Palmolive, Seattle, Washington 10/72 to 6/74

MERCHANDISER. Called on drug and grocery accounts, taking orders, creating displays and stocking as needed. Opened up Skaggs for the first time to the full line of Colgate Palmolive products.

167

CAREER CHANGERS

I really applaud people making career changes. Career changers can find greater job satisfaction, a lifestyle more in tune with their current values, and depending on several variables, more money. Career changers, however, have the most difficult and frustrating experiences with resumes. Used in the traditional way of mailing out one hundred or more resumes, career changers experience very little success. A resume is still a necessity but *must* be used in a way that takes advantage of the hidden job market.

Determine the type of position you'll be seeking. Your job is to pick out every experience even remotely related to that line of work and insert it in some form in the resume. The Qualifications section is often an excellent place to do this.

When you start describing your employment, you have two main functions: (1) show you were successful at what you did, and (2) emphasize any parts of your jobs which are related to your current objective. Success is important. Employers are dubious enough about hiring a career changer; they certainly want a person with a proven record of success. Essentially you'll be saying through your resume, "I've been successful in the past, and I'll be successful for you, also." Emphasizing related experience in each job is important. In most cases you should provide an adequate and accurate overview of your entire job, but that can usually be covered in one or two sentences. The remaining space should cover those functions which are related to your objective. In other words, duties which took up only ten percent of your time may get ninety percent of the space.

Career changers tend to have longer Qualifications sections than those who have years of experience in the same field. Review the Qualifications sections in a number of resumes and notice how you can best utilize that section in your own resume.

Career changers sometimes do better with a functional resume. Read pages 106 to 111 for a full explanation and several examples.

PAULA PROJASKA
2531 Sealdn Avenue #26
Danbury, Connecticut 06816
(203) 752-9628

JOB OBJECTIVE: Sales

QUALIFICATIONS

Proven ability to sell products and services. Quickly develop product knowledge and relate very well to people at all levels.

Strong track record. The Four Winds Hotel increased its revenue 70% in six years without remodeling or advertising more heavily--the staff simply cared more and gave more.

EDUCATION

B.A. - Public Relations, Wesleyan University (1975)

EMPLOYMENT

Bravos Restaurant, Danbury, Connecticut 1983

RESTAURANT CONSULTANT - For a new restaurant which was failing, provided consulting services which increased revenues 50% in five months. Retrained and cross trained the staff, introduced a new and unique menu and created excellent media coverage. Sold banquet services to businesses and associations and increased banquet revenues by 110%.

Four Winds Hotel, Danbury, Connecticut 1976 to 1983

EXECUTIVE ASSISTANT (1981 to 1983). Raised guest service to the highest level found anywhere in Danbury. Increased communication and cooperation between departments and implemented an effective cross training program. Kept the hotel and restaurants operating at capacity. Worked closely with the Chamber of Commerce and continually performed PR functions with other businesses and organizations.

FOOD SERVICES COORDINATOR (1978 to 1981). Introduced new food and room services which created a 20% increase in room revenue and a 22% increase in food and beverage revenue. Supervised a staff of sixty.

ASSISTANT FOOD SERVICES COORDINATOR (1976 to 1978). Coordinated all food services including room service, coffee shop, dining room, lounge, and meeting rooms. Supervised a staff of twenty. Designed a new training program which instilled more professionalism in the staff. Annual turnover was cut from 20% to 5%. As service improved, room revenue and food and beverage revenue each increased 40%.

ROSALYN RODRIQUEZ
2315 Dixie Avenue
Charleston, South Carolina 29406
(803) 976-4204

OBJECTIVE: Position in Training and Development

QUALIFICATIONS

Broad background in planning and developing programs. Skilled in determining program needs through task analysis. Planned and organized numerous programs, including the Council for Exceptional Children 1982 State Conference.

Extensive knowledge and experience in determining needs, setting behavioral and learning objectives, and developing assessment tools. M.A. in Curriculum and Program Development.

Expertise in selecting appropriate teaching techniques to match the audience. Quickly establish rapport with groups.

Outstanding record in teaching.

Evaluated and selected speakers and consultants for educational topics and conventions.

Able to design on-the-job training programs.

Extensive budgetary and purchasing experience with instructional materials.

Excellent writer.

Able to interpret achievement tests and other test scores. Extensive use of statistics.

Interviewed, hired, and evaluated teacher's aides.

Strong abilities in performing and graphics arts. Directed, stage-managed, and designed sets and costumes for numerous theatrical productions.

Designed brochures, advertising, and posters.

Experienced with most audio-visual equipment, including video tape systems.

EDUCATION

M.A. - Curriculum and Instruction, University of South Carolina (1976)
B.A. - Art, Arkansas State Teachers College (1966)

EMPLOYMENT

Teacher, Charleston Public Schools, Charleston, South Carolina 9/76 to Present
Teacher, Greenville Public Schools, Greenville, South Carolina 9/66 to 9/76

ASSOCIATIONS

Member - American Society for Training and Development
Member - Council for Exceptional Children, State Bylaws Chairperson (1980 to
  Present, Chapter President 1979, Chapter Vice President 1978).

BRUCE GARNETT
3219 Puget Way North
Tacoma, Washington 98405
(206) 785-2319

OBJECTIVE: Purchasing

QUALIFICATIONS

Four years of successful sales, selling to wholesalers and retailers. Extensive experience with Buyers and Purchasing Agents. Understand the techniques for obtaining high
quality products for a reasonable price.

Detail-oriented person. As a salesman, carefully monitor inventory levels and ensure
deliveries are made as scheduled. Conducted numerous fisheries studies involving
collecting, computing and analyzing biological data.

Strong technical background. Able to repair and maintain mechanical and electrical
systems. Extensive training and experience in chemistry, biology and many types of
laboratory testing. Able to perform quality assurance tests.

Strong background in planning, organizing and coordinating research and statistical
analysis. Skilled in design and implementation of sophisticated surveys. Coursework
in BASIC and FORTRAN.

EDUCATION

B.S. - Fisheries Management, University of Washington (1972 to 1976)

PROFESSIONAL EXPERIENCE

Simms-Simpson Company, Inc., Tacoma, Washington 1980 to 1983

FOOD SALES. Increased market penetration of food lines through creative merchandising and effective use of advertising and discounts. Increased distribution of food
lines over 20%.

National Marine Fisheries Service, Seattle, Washington 1976 to 1980

FISHERIES BIOLOGIST. Conducted resource assessment surveys of Bering Sea fish
populations. Collected, computed and analyzed biological data and prepared scientific
reports. Co-authored three published articles on the development of several fish
species.

U. S. Navy 1963 to 1972

SURVIVAL INSTRUCTOR 1969 to 1971. Developed and administered a highly successful survival training program for military and civilian flight personnel using new and
creative techniques. Published an article in Approach Magazine describing survival
methods at sea.

EQUIPMENT TECHNICIAN 1963 to 1969. Repaired and maintained ejection seats,
oxygen systems and parachutes. Provided demonstrations and lecture tours covering
survival equipment to visiting civic organizations.

ADDITIONAL SAMPLE RESUMES

The following resumes may prove helpful as guides. See pages 124 and 125 for an index of the resumes contained in *Resume Power.*

ACCOUNTANT/CONTROLLER

KENT PULSEN
1280 7th Avenue North
Portland, Oregon 97225
(503) 681-2132

OBJECTIVE: Controller/Senior Accountant

QUALIFICATIONS

Strong background in Accounting with excellent Management experience. Broad experience in implementing computerized accounting systems and designing more effective manual systems.

EDUCATION

B.A. - Business Administration, Accounting Major, Whitman College

EMPLOYMENT

Old Federal Financial Services, Portland, Oregon 6/81 to 10/83

CONTROLLER 1/82 to 10/83. Responsible for all accounting functions for this finance company with 15 branches throughout Washington, Oregon, Idaho and California. Made all long and short term investments and successfully maintained high returns. Oversaw office and car leasing and the purchase of office equipment.

Researched time sharing systems and worked closely with a vendor to automate the manual financial system. Developed custom software and implemented the General Ledger, AP/AR, and Budgeting System which has exceeded expectations. Responsible for monthly and year-end financial statements, Federal and State taxes, budget reports, branch activity reports and numerous financial and statistical reports. Established accounting procedures which significantly reduced errors and duplication of effort.

ACCOUNTANT 6/81 to 1/82. Produced financial statements, budget reports and audited branch offices.

Steel Jensen & Associates, Multnomah, Oregon 7/80 to 4/81

SENIOR STAFF ACCOUNTANT - Performed reviews, compilations, audits and tax reporting for client firms. In-charge on numerous audits.

Kregle & Associates, Portland, Oregon 11/77 to 7/80

SENIOR STAFF ACCOUNTANT - Performed reviews, compilations, audits and tax reporting. In-charge on numerous audits. Converted several manual bookkeeping systems to computerized systems.

Multnomah School District, Multnomah, Oregon 10/76 to 11/77

AUDIT ASSISTANT - Produced financial and operational audits at the 22 schools within the district. Trained school employees to comply with new state accounting regulations and identified accounting and operational irregularities. Researched IRA and Insurance Benefits programs for teachers and brought about higher interest paid on IRA's and decreased the district's paperwork.

ACCOUNTANT/CONTROLLER

PAUL HUSTED
406 Ash
Boise, Idaho 83702
(208) 361-2918

OBJECTIVE: Senior Accountant

QUALIFICATIONS

Fifteen years accounting experience with a strong background in auditing,
business and individual taxes and cost control programs.

Excellent management experience. Consistently obtain high productivity from
employees.

Implemented computerized accounting systems and supervised computer
installations.

LICENSES

CPA, Idaho State Certification (1969)

EDUCATION

B.A. - Accounting, University of Idaho (1968)

EMPLOYMENT

Brandon Refrigerated Service Inc., Boise, Idaho 3/81 to 10/83

CONTROLLER - For this refrigerated freight hauler, prepared financial
statements and supervised payroll, rate, billing and AP/AR personnel.
Extensively involved in customer relations, establishing credit ratings,
approving credit, reviewing and approving customer claims and making
collections. Managed the cash flow of the company. Developed a major cost
control program and implemented portions which cut overhead 15%. Maintained
the smooth functioning of a sophisticated computerized accounting system.

Bestway Freight Lines, Boise, Idaho 8/77 to 3/81

CONTROLLER - Responsible for financial statements and tax preparation.
Supervised ten employees handling rates, billing, payroll, claims and AP/AR.
Oversaw the payroll system covering six separate union agreements. Developed
the company's first cost studies and identified areas for substantial savings. Cut the shop force from 21 to 11 with no reduction in work completed.
Worked closely with vendor and contract programmer while installing a computerized accounting and payroll system. Implemented a computerized system
to track commodity transactions which reduced required staff time each month
from 180 to 6 hours.

Robert Perkins, CPA, Boise, Idaho 6/68 to 8/77

STAFF ACCOUNTANT - Performed audits and developed financial statements for a
wide variety of clients. Handled state and federal taxes for individuals,
trusts, estates, partnerships and corporations. Provided management services
and designed cost control programs.

174

BANKING MANAGER

DOROTHY MICKULIN
9103 Union
Kansas City, Missouri   64133
(816) 276-4217

OBJECTIVE: Operations Management

QUALIFICATIONS

Eight years in Branch Operations Management as a highly respected Officer
within Kansas City Trust & Savings. Repeatedly given responsibility for
Branch Operations in branches with morale problems. Consistently improved
situations by strengthening training and working closely with individual
staff members. Reduced operations charge-offs, absenteeism and turnover.
Through extensive cross training increased productivity, reduced overtime and
always worked within the budgeted complement. Very effective in training
staff to sell banking services and maintain customer loyalty.

EMPLOYMENT

Kansas City Trust & Savings 6/72 to 12/81

BRANCH OPERATIONS MANAGER 8/79 to 12/81. Responsible for the smooth
functioning of branch operations, while supervising 20 employees. Produced
many weekly, monthly and annual reports, including Charge-off, Dormant Control, Expense Accounts, Full Time Equivalent, Methods and Analysis Branch
Study, Suspense, Internal Certification on Branch Accounts, and Budget and
Profit Plan.

As Branch Operations Manager of two branches, overcame morale problems.
Worked closely with the staffs and significantly improved morale through
better training and supervision. At each branch absenteeism, turnover and
operations charge-offs were significantly reduced. Customer service and
marketing of bank services were strengthened.

RELIEF SUPERVISOR 7/78 to 8/79. Functioned as Branch Operations Manager at
five branches. Supervised 8 to 20 employees.

BRANCH OPERATIONS SUPERVISOR 6/72 to 8/79. Performed same function as Branch
Operations Manager. Supervised and trained 15 to 16 employees. Elected
Corporate Banking Officer by Board of Directors in 1975.

Prior Employment:

Savings Bank of St. Louis, St. Louis, Missouri

OPERATIONS SUPERVISOR 1/70 TO 6/72
MANAGEMENT TRAINEE 1/69 to 1/70
NOTE TELLER 10/67 to 1/69

PURCHASING AGENT

WILLIAM SAXTON
641 Arastradero
Palo Alto, California 94306
(415) 881-9595

OBJECTIVE: Buyer/Purchasing Agent

QUALIFICATIONS:

Over eight years of extensive experience in developing and improving buyer
resources and purchasing systems.

EDUCATION

B.A. - Geography, San Jose State University (1970)
      Minor - Business Administration

EMPLOYMENT

Rapsody Clothing, Palo Alto, California 7/79 to 6/83

DIRECTOR OF CORPORATE SERVICES 7/81 to 6/83. Assigned responsibility for
the departments of Purchasing; Facilities Repair, Maintenance and Operations;
Communications and Copying; Central Supply, Mail Room; and Shipping/Receiv-
ing. Reduced staff personnel 15% while improving response time and communications between corporate services and other departments within the company.

Planned, coordinated and supervised a $6.0 million national inventory sale.
Handled all logistics as Rapsody inventory was moved for blitz sales in
seven major cities. Responsible for negotiations of site locations, contracts, banking locations, personnel needs, materials and equipment trans-
porting, telephones, utilities, hotels, and airline schedules. Accomplished
all corporate goals within a tight schedule.

DIRECTOR OF PURCHASING 7/79 to 7/81. Eliminated duplication of supplies,
increased buying power and reduced cost on items purchased by 15-35%. Saved
$20,000 annually on continuous data processing forms and increased copying
efficienty 50%. Developed and implemented a departmental charge back system
for supplies.

Administered all aspects of national and local trade shows including planning, purchasing new exhibits, contracting with trade people, obtaining sites
and floor spaces, purchasing materials, and handling transportation. Met all
deadlines and reduced costs $75,000 over a two year period.

Ryans Department Stores, Los Angeles, California 7/74 to 12/78

DIRECTOR OF PURCHASING - Negotiated, awarded, and administered contracts with
vendors for the procurement of over 500 different items. Personally redesigned gift boxes and saved $150,000 annually in production and storage
costs. Developed a unique automated packing material system which reduced
labor and handling costs and saved $20,000 annually. Planned and managed an
increased volume of purchasing from $1.1 million to $3.2 million as the chain
increased from six to fourteen stores in three years. Managed the paper
stock warehouse and in-plant print shop.

PURCHASING MANAGEMENT

TERRY PROHASKA
4047 Westavia Drive
Raleigh, North Carolina 27612
(919) 971-3242

QUALIFICATIONS

Strong experience in implementing cost saving purchasing programs. Extensive background in developing and introducing data processing systems to aid in cost reductions. Established reputation as excellent negotiator.

EDUCATION

B.A. - Business Administration, Oakwood College, Huntsville, Alabama (1965)

EMPLOYMENT

Conway Inc., Raleigh, North Carolina 10/75 to Present

MANAGER, FACILITIES PURCHASING 6/80 to Present. Department annually purchases $80 million dollars of supplies, parts and equipment for Maintenance, Repair and Operation of Conway facilities. Manage a staff of twelve buyers and four clerical personnel. Review and approve all purchases over $40,000 and resolve discrepancy reports. Developed and implemented a major program to reduce inventory and operating costs. Since April inventory has been reduced from $5.4 million to $2.9 million, with documented savings of $1.1 million. Continuing to implement additional cost savings measures.

SUPERVISOR, CORPORATE PROCUREMENT 10/75 to 6/80. Negotiated, awarded and administered contracts with vendors for the procurement of over 20,000 different standard parts. Worked closely with company plants throughout the country to calculate future needs for stocked parts. Improved coordination led to larger orders and decreased costs. Aggressively sought out new vendors desiring Conway business in order to tap innovative equipment and methods they possessed. Full procurement program led to $15 million in documented savings in four years on purchases of $70 million.

Nova Co., Valdez, Alaska 8/72 to 10/75

PROCUREMENT ADMINISTRATOR - Installed a catalog list purchasing system and purchased all electrical equipment and hardware for this electrical contractor on the Hunt Oil Refinery. Developed procurement policies and procedures which led to significant savings and introduced volume procurement. The previous small order system resulted in parts delays and higher prices. Worked closely with the architect on this design-build project to predict future needs, then purchased the materials necessary to complete entire sections of the project.

Bronka Industries, Birmingham, Alabama 8/69 to 8/72

MATERIEL ADMINISTRATOR - Developed a solid foundation in the principles of purhasing. In 1970, with a task force of four people, designed and implemented a Stockless Purchasing System which is still used throughout Bronka. System reduced PO's by 75%, enabled the reduction of the buying group from sixty to twenty-five and reduced administration costs 22%. Oversaw the system and continued to handle purchasing duties.

177

FEDERAL GOVERNMENT

LAURA DONOHUE
401 Eastman West
Arlington Heights, Illinois   60005
(312) 871-2652

QUALIFICATIONS

Excellent organizational ability. Successfully developed new systems which
have increased productivity and quality of work.

Excellent speaker. Frequently speak before groups of 100-400 people. Received a standing ovation at an annual convention for making a difficult
subject easily understood.

Outstanding public relations ability. Work very effectively with organizations and individuals while solving problems and explaining policies.
Quickly gain the respect of all parties.

Highly competent. Increased the effectiveness and level of professionalism
in each position held.

EDUCATION

Graduated - Colville High School, Colville, Washington   (1970)

EMPLOYMENT

United States Railroad Retirement Board, Chicago, Illinois   11/74 to Present

Contract Representative 10/77 to Present. Explain and interpret complex laws
and regulations related to retirement, disability and unemployment benefits.
Interview claimants, obtain necessary documents and substantiating evidence
and determine eligibility and amount of benefits. Provide training sessions
for union and management groups to bring them up to date on changes in the
law and regulations. Successfully introduced a group interview procedure for
explaining unemployment compensation when claims rose from 250 to 2000 per
month. Developed numerous systems which decreased backlog and increased
services and staff morale. Job involves 25% travel.

Unemployment Claims Examiner 11/74 to 10/77. Interviewed claimants and
former employers to determine eligibility for benefits. Monitored job finding efforts of claimants and assisted in obtaining new positions. Developed
a new system for coding claims and won the Region Accuracy Award in 1976.

Social Security Administration, Chicago, Illinois   6/70 to 11/74

Service Representative 11/73 to 11/74. Provided assistance and technical
information about Social Security, Medicare and Supplemental Security Income
to beneficiaries and the general public. Resolved problems, untangled red
tape and helped make the system work. Received a cash bonus award for
suggesting improvements in Social Security forms. The change is used nationwide.

Secretary 6/70 to 11/73. Ensured offices ran smoothly, answered correspondence, compiled statistical reports, typed and answered phones.

178

PROPERTY MANAGEMENT

DON ABRAHMS
6317 Avery Road
Fairfax, Virginia 22033
(702) 282-1971

QUALIFICATIONS

Broad experience in all phases of Property Management and Building
Management. Able to keep occupancy rates high and tenants satisfied.

Strong ability in negotiating new and renewal leases.

Creative problem solver. Able to negotiate solutions to the satisfaction of
all parties.

Able to identify new methods for cutting operating costs while increasing
tenant services.

EDUCATION

A.A. - General Studies, Whipple Community College (1970)

EMPLOYMENT

Bridgeport Property Management, Fairfax, Virginia 6/72 to Present

PROPERTY MANAGER 8/79 to Present. Property Manager for Southfield Office
Park and other commercial/industrial properties in Fairfax County. Negotiate
new and renewal leases, resolve tenant problems and oversee the maintenance
of the buildings and grounds. As General Contractor, completed a major
renovation of 10,560 square feet of office space at 18% under the estimated
cost. Increased square footage rates 22% during the last year and a half and
increased the occupancy rate from 92% to 97%. Using a long term, no interest
federal government loan, initiated an energy management system which will
reduce energy costs 20%. Actively involved with budget planning and instituting cost controls.

BUILDING MANAGER 5/75 to 6/79. Managed all maintenance functions at
Southfield Office Park and acted as General Contractor for tenant alterations
and improvements. Worked closely and effectively with subcontractors and
consistently completed projects on schedule and within the budget. Planned
and initiated an in-house HVAC mechanical department - maintenance costs were
reduced and tenant satisfaction increased. Obtained excellent results from
janitorial and security services. Personally performed many repairs.

FIELD SUPERVISOR 6/72 to 5/75. Supervised grounds crews of up to 22
employees while constructing the Southfield Office Park. Operated cranes,
cats, and other heavy equipment while supervising the land reclamation, and
the construction of building sites, streets, parking lots and utility
systems.

MANUFACTURING MANAGEMENT

JON ARNETT
19112 Edgecliff Drive
Cleveland, Ohio 44119
(216) 726-3982

OBJECTIVE: Manufacturing Management

QUALIFICATIONS

Strong background in all phases of production supervision in the electronics
industry including job scheduling, quality assurance, inventory control,
purchasing, customer relations, and supervising and training up to twenty-
eight production workers. Consistently able to increase on time deliveries
while increasing quality and reducing rejections.

EDUCATION

Business - Dennison Community College, 66 credits (1974 to 1977)

EMPLOYMENT

Advanced Circuits, Cleveland, Ohio 11/79 to 8/83

PRODUCTION MANAGER - Supervised five to seven shop personnel in the production of prototype circuit boards. Handled cost estimating, job scheduling, production control, and inventory control. Reduced turnaround time on
orders from three weeks to one week without adding staff or increasing overtime. Quality increased substantially as rejections were reduced 65%. Significantly reduced purchasing costs through a more effective inventory control program.

Digital Systems, Ashtabula, Ohio 5/78 to 11/79

DRILLING AND FABRICATION SUPERVISOR - Supervised twelve production workers
operating computer numerically controlled drilling and fabrication machines.
Also supervised the machine programmers and personally did some programming.
Developed a new job scheduling system which reduced late deliveries by 30%.
Researched inventory needs for raw materials and supplies and determined lead
times. Data allowed the company to reduce inventory on numerous items and
reduced work stoppages due to lack of parts or supplies. As part of a team,
investigated various machines and made recommendations for purchase. Shipped
$300,000 in printed circuit boards monthly.

Hudson Manufacturing, Akron, Ohio 3/74 to 5/78

LEAD PRODUCTION SUPERVISOR 11/76 to 5/78. Supervised two supervisors, four
leads, and thirty-five production personnel. Implemented a job scheduling
system which increased on time deliveries 40% with an average of 150 shipments monthly. Heavily involved in the design of a new facility and planning
the actual move.

SHOP LEAD 9/75 to 11/76. Assigned jobs to eighteen production workers in
drilling, screening, plating, fabricating, and camera work. Developed a
maintenance program which reduced production losses due to breakdowns 70%.

SILKSCREENER 3/74 to 9/75. Hand screened circuitry, bakeable and UV curable
solder mask, and sheet metal front panels.

QUALITY CONTROL MANAGEMENT

TED INGALLS
1887 Hamlin Drive
Dayton, Ohio 45414
(513) 623-7122

OBJECTIVE: Manufacturing Management

QUALIFICATIONS

Strong knowledge of manufacturing practices and procedures.

Developed Quality Control and Material Control procedures which significantly reduced rejects and improved procurement and flow of materials.

Able to strengthen working relations between departments and with vendors.

Consistently produced results beyond expectations of supervisors.

EDUCATION

B.A. - Business Administration, University of Notre Dame   (1979)

TRAINING

Metallurgy, 5 credits, Burlington Community College (1982)
Blueprint Reading, 5 credits, Burlington Community College (1982)
Management by Objectives, 12 hours, Embarco (1981)

EMPLOYMENT

Embarco Manufacturing, Dayton, Ohio 6/79 to 4/83

QUALITY ENGINEER 4/81 to 4/83. For this manufacturer of deck machinery and fishing gear, responsible for quality and material control. Developed QC policies and procedures, including heat treatment requirements, storage procedures, methods to reduce product liability exposure, and raw material and casting specifications. Significantly increased consistency in design specifications of like parts. Handled Process Review and Process Control duties. Reviewed all discrepant work orders and identified sources of problems in-house and with vendors. Through vendor surveillance developed a list of approved vendors. Analyzed all rejected parts and determined the most cost effective means of disposition.

Developed material control policies and procedures and helped redesign the inventory control system. New procedures significantly reduced delays due to out of stock parts. Developed new procedures for procurement of raw materials and castings which reduced discrepant work orders. Analyzed data processing requirements for material control.

EXPEDITER/SCHEDULER 6/79 to 4/81. Expedited parts through machine shops, vendors, and assembly. Issued work orders, scheduled machine shop operations, and participated in the fiscal inventory.

181

TEACHER

SUSAN MAZARA
5211 Swan Avenue
Pittsburgh, Pennsylvania 15211
(412) 276-1954

QUALIFICATIONS

Broad assessment and observational experience.

Proven ability to successfully plan, implement and evaluate educational
programs.

Highly effective with parents. Able to actively involve parents in
Individual Education Plans and provide valuable counseling to them.

Strong background in coordinating support personnel to enhance education for
the profoundly retarded.

Perceptive and sensitive to the special needs students.

EDUCATION

M. ED. Special Education - University of Pittsburgh (completion Fall 1982)

B.A.   Early Childhood Education - University of Pittsburgh (1976)

TEACHING EXPERIENCE

University of Pittsburgh, Pittsburgh, Pennsylvania 9/80 to 6/82

PRACTICUM SUPERVISOR/INSTRUCTOR - Arranged practicum experiences and observed
and supervised twenty-six students. Motivated students to develop their own
professional skills. Taught a senior seminar covering practical issues in
special education including behavioral objectives, lesson plans and
Individual Education Plans.

Simpson Institute, Pittsburgh, Pennsylvania 6/81 to 9/81

TEACHER - Involved with the development of innovative curriculum, educationl
activities and behavior management techniques as a teacher of moderately and
severely retarded adults.

Fircrest School, Pittsburgh, Pennsylvania 9/76 to 8/80

TEACHER - Planned and implemented individualized educational programs for the
profoundly retarded student. Informally assessed their progress and adapted
their programs accordingly. Emphasized the skill areas of self help, social-
ization, communication, pre-vocation and home living. Developed thorough
Individual Education Plans while using effective communication skills with
parents. Highly involved with the coordination of support personnel in
program development.

Butler School District, Butler, Pennsylvania 3/76 to 6/76

STUDENT TEACHER - Demonstrated the ability to motivate the kindergarten child
while teaching all classroom subjects.

FLIGHT ATTENDANT

RACHEL HUANG
4215 West Pinegrove Drive
Madison, Wisconsin 54709
(608) 272-1945

OBJECTIVE: Flight Attendant

QUALIFICATIONS

Excellent experience gained as a Waitress, Salesperson and Assistant Store
Manager. Deal very tactfully and effectively with difficult customers.
Handle emergencies and crises smoothly and efficiently. Develop rapport and
respect among customers and fellow employees.

Always a valued employee. Recognized as cooperative, friendly, cheerful,
self-confident, poised and sincere.

Service oriented person. Received many compliments from store and restaurant
customers for going far beyond the norm.

EDUCATION

A.A. Brunswick Community College (1977-1979)

TRAINING

Customer Service, Daytons, 16 hours (1982)
Achieving Your Potential, The Pacific Institute (Louis Tice), sponsored by
   Daytons, 12 hours (1982)

WORK EXPERIENCE

Daytons, Madison, Wisconsin 1/82 to Present

RETAIL SALES - Sell women's clothing and shoes in an environment where the
customer and service to the customer is first and foremost. Obtained outstanding training in customer service with an emphasis on professionalism.
Received many letters and words of thanks from satisfied and appreciative
customers.

Silver Shell, Madison, Wisconsin 2/80 to 1/82

ASSISTANT STORE MANAGER - In ten months moved from Salesperson, to Head
Cashier to Assistant Manager for this women's fashions store. Handled payroll, developed weekly and monthly sales reports, scheduled staff and trained
new personnel. Created store and window displays and helped coordinate
fashion shows.

Satin Turtle Restaurant, Milwaukee, Wisconsin 6/79 to 10/79

WAITRESS - Became an excellent waitress and received many compliments for my
service, helpfulness and friendliness. Developed a knack for sensing when
additional help was needed at a table.

PERSONAL DATA

Birthdate: 8/15/58   Excellent Health - No limitations
Single   5'8", 129 pounds
Will relocate

RETAIL STORE MANAGEMENT

PERRY CARLTON
13922 Navajo Court
New Bedford, Massachusetts 02740
(617) 823-7947

QUALIFICATIONS

Strong store management background. Received rapid promotions by consistently obtaining results exceeding expectations.

EDUCATION

B.A. English Literature, Massachusetts State University (1977)
      (Business 30 credits)

Graduate Gemologist, Gemological Institute of America (1982)

EMPLOYMENT

Werner Jewelers - May 1978 to Present

MANAGER (2 years) - Responsible for maintaining profitable store operations,
supervise and schedule nine employees; control all special ordering and con-
signment goods; oversee mark-up on special orders, shop repairs and instore
repairs; perform daily, weekly and monthly bookkeeping of all store sales and
payroll. Increased sales 29% over two years in the chain's number two store
by implementing a comprehensive sales training program and selecting better
merchandise.

ASSISTANT MANAGER (2 years) - Assumed responsibility of sales training and
scheduling. Promoted to store manager for adding a "spark" of service-
oriented enthusiasm to each of three stores served. Supervised yearly inventory and maintained inventory control of the watch and stone ring departments.

SALES (9 months) - Rose to the top ten in sales among 150 salespeople in
only six months. Through excellent time-management, outstanding sales, and
rapid assimilation of product and industry knowledge, was promoted to Assistant Manager after nine months' employment.

INTERESTS

Enjoy golf, skiing, and baseball.

MEGAN HATHAWAY
2401 Belle Haven Road N.W.
Roanoke, Virginia 24019
(703) 829-7913

OBJECTIVE: Retail Management

QUALIFICATIONS

Experienced in all phases of retail marketing, merchandising and sales.

Quickly promoted from sales to Department Manager.

Received numerous compliments for creative displays and effective layout of merchandise.

Supervise employees very effectively. Obtained excellent results from a young sales staff.

EDUCATION

AA - Merchandising: Fashion Institute of Design and Merchandising; Los Angeles, California   GPA 3.96 (3/79 to 9/80)

EMPLOYMENT

Brodericks, Roanoke, Virginia 9/81 to 1/84

DEPARTMENT MANAGER Managed the luggage and young men's departments with a staff of ten. Responsible for displays, merchandising, scheduling, price changes, merchandise transfers and twice yearly inventories. Interviewed, hired and trained new employees and wrote performance reviews.

Worked closely with store buyers and manufacturers representatives to maintain high quality merchandise. Remained number one in luggage sales within the chain. Significantly improved the look of the young men's department through creative displays and new merchandising techniques. As Lead Salesperson sold handbags, accessories, young ladies' clothing and functioned as Assistant Department Manager.

Brentanos Department Stores, Los Angeles, California 9/80 to 9/81

ASSISTANT DEPARTMENT MANAGER - Sold handbags, wallets, accessories and designer ready-to-wear clothing. Supervised and trained a staff of ten salespeople.

TRAFFIC MANAGER

KYLE BAUMGARTNER
814 Horgen Avenue
Orlando, Florida 32807
(305) 981-4660

OBJECTIVE: Physical Distribution/Traffic Management

QUALIFICATIONS

Experienced in all phases of Traffic Management. Developed two traffic
departments into smooth functioning, money saving organizations.

EDUCATION

A.A. - Transportation Management, Saltwater Community College (1974)

WORK HISTORY

Traffic Manager   Webber Industries
8/79 to 12/83   Orlando, Florida

Managed the Traffic Department of this $25 million appliance parts manu-
facturer. Annual freight costs total $1.5 million. Set policies for freight
handling, routed all orders, negotiated rates and contracts with carriers,
maintained compliance with transportation laws, filed freight claims,
mediated customer problems and complaints, and audited freight bills for
payment.

Negotiated freight rates with a major carrier, cutting the rate in half and
saving $175,000 per year.

Introduced a routing and consolidation program, saving $80,000 per year
through multi-bill consolidations, utilizing carrier discounts, consolidating
orders, and carrier selection.

Negotiated a product classification change for California freight, saving
$12,000 annually.

Traffic and Distribution Manager   Custer Distributors
6/74 to 8/79   Orlando, Florida

Managed the Shipping and Receiving and Distribution departments for this $28
million distributor of retail products. Annual freight costs totaled one
million dollars. Set up and managed a private trucking operation, saving
$35,000 annually. Introduced new procedures which increased productivity and
created annual cost savings of over $45,000.

186

PERSONNEL ADMINISTRATOR

CHARLES PARSONS
1226 3rd Avenue N.W.
Minnetonka, Minnesota 55343
(612) 378-5162

QUALIFICATIONS

Over eighteen years of progressively responsible experience in all areas of
Human Resources Management.

Repeatedly successful in planning, organizing, and coordinating a wide variety of Human Resources Development programs.

EDUCATION

M.P.A. - Public Administration, Tufts University (1965)
B.A.   - History, Western Kentucky University (1963)

EMPLOYMENT HISTORY

PERSONNEL MANAGEMENT ADVISOR   U.S. Office of Personnel Management
9/76 to Present   Minneapolis, Minnesota

Responsible for promoting Human Resources Management practices with State and
Local governmental organizations in Minnesota, Iowa, and Wisconsin. Plan,
design, and implement Human Resources systems including policies, procedures,
job evaluation, compensation, benefits, recruitment, selection, employee
relations, employee development, management information systems, organizational development, and safety. As project manager develop and adhere to
budgets, supervise and train staff, and coordinate activities with client
agencies. Most recommendations have been adopted, with agencies experiencing
improved quality of service, increased morale, and greater productivity.

CLASSIFICATION AND PAY MANAGER   Hennepin County
9/71 to 9/76   Minneapolis, Minnesota

Developed, implemented, and directed the classification and pay function for
a totally new, comprehensive personnel management system. Trained and motivated the Classification staff to the point that they became a highly respected part of the County Office of Personnel. Designed and developed the
County's first uniform pay system. Promoted, planned, and coordinated a
Personnel Management Information System which significantly increased personnel data needed for management decisions. Improved service delivery 35% by
instituting a personnel generalist approach.

SUPERVISOR OF CLASSIFICATION AND PAY State of Minnesota Merit Employment
4/69 to 9/71   St. Paul, Minnesota

Selected, trained, and supervised the professional staff which maintained and
improved the State classification and pay systems. Developed improved classification and pay policies.

ADMINISTRATIVE CONSULTANT   Public Administration Service
7/65 to 4/69   Chicago, Illinois

Provided administrative, organizational, and personnel management consulta-
tive services to state and local governments nationwide for this highly
respected, non profit consulting organization established in 1933.

COUNSELOR

ADELLE CLEVELAND
3619 N.W. 42nd Street
Malden, Massachusetts 02148
(617) 485-9150

QUALIFICATIONS

Consistently enable clients to function more effectively.

Able to research and develop courses and programs relating to human growth
and development. Have always received high student ratings for knowledge,
enthusiasm and overall effectiveness.

Knowledgeable of local resources. Able to assess problems and connect people
with agencies which have proven helpful.

EDUCATION

M.A. - Counseling, Brandeis University (1977-1979)
B.A. - English Literature, Radcliffe University (1970-1973)

PROFESSIONAL EXPERIENCE

Creative Parenting, Inc., Boston, Massachusetts 1981 to Present

COUNSELOR/INSTRUCTOR - Design, research, organize and teach classes for parents in parenting, discipline and sibling relations. Provide group, family
and individual counseling.

Boston Youth Services, Boston, Massachusetts 1980 to 1981

COUNSELOR/INSTRUCTOR - Counseled families and individuals regarding such
issues as conflict resolution, behavior problems and drug and alcohol abuse.
Publicized and presented "Positive Parenting" classes and co-led adult growth
groups.

Boston Big Sisters, Boston, Massachusetts 1979 to 1980

COUNSELOR/SUPERVISOR - Assessed the needs of young girls and their parents
and matched them with the appropriate Big Sister. Monitored the relationships, offered support and provided crises counseling. Developed recrea-
tional, cultural and educational programs for clients. Designed and co-led
career exploration workshops. Heavily involved in recruiting volunteers and
clients.

Environmental Works, Boston, Massachusetts 1973 to 1977

COMMUNITY ASSISTANCE - Developed and implemented an information and referral
service for consumer complaints and solid waste recycling. Developed an
audio-visual public information program for schools and organizations.
Designed, wrote and produced information booklets on recycling, nutrition and
organic gardening.

TRAINING AND DEVELOPMENT SPECIALIST

DEBRA SLAWSON
1503 Adrian
Minneapolis, Minnesota 55102
(612) 281-6964

QUALIFICATIONS

Broad experience in designing, teaching, and supervising training programs in a large training department.

Consistently able to develop a team and maintain high morale and a sense of commitment.

EDUCATION

M.S. - Curriculum Design Administration, University of Minnesota (1971)
B.S. - Education, Moorhead State University, Minneapolis, Minnesota (1963)

PROFESSIONAL ORGANIZATIONS

Treasurer - American Society for Training and Development, Twin Cities
        Chapter (1981-1982)

American Society for Health Education and Training (ASHET)

EMPLOYMENT HISTORY

Prodigital, Inc., Minneapolis, Minnesota 10/80 to Present

MEDICAL TRAINING ADMINISTRATOR (10/82 to Present)

Responsible for designing and implementing workshops nationwide which train medical professionals in the uses and benefits of digital radiography.

Consult with Prodigital subsidiaries to assess training needs and help them establish training departments.

Developed a comprehensive program to train the fifteen member technical training staff in effective teaching techniques. Ratings from customers after equipment installations have improved 40% since the program was implemented.

CLINICAL APPLICATION TRAINING SUPERVISOR (5/81 to 10/82)

Administered and monitored week-long training workshops for domestic and international customers. These workshops have firmly established Prodigital's reputation for providing excellent service and training after the sale. Developed programs for introducing new product lines to the national sales force. Hired, trained, and supervised a staff of three medical trainers.

TRAINING SPECIALIST (10/80 to 5/81)

Designed and created one week product orientation courses for customers. Due to the success of the courses, the format and procedures were adopted for all training courses.

Thompson Manufacturing Co., St. Paul, Minnesota 9/76 to 10/80

TRAINING SUPPORT MANAGER (7/79 to 10/80)

Developed sales training courses and materials for new and experienced sales people. Took highly technical data and constructed practical, understandable courses.

TECHNICAL TRAINING SPECIALIST (1/79 to 7/79)

Identified needs and designed a five week technical training program for domestic and international specialists. The program became the model for other workshops within Thompson.

ADMINISTRATIVE ASSISTANT TO PRODUCT PLANNING MANAGER (9/76 to 1/79)

Researched market trends and studied products and marketing plans of competitors.

PRIOR EXPERIENCE

School Principal (1972 to 1976), School Supervisor (1971 to 1972), Teacher (1963 to 1971)

CONSTRUCTION MANAGEMENT

MARSHALL TREVES
924 Durhamtree Place
Louisville, Kentucky 40229
(502) 666-2413

QUALIFICATIONS

Coordinate well with contractors and subcontractors. Able to resolve
problems and maintain friendly and effective relations.

Extremely analytical and inventive. Consistently come up with unique
solutions to construction problems.

Proven ability to get projects completed ahead of schedule and under budget.

Able to get the most and best from each worker.

Experienced in all phases of construction.

Calculate very accurate estimates.

EMPLOYMENT

Blouton Ceiling Installation, Louisville, Kentucky 7/80 to 7/83

JOB SUPERINTENDENT - Oversaw and worked on numerous projects for this ceiling
subcontractor, including the First National Building, the remodeling of
eighteen Louisville schools, and the Westgate Mall. As Job Superintendent
for the First National office building, supervised a crew of four men and
coordinated with the contractor and subcontractors to handle the many changes
in the smoothest way possible.

While functioning as foreman of a crew remodeling schools in Louisville,
developed a system which speeded up the work and allowed the project to be
completed under budget and ahead of schedule.

As Job Superintendent on the sixty-five shop Westgate Mall, took a project
that was over budget and behind scheule and turned it around. Developed an
excellent working relationship with the contractor, raised morale, organized
the work more effectively, and created a highly motivated crew. The project
was completed under budget and ahead of schedule.

Treves Construction, Louisville, Kentucky 2/71 to 7/80

OWNER/MANAGER - Provided subcontracting work in framing, finishing, dry wall,
insulation, metal stud framing, aluminum siding, and soffits. Gained expertise in estimating, bidding, and purchasing. Developed a reputation for high
quality work.

Prior Experience: Carpenter 6/65 to 2/71

EDUCATION

Attended Kentucky State University (1963-1965) 105 Credits
Major: Electrical Engineering

FIELD ENGINEER

MARVIN GALUSKA
7212 Lundy Drive
Florissant, Missouri 63031
(314) 682-3099

OBJECTIVE: Field Engineer

QUALIFICATIONS

Strong technical ability in troubleshooting and repairing computer systems
including peripherals and mechanical devices.

Heavily involved in critical customer responsibility. As an on-call field
engineer have developed excellent relations with customers by showing genuine
concern for their problems and by keeping downtime to an absolute minimum.

EDUCATION

Certificate - Radio/Television Servicing, G.W. Mohan Vocational Technical
    Institute (9/76 - 3/78)

CERTIFICATES

Certified Electronic Technician (1977)

EMPLOYMENT

Control Data Corporation, St. Louis, Missouri 4/79 to Present

FIELD ENGINEER - Provide on-site maintenance of many types of computer
equipment including minicomputers, disk drives, magnetic tapes, printers and
communications devices. Perform preventive maintenance and diagnosis/fault
isolation at the component and board level. Responsible for repairing all
mechanical devices and peripherals.

Personally installed several small minicomputer systems. Was lead over two
to three other field engineers on larger installations. Involved with installing several mainframes. Frequently relocate systems.

As Site Engineer for McDonnel Douglas (6/79-6/80) drastically reduced response time and downtime. Analyzed inventory needs and reduced significantly, saving Control Data thousands of dollars.

For the Midwest branch responsible for monitoring factory change orders and
ensuring changes are made at all customer sites. Assist Inventory Control
Manager in keeping branch inventory and site inventories at proper levels.

N.C.R. Corporation, Indianapolis, Indiana 7/78 to 4/79

FIELD ENGINEER - Maintained financial processing equipment on-site, including
check processors and c.o.m. units. Worked closely with customers to solve
their problems.

L.F.N. Electronics, Inc., Indianapolis, Indiana 3/78 to 7/78

ELECTRONICS TECHNICIAN - Performed bench repair and calibration of all
varieties of mechanical and electronic UHF/VHF tuners used in televisions.
Handled inventory control duties.

TRAINING

Mag Tape/Controller Maintenance, Control Data, 80 hours (1983)
Disk Drive/Controller Maintenance, Control Data, 120 hours (1982)
Inventory Management, Control Data, 40 hours (1982)
Minicomputer Maintenance, Control Data, 40 hours (1982)
Line Printer Maintenance, Control Data, 40 hours (1982)
Terminal Systems, Control Data, 40 hours (1980)
Data Communications, Control Data, 40 hours (1979)
Minicomputer Maintenance, Control Data, 160 hours (1979)
Mag Tape Maintenance, Control Data, 40 hours (1979)
Data Products/Line Printer Maintenance, Control Data, 40 hours (1979)
Disk Drive Maintenance, Control Data, 80 hours (1979)

FIELD SERVICE MANAGER

JOSE LEANDRO
13224 Caroline Avenue
Syracuse, New York 13209
(315) 454-2906

OBJECTIVE: Project Manager, Field Service Manager

QUALIFICATIONS

During eight years of installing and maintaining computer systems created an
excellent record for smooth deliveries and installations. Noted for ability
to solve hardware and software problems before installation.

Develop effective working relations with customers, software engineers,
hardware engineers, and field service engineers.

Provide outstanding training for technicians and field service engineers.

EDUCATION

Certificate - Electronics, Blue Sky Community College (1975)

TRAINING

Diablo Disc Drive Maintenance, 80 hours (1975)
Honeywell Computer Repair, 80 hours (1975)

EMPLOYMENT

Distol Engineering Corporation, Syracuse, New York 9/78 to Present

SYSTEMS APPLICATION ENGINEER - Prepare, install and maintain real time process control computers designed for use in the pulp and paper industry.
Using system specifications and functional descriptions, integrate hardware
into proper system configurations. Construct system block diagrams, system
cabling diagrams, and design cables necessary for final installation. Com-
pile proper documentation packages for each system.

Check out individual items and prepare computer systems for in-house acceptance. Supervise the installation of power and signal cables and peripherals.
Train mill personnel in the operation and maintenance of the systems. Assist
in debugging application software and write programs used in the check out of
all systems. Troubleshoot and repair systems after installation.

Interface between customers, project managers, software engineers, and hardware engineers during all phases of system development and installation.
Highly successful in recognizing potential problems and working them out
before installation.

Compudata, Inc., Long Beach, California 6/75 to 9/78

FIELD SERVICE ENGINEER - Repaired and serviced computer systems at customer
sites. Assembled, checked out, and installed computer systems and peripherals.

194

MECHANICAL ENGINEER

RANDY BURKOVSKY
2216 Viewcrest Drive S.E.
Portland, Oregon 97222
(503) 761-2971

OBJECTIVE: Mechanical Engineering

QUALIFICATIONS

Strong design background. Extensive experience in sizing and selecting pumps as Lead Engineer, designing and laying out process piping and plumbing systems, and computer pipe stress analysis.

Excellent writer. Wrote operation, construction acceptance, and maintenance manuals and reports.

EDUCATION

B.S. - Mechanical Engineering, University of Oregon (1970-1975)

EMPLOYMENT

Harcourt Engineers, Portland, Oregon 3/80 to 12/83

MECHANICAL ENGINEER - Worked on large-scale chemical wastewater recovery systems for electric utilities including the Bonneville Power Administration and the Grant County P.U.D. Responsibilities included pump sizing and selection, air compressor installations, vacuum system design, tank and mixer design, clarifier modifications, process piping design, and plumbing and drainage system design for buildings. Also wrote operation, construction acceptance, and maintenance manuals.

Barclay Engineers, Portland, Oregon 5/78 to 3/80

MECHANICAL ENGINEER - Responsibilities included pump sizing and pipe stress analysis for a Pittsburgh and Midway coal mining project, and cost estimating and piping design for a U.S. Army underground heating system at Fort Lewis. Spent six months at the Weyerhaeuser Kraft Mill in Everett as a Project Engineer. Projects included filtrate, white liquor and polyphosphate tank design, couch lumpbreaker roll lift mechanism design, installation of mudwasher mist eliminator, and piping systems for chlorine and hydrochloric gas.

Dayton Company, Portland, Oregon 7/75 to 5/78

PIPING ENGINEER - Duties included cost estimating, piping design, and pump sizing for a Weyerhaeuser pulp and paper modernization project in Longview, Washington. Also, did piping design on a Crown Zellerbach pump and paper project.

ELECTRONICS ENGINEER

JOHN MYERSBY
1487 Laurel Hill Road
Detroit, Michigan 48103
(313) 576-2191

OBJECTIVE: Electronics Engineer

QUALIFICATIONS

Excellent engineering background including experience with
microprocessing design.

EDUCATION

B.S. - Electrical and Computer Engineering, University of
Michigan (1976)

EMPLOYMENT

General Motors, Detroit, Michigan 10/80 to Present

SENIOR ENGINEER - As part of a team of Software Quality Assurance Engineers, evaluate CAD/CAM software and make recommendations for improvements before software is made available to
users within the company. Review functional specifications to
ensure all portions are testable and fully meet user needs.
Analyze test results, identify problem areas, and make final
recommendations.

Performed a cost improvement study which documented savings
through the Software Quality Assurance Program of $400,000
annually. Program has eliminated duplication of testing, produced a more organized software development process, and resolved problems at earlier stages.

Mutual Signals, Ann Arbor, Michigan 6/74 to 10/80

MANAGER OF ENGINEERING SERVICES 6/76 to 10/80. For this firm
which designs, sells, and installs industrial and municipal
signaling and alarm systems, designed systems and oversaw installations. Analyzed job specifications to determine necessary equipment, did takeoffs from blueprints for bids, modified
or designed/built equipment, and provided technical support on
sales calls. Oversaw installations and tested large systems
upon completion.

ELECTRONICS TECHNICIAN 6/74 to 6/76. Installed and tested
systems and did takeoffs from blueprints, as well as supervised
technicians at installation sites.

QUALITY CONTROL INSPECTOR

RITA SAWYER
1202 Guthrie Avenue South
Tulsa, Oklahoma 74119
(918) 693-4217

OBJECTIVE: Quality Control Inspection

QUALIFICATIONS

Excellent training and experience in all phases of quality control inspection. Highly valued by each employer for quality of work. Work hard and
produce excellent results. Work well with engineers, production supervisors,
production workers and vendors.

Broad experience with many measuring devices, including Vernier calipers and
scales, micrometers, sineplates, air gauging equipment, durometer and Rock-
well hardness testing, XYZ coordinate measuring machines, optical comparators, roughness measurement equipment and height gauges. Experienced in
surface plate inspection.

EDUCATION

Graduated - Keota High School, Keota, Oklahoma (1979)

TRAINING

Advancetech, Certificates in: D.C. Electronics, A.C. Electronics,
Semiconductor Devices, Digital Technology, Geometric Tolerancing

EMPLOYMENT

Advancetech, Inc., Tulsa, Oklahoma 10/82 to 10/83

QUALITY CONTROL INSPECTOR - Responsible for all first article inspections and
final inspections for this sheet metal fabricator. Using blueprints calculated dimensions and bend factors to check and approve flat pattern layouts.
Verified proper sequencing of production plans. Received and logged incoming
sheet metal and other products. When parts did not meet customer's specifications, worked closely with engineers to discover if the fault was in the
original design or in the fabrication process. With discovery of fault,
worked with engineers to correct it.

Electrotech Laboratories, Oklahoma City, Oklahoma 6/81 to 10/82

QUALITY CONTROL INSPECTOR - As Source Inspector (7/82 to 10/82) inspected
sheet metal fabrications at vendors' sites. From 6/81 to 7/82 inspected
incoming vendor supplied sheet metal and small precision parts. Used hand
measuring devices as well as XYZ measuring machines and optical comparators.
Inspected for conformance to geometric tolerances. Inspected and tested
electrical components and electrical subassemblies.

K & I Industries, Muskogee, Oklahoma 4/80 to 6/81

MACHINE OPERATOR - Set-up, operated and maintained six Brown & Sharp and two
Traub single spindle screw machines. Inspected manufactured parts and
recorded set-up procedures for ease of manufacturing the part in the future.

MACHINE OPERATOR

PAUL YOKIHANA
13097 Mona N.E.
Honolulu, Hawaii 96821
(808) 292-3724

OBJECTIVE: Machine Operator

  Strong mechanical, tool and woodworking ability.

  Excellent knowledge of the working characteristics of a variety
  of hardwoods.

  Easy to get along with. Cooperative. Flexible.

EDUCATION

  Wood working, Kauai Community College, 60 credits
  (1977 to 1979)

EMPLOYMENT

Exotic Woods Inc., Honolulu, Hawaii 6/79 to 7/83

  MACHINE OPERATOR - Responsible for production of domestic and
  exotic hardwood molding for this small picture frame manufacturer. Handled all operations including selecting wood, rip-
  ping, rabbeting, shaping, rough sanding, finish sanding, stain-
  ing and oiling. Set up and operated jointer, table saws with
  and without power feed, wide belt sander, molder-planer, radial
  arm saw and wood shaper.

  Duties included operation of hand sanders and chopsaws. Occasionally finished and assembled frames. Trained new employees
  and ensured smooth operations in the shop. Produced a very high
  quality product which enabled the firm to double its business
  between 1980 and 1983.

Previous Employment

  Maintenance, CST Inc., Honolulu, Hawaii 6/78 to 6/79
  Waiter, Spring Winds Resort Hotel, Kapaa, Hawaii 5/76 to 6/78

DIRECTOR OF NURSING SERVICES

ELEANOR SIEVERS
3116 Indale Avenue
Athens, Georgia 30606
(404) 643-8014

OBJECTIVE: Director of Nursing/Administrator for Nursing Services

QUALIFICATIONS

Very strong nursing administration experience.

EDUCATION

M.A. - Hospital Administration, University of Southern California (1974)
B.S. - Nursing, University of Texas (1962-1966)

PROFESSIONAL EXPERIENCE

University Hospital, Athens, Georgia 7/77 to Present

ASSOCIATE ADMINISTRATOR FOR NURSING SERVICES 4/82 to Present. Directed the
activities of a 520 FTE nursing staff with a $14 million budget in a 280 bed
medical center. Responsible for all inpatient units including medical, sur-
gical and cardiac intensive care units, an eight room operating suite, and
a level one trauma/emergency department. Worked directly with four Division
Directors and twelve Nursing Supervisors.

Developed new standards for care and set up daily mechanisms to assure
compliance. Established more effective budgetary and staffing monitoring
systems which saved $400,000 over the previous year. Opened six critical
care beds and added a head nurse.

DIVISION DIRECTOR, ACUTE CARE 1/80 to 3/82. Responsible for this eight unit
division with a 205 FTE nursing staff - 190 beds, $5.3 million budget. Es-
tablished workable and effective budgetary controls. Installed and coordinated a capital equipment purchasing system which saved $45,000. Implemented
two medical services. Established, trained and supported a service for
ventilator dependent quadriplegics in the Rehabilitation unit. Trained staff
in troubleshooting ventilators and working with patients.

NURSING ADMINISTRATIVE SUPERVISOR, MEDICAL/SURGICAL 7/77 to 1/80. Had re-
sponsibiliy for two 24-bed units with a 69 FTE staff. Established a six bed
telemetry unit and a cardiac patient teaching program. Developed a primary
nursing care model and upgraded the staff from mostly aides to mostly RN's.
Increased the role of head nurses by giving them greater budgetary and administrative responsibilities. Established preoperative standards.

The Methodist Hospital, Houston, Texas 6/66 to 7/77

NURSING ADMINISTRATIVE SUPERVISOR, ACUTE MEDICINE 6/74 to 7/77
Administered two medical units with 62 beds and a 65 FTE staff. Trained new
staff as the units moved from mostly aides to a staff of RN's. Worked with
head nurses as they were given more managerial responsibility.

INSERVICE INSTRUCTOR 3/70 to 6/74. Provided orientation and continuing
education of RN staff and skills training for nurses assistants.

HEAD NURSE, Cardiac Unit 2/68 to 3/70

STAFF NURSE, Intensive Care Unit, Cardiac Unit 6/66 to 2/68

199

REGISTERED NURSE

PETER SIMMONS
1527 Broadway #217
Irvine, California 92713
(714) 523-7615

OBJECTIVE: Emergency Room Nursing

QUALIFICATIONS

Highly trained and experienced. Considered by supervisors to be an excellent
emergency room nurse. Strongly motivated, provide quick, accurate assessments, and work effectively with doctors and other ER staff. Develop excellent rapport with patients.

EDUCATION

Diploma, School of Professional Nursing, St. Lukes Methodist Hospital, Cedar
  Rapids, Iowa (1975)
Certificate - Emergency Medical Technician (1975)

EMPLOYMENT

University of California, Irvine Medical Center, Orange, California 10/81 to
  9/83.

STAFF R.N., EMERGENCY ROOM - In this busy, twenty-two bed emergency room,
worked with up to sixty patients per shift. As the triage nurse on the seven
nurse staff, stabilized patients, made critical decisions, and handled the
flow of patients. Received a high number of trauma patients.

Scripps Memorial Hospital, San Diego, California 6/79 to 10/81

STAFF R.N., EMERGENCY ROOM - Night shift charge nurse for this eight bed
emergency room. Worked with a lot of cardiac, respiratory, and psychiatric
emergencies. Independently assessed patients and initiated diagnostic procedures. Ordered x-rays and lab tests. Consulted with patients by telephone
and determined appropriate actions.

Las Cruces Memorial Hospital, Las Cruces, New Mexico 5/77 to 4/79

STAFF R.N., EMERGENCY ROOM - Performed all emergency room functions at this
sixteen bed emergency facility. Trained nursing students and supervised the
outpatient methadone treatment program. Also assisted in the minor surgery
department and the bronchoscopy department.

Mercy Medical Center, Roseburg, Oregon 6/75 to 4/77

STAFF R.N., EMERGENCY ROOM - Treated many motor vehicle and sawmill accident
trauma patients at this twelve bed emergency room. Charge nurse last ten
months. Also functioned as mobile intensive care nurse working by ambulance
with an EMT and respiratory therapist. Taught IV therapy, CPR, and assessment skills to EMT's as part of an extensive training program.

MEDICAL RECORDS MANAGEMENT

JAMA COLERIDGE
126 Bridge Street S.E.
Titusville, California 92171
(714) 762-1724

QUALIFICATIONS

Excellent Medical Records background. Strong ability in all areas, including medical terminology, transcribing, coding, abstracting, chart assembly, chart analysis, committee work, medical/legal, confidentiality, testifying in court, risk management, and CRT retrieval.

Strong ability to organize and simplify office procedures, and keep morale and productivity at peak levels.

Able to instill in employees the need for accuracy and attention to details.

Develop close working relations with subordinates and work very effectively with hospital administrators.

Able to cut costs without cutting service.

EDUCATION

A.A. - Medical Record Technology, Riverside Community College (1974)

EMPLOYMENT

Titusville General Hospital, Titusville, California 6/74 to 4/83

ASSISTANT DIRECTOR OF MEDICAL RECORDS 5/77 to 4/83

Supervised and trained a staff of sixteen. Maintained very low turnover and low use of sick leave. Continually streamlined policies and procedures to make the workload more reasonable. When work became heavy, would code, transcibe, assemble charts, or help wherever the need was greatest. Worked hard to keep morale up during many difficult times.

To improve quality and training, created job descriptions, responsibility statements, and standards for each position. A cross-training program resulted in greater productivity and the ability to cover for people on vacation. Ways to cut costs were constantly being implemented. Office supplies were reduced $5,000 in 1980 through very tight monitoring of needs.

MEDICAL RECORD ANALYST 6/74 to 5/77. HICDA coding, PAS-MAP abstracting, assembled and analyzed medical records.

Prior Employment:

Medical Record Clerk, Mercy Hospital, 5/72 to 6/74
Dietician's Aide, Mercy Hospital, 2/71 to 5/72
Cashier, Savmor, Inc., 8/70 to 2/71

LAW ENFORCEMENT INVESTIGATOR
POLICE OFFICER

BRAD PIERSON
219 Diehl Street
Raleigh, North Carolina   27608
(919) 688-4216

OBJECTIVE: Law Enforcement/Investigation/Internal Security

QUALIFICATIONS

Thirteen years of strong and varied law enforcement experience.

EDUCATION

B.A. - Business Administration, North Carolina State University, 3.5 GPA
(1980-1982)
A.A. - Police Science, Raleigh Community College, Graduated with Honors
(1970-1973)
North Carolina State Training Commission Police Academy, Graduated #1 in
graduating class (1971)

LAW ENFORCEMENT TRAINING

DWI Enforcement, Northwestern University Traffic Institute, two weeks (1978)
Accident Investigation, Northwestern University Traffic Institute, two weeks
(1977)
SWAT School, FBI, two weeks (1976)
Drug Enforcement, Drug Enforcement Administration, two weeks (1974)
Homicide Investigation, North Carolina State Training Commission, one week
(1974)
Advanced Law Enforcement, North Carolina State Training Commission, one week
(1974)

EMPLOYMENT

Wake County Prosecuting Attorney, Raleigh, North Carolina   4/80 to Present

As part of this very aggressive prosecuting team, increased conviction rate
from 48% in 1979 to 74% in 1981. From 10/80 to 1/82, member of the experi-
mental Career Criminal Unit. Met and exceeded goals of keeping repeat
offenders incarcerated until trial, bringing cases to trial quickly, and
obtaining maximum sentences. Unit had a 98% conviction rate.

INVESTIGATOR 4/80 to Present. Assist deputy prosecutors in case preparation,
research, and courtroom preparation. Involved in most major cases and homicides. Was chief investigator for the office in the recent Chet Thurston
triple homicide trial. As illustrator, draw crime scene diagrams, sketches,
and illustrations for use in trials.

POLICE LIAISON OFFICER 4/80 to Present. Maintain open communications with
Federal, State, and Local law enforcement agencies. Keep individual officers
informed of progress in cases they investigated and made arrests in. Have
developed excellent relations with all departments.

PUBLIC INFORMATION OFFICER 1/82 to Present. Work with'the media to keep them
informed of progress and developments in cases. Handle all press inquiries,
hold press conferences, and prepare press releases.

Raleigh Police Department, Raleigh, North Carolina 1/69 to 4/80

PATROL OFFICER (6 years) Handled all types of cases including shop lifting, burglaries, robberies, con artists, and traffic accidents. Worked closely with Pennys, Jarvis Stores, and Sears to break up a four state shoplifting ring. Handled numerous internal fraud and theft cases with large companies. One of three officers on-call to investigate traffic fatalities. Received very high interdepartmental ratings and received many letters of commendation from individuals, businesses, and agencies. Member of SWAT team.

SPECIAL INVESTIGATIONS (3 years) Specialized in narcotics investigations including undercover assignments. Involved in several major narcotics arrests including breaking up a large heroin distribution ring. Investigated homicides, burglaries and frauds as well.

STAFF SERVICES (2 years) Performed comprehensive background checks on police department applicants and screened out those unsuitable. Established a more extensive in-service training program and personally taught many workshops.

U.S. Army 12/65 to 12/68

CREW CHIEF - Served as helicopter crew chief and maintenance supervisor. Decorated for service in Vietnam. Honorable discharged as a Sergeant E-5.

INSTRUCTING

Presented several one and two day lectures for the North Carolina State Training Commission Police Academy and Police Science departments at Community Colleges. Topics have covered accident investigation, crime scene drawing, firearms, and narcotics investigation.

203

SECRETARY

MARY BLAIR
1199 - 7th Avenue S.
Tucson, Arizona 85701
(602) 426-6197

OBJECTIVE: Executive Secretary/Office Manager

QUALIFICATIONS

Considered outstanding in organizational ability, office efficiency and time management. Type 70 wpm, shorthand 90 wpm. In current position have been told I am the best person they've ever had. Very cheerful, get along well with everyone, and always complete work on schedule. Excellent public relations and customer contact ability.

EDUCATION

Certificate - Secretarial Program, Simpson Business College, Tucson, Arizona (1963-1964)

EMPLOYMENT

Randolph Machinery, Tucson, Arizona 1/81 to Present

SECRETARY - Secretary to the Support Manager of Manufacturing Research and Development. In addition to typing and other secretarial functions, work with up to twelve executives to schedule frequent manufacturing meetings at times acceptable to all. Update log books and determine status and progress of R&D projects. Timekeeper for forty engineers.

Fuller Custom Building, Tucson, Arizona 2/79 to 12/80

OFFICE MANAGER - Purchased lumber, moulding, and hardware; supervised one clerk; and handled payroll, accounts payable, and accounts receivable. Significantly increased the efficiency and professionalism of the office.

Hydro-Pump, Tucson, Arizona 5/70 to 7/72

EXECUTIVE SECRETARY - Secretary to the Vice President of Production. Typed, took dictation, kept the office running smoothly, and arranged all business travel for the Production Department.

Prior Employment

STENOGRAPHER - North American Insurance, Tucson, Arizona 10/67 to 7/69
STENOGRAPHER - Bryer Insurance Agency, Tucson, Arizona 6/64 to 10/67

SECRETARY

HARRIET GUERRERA
1326 S. Denby
Toledo, Ohio 43615
(419) 763-2142

QUALIFICATIONS

Experienced in all facets of office work and capable of handling a great deal of responsibility.

Detail oriented person with strong organizational abilities. Very accurate in all areas of work.

Work very effectively with customers and co-workers.

Highly regarded by all employees for friendliness, hard work and the ability to learn new procedures very quickly.

EDUCATION

Johnson Business College, Toledo, Ohio (1976)

EMPLOYMENT

Totem Cycle, Toledo, Ohio 5/81 to 9/83

SECRETARY - Organized and filed customer files; typed contracts, titles and letters; balanced end of month books; coordinated with banks on credit applications; handled bulk mailings; wrote and posted invoices; purchased shop and office supplies; inventoried parts; responsible for petty cash; balanced till sales against invoices. Functioned as office manager in absence of owner.

Bronking Electronics, Toledo, Ohio 10/80 to 5/81

ASSISTANT PRODUCT MANAGER - Posted all product transactions to maintain a proper inventory of electronic components. Handled telex orders and confirmed product availability. Worked closely with other branches when seeking parts. Used computer terminals and manual systems to locate products and post transactions.

Touche Ross and Company, Toledo, Ohio

FILE LIBRARIAN - Checked out audit materials on client firms to the company's CPA's and ensured proper filing when returned. Located and filed microfiche audit information.

ADMINISTRATIVE ASSISTANT

ANGELA MENDOZA
1206 Capistrano Way
Los Angeles, California 90063
(213) 871-5239

OBJECTIVE: Office Manager/Administrative Assistant/Executive Secretary

QUALIFICATIONS

Extremely well organized and efficient. Quickly learn procedures and methods. At each position have become the department's resource person because of thorough knowledge of the system and the people within it.

Consistently able to develop new forms, systems and procedures to increase the efficiency and effectiveness of an office, yet also able to keep intact those parts which continue to work well.

Excellent supervisor of office staff. Provide effective staff training. Able to produce a well motivated staff and have successfully turned problem employees into excellent workers.

EDUCATION

East Los Angeles College, Business courses, 36 credits (1964-1965)
Woodrow Wilson High School, Los Angeles, California (Graduated 1964)

EMPLOYMENT

Los Angeles County 6/62 to 6/83

SUPERIOR COURT CLERK 1/79 to 6/83. Responsible for ensuring a smooth flow of cases through the Los Angeles County court system. Continually updated the master calendar for two civil judges and tracked the progress of trial and pre-trial motions and appeals and the overall status of up to 150 cases at a time. Coordinated between the judges and 300 attorneys in order to get cases through the court system as efficiently as possible. Attended all jury and nonjury trials and handled numerous responsibilities. Produced daily reports for each trial and made sure documents and evidence were properly handled.

ADMINISTRATIVE ASSISTANT 9/72 to 1/79. As Administrative Assistant to the County Clerk, supervised seven secretaries and typists and made sure the dozens of forms and documents were processed properly. Had frequent contact with foreign consulates and the office of the California Secretary of State. Developed a secretary's manual which explained hundreds of procedures and significantly reduced clerical errors.

SENIOR STENOGRAPHIC SECRETARY 6/68 to 9/72. As Senior Secretary in the Department of Personnel, supervised five clerk-typists in the processing of performance evaluations, certifications, and all other matters pertaining to the Employee Development Division. Developed evaluation forms for specific jobs and edited and proofread job descriptions written by job analysts.

SECRETARY 5/65 to 6/68. As a Secretary in the Sheriff's Department worked directly with Deputies, Patrol Officers and Detectives. Took dictation on all types of crime reports and intelligence reports.

BOOKKEEPER/OFFICE MANAGER

JANE PETERSON
3126 Larado Drive
Fargo, North Dakota 58103
(701) 923-6541

OBJECTIVE: Bookkeeper/Office Manager

QUALIFICATIONS

Strong Bookkeeping and Office Management experience. Full-charge bookkeeper with broad experience organizing office functions and supervising office
staff.

EDUCATION

Bookkeeping Certificate, Berkeley Business College, Tulsa, Oklahoma (1972-
1973)

EMPLOYMENT

Coca-Cola, Fargo, North Dakota 9/79 to 2/83

ROUTE ACCOUNTANT - Computed sales and cash receipts data for 220 routes,
and converted data for computer input. Maintained very accurate records and
completed work at twice the rate of the next fastest Route Accountant.

Bend Showcase Company, Fargo, North Dakota 7/75 to 9/79

BOOKKEEPER/OFFICE MANAGER - For this manufacturer of fine wood store
fixtures, supervised an office staff of three. Handled payroll for 250 employees
represented by thirty different unions, and reconciled bank accounts.
Developed a report used by estimators which enabled them to calculate labor
costs more accurately. Assisted in the installation of an automated data
processing system.

Kennecott Die & Mold, Tulsa, Oklahoma 6/73 to 5/75

BOOKKEEPER/SECRETARY - Full-charge bookkeeper for this manufacturer of
industrial dies and molds. Duties included general ledger, trial balance, bank
reconciliation, tax returns, financial statements, costing, accounts payable,
accounts receivable, and payroll. Purchased all raw materials, tools and supplies.

ACTIVITIES

Enjoy gardening, crossword puzzles, and creative writing.

OFFICE MANAGER/BOOKKEEPER

BRENDA BURNS
4603 Corporal
Boise, Idaho 83706
(208) 263-5974

OBJECTIVE: Office Manager/Full Charge Bookkeeper

QUALIFICATIONS

Broad experience in all phases of Bookkeeping including General Ledger, AP/AR, Journal Entries, Cash Receipts, Bank Deposits, Reconciliation, Invoicing, Vouchers, P and L Statements, and Taxes. Totally enjoy all aspects of Bookkeeping.

Excellent Supervisor. Create an open, friendly, relaxed environment where all work and assignments are completed on time.

Efficient, hard working, very accurate, methodical, love the challenge of balancing.

EDUCATION

Graduated Bush High School, Bush, Idaho (1978)
Major Courses: Bookkeeping, Typing

EMPLOYMENT

Wentworth Construction Co., Boise, Idaho 7/78 to 6/83

OFFICE MANAGER/BOOKKEEPER - For this builder of dams, bridges, and highways, handled the books for three companies simultaneously. Responsible for full set of books including AP/AR, Cash Receipts, Bank Deposits, Reconciliation, Invoicing, Vouchers, Journal Entries, and General Ledger. Maintained a payroll system that accommodated 20-250 employees. Supervised two clerical staff. Computed and filed all federal, state, county, and city taxes and maintained all necessary records. Responsible for all phases of bookkeeping through Profit and Loss Statements.

For Gorge Developments, a newly created investment company, set up a complete set of books, consolidated many procedures to avoid duplication of effort, wrote a procedures manual, and computerized the transmittals of cash and sales.

THE SYSTEMATIC JOB SEARCH

Many people are startled to discover that only two of every ten job openings are ever advertised or listed with employment agencies. The other eight jobs have become known as "the hidden job market." This fact of life necessitates a job-finding strategy far different from the one used by the average job seeker. The typical job-finding strategy consists of mailing out dozens of resumes, visiting a handful of employment agencies, and religiously reading the want ads. While twenty percent of all people do find jobs this way, there are many for whom this strategy simply does not work.

Relatively few job openings are ever advertised since advertising is often a last resort. When a position opens up the supervisor immediately begins considering people she knows, including people who took the initiative to meet her. If no one comes to mind, the supervisor may ask people in the department to refer their friends or contacts. If that doesn't work, she may contact business associates for referrals. Finally, the supervisor may contact personnel. Personnel may then choose to advertise or list the opening with an employment agency. But most jobs are filled before the need to advertise arises.

Many companies search first in their own ranks when filling a position, and it's not uncommon for this process to take a month. If you happen to call or show up at just the right time, or get referred by someone, you may become the only outsider to be interviewed.

Finding the right job, one that provides growth and satisfaction, requires the right strategy. It takes considerable amounts of thought, time, and energy, but the payoff is tremendous. You're going to tap into the hidden job market with The Systematic Job Search strategy. These are the requirements:

Focus—Know exactly what type of work you want and the type of organization you want to work for. Identify your strengths so that you'll know you can do an outstanding job.

Resume—Develop a resume that really sells you, one that accurately describes your accomplishments and potential.

Employer Research—Develop a list of fifty to two hundred prime organizations that match your requirements for industry, location, size, growth, and any other factors. Break the list into groups of twenty, categorizing them by desirability. Group A has the highest priority, Group B the second highest, and so forth. When an interview is arranged, review the research you did on that company and go prepared.

Contacts—Send your resume to friends, relatives, and business contacts, and then talk to them about what you're seeking. Your network of contacts will keep their eyes and ears open for you; when positions open up in their companies (or in *their* friends' companies), they can supply you with the names of people to contact.

Calls—In the first week call each of your top-twenty organizations and ask for the name of the person with the power to hire you. That person is usually one or two levels higher than the position you would fill. Call those people and ask for ten or fifteen minutes of their time; explain that you understand that they probably don't have any openings at the moment. Make your calls either before or after sending your resume. You may prefer to simply sell yourself over the phone. If you mail your resume first, state in your cover letter that you will call next week to set up a brief meeting.

Interviews—Your calls will result in interviews forty to eighty-five percent of the time. Before each interview, research the organization. During the ten- to fifteen-minute interview you will learn more about the organization and what they look for in their employees. Ask intelligent questions and explain how your background could be helpful to them. Create a favorable impression of yourself and cause the person to think, "If I had an opening, that's a person I'd like to have on board." At the end of your meeting, ask for referrals to the key people in other top-twenty organizations.

Followup—After each interview send a thank-you note and express your interest in the organization. This causes the person to think favorably of you once again. Three weeks later call to see if any jobs have developed. If not, make a brief call every four weeks. After two or more calls, the person who interviewed you may refer you to someone else in the organization, perhaps even his secretary; as long as that person will be aware of openings, everything is fine.

More Interviews—After talking to key people in most of your top-twenty organizations, you have several options: (1) you can repeat the process with your next group of twenty; (2) you can mail resumes to all the other organizations and wait for interview offers; (3) you can mail resumes to the remaining organizations and follow up with phone calls to set up meetings even if no current openings exist; (4) you can mail resumes to the remaining organizations and set up interviews only for current openings; (5) you can call the remaining organizations and ask if openings exist.

Hunting jobs in the hidden market will require hard work and endurance, but it can be exciting and very rewarding. There may be frustrations and down times, but nothing compared to what most people experience.

Let's look at the points just covered, but in more detail.

FOCUS

First you need focus. Focus means you have narrowed your choices to one or two main fields. Within those fields there may be several job titles to consider, but they will all be interrelated. Occasionally someone can handle as many as three or four fields, but that requires a lot more effort than most can devote and often dilutes energy. The person looking at four different fields may spread himself too thin and not do justice to the job search in any.

People looking for the same job with a different company or a promotion to the next level in their field already have this basic kind of focus. The person making a career change or the person who has merely held jobs but never a career often lacks this type of focus. Their tendency is to depend on the want ads as their only source of job leads. An attitude of, "I don't know what I'm looking for, but when I see it in an ad, I'll recognize it" will rarely lead to a high-quality job. Professional assistance in career counseling can help such people develop focus.

Some people are fortunate enough to discover at a fairly young age what type of work they like to do. Others fall into a job somewhat by accident and find that they basically enjoy it and do it well. Some find it very difficult to select an occupation they really like and bounce from job to job. Still others have been in one field for several years but realize they need a change—the challenge may be gone, their specialty may have become obsolete, or perhaps their values have changed. The last two types of people have the most difficult time achieving focus in their job search.

If you are a person who has had jobs but never a career, or if you've had a career which now must be altered, you are the best candidate for professional assistance. I suggest you read *The Three Boxes of Life* by Richard Bolles to start. You can find it in most book stores. *The Three Boxes of Life* will take you through the steps of making sound career decisions and is the best written among several books on the market.

After reading it you may want to consider taking a career exploration class at a community college or work through your exploration with a private career counselor. Private firms offer group workshops, individual guidance, or a combination of the two. Most will offer you a free introductory workshop or a free introductory individual session. Costs can vary from two hundred to over two thousand dollars. Most will also assist you with your job search and they will teach you how to use the hidden job market to your benefit. The more expensive ones are not necessarily more effective than the less expensive ones; choose carefully.

With a good firm you will have made an excellent investment even at costs of over one thousand dollars. When you consider the value of having a job you enjoy and one you do well in, it will no doubt pay for itself very quickly. If it helps you find the right job faster than if you had not sought assistance, it has paid for itself again. If they help you identify your strengths and prepare you for interviews, you will sell yourself better and be offered a higher salary than otherwise. By working in a job that utilizes your strengths you will move up faster and get more money for your efforts.

Once you have focused on one or two fields, read everything you can about them. A good textbook is often the place to start. One of my clients has been in sales for three years but was interested in purchasing. He had dealt with purchasing agents, but he knew relatively little about the technical aspects of the job. He found an introductory college textbook extremely helpful; it was organized well and gave him a good grasp of all the basic concepts. Since he wasn't studying for a grade he read it fairly quickly with the goal of getting the main ideas. Next he visited the library and found they had a trade journal for purchasing agents, which discussed the latest trends in the field.

Trade journals are simply magazines designed for specialists. They exist because companies find it cost effective to advertise their products or services exclusively to the people who need what they provide. Virtually every industry and occupation has a trade journal. Their main advantage for job seekers is that they cover current practices as well as new ideas being tested. They'll give you a sense of what the field is *really* like, because the articles are written not by theoreticians or academics but by people who are out in the market place. You'll also pick up the jargon; when you start interviewing you'll be able to converse intelligibly with the employer. Since it is common for employers to ask you what you think about a particular issue, it helps to be familiar with it.

In addition to textbooks and trade journals you should use your library to locate occupational books about your chosen career field. Don't hesitate to ask your librarian for assistance. The books are usually written by people who have worked in the field and have an intimate knowledge of its advantages and disadvantages. They'll describe what the work is like, how to get into the field, and the career options available.

Eventually there is no substitute for talking to people in your chosen field. As helpful as textbooks, occupational books, and trade journals are, there is nothing like a face-to-face conversation with a knowledgeable person.

Talk

Once you've narrowed your choices down to a few occupations and done your reading, begin talking to people who already work in your chosen field. Learn the positives and negatives about the field, get advice, find out which are the best companies to work for, and get referrals.

People are generally easy to talk to and they like to be helpful. If you wanted to be a buyer for a clothing store you could begin by calling a store and asking for the name of a buyer, or you might simply ask for the buying department. Explain that you are seriously considering buying as a profession, have done some reading about it, and need to talk to several buyers before you can really make a final decision. Then ask for twenty minutes of their time. If you are pleasant on the phone, I guarantee that ninety percent of the people you call will give you some time. Of course some will be more helpful than others.

The biggest problem people face is their fear of rejection. Don't let that stand in the way. If someone is unwilling to give you some time, assume that she would not have been very helpful anyway. Remember, you're not asking anyone to do something you wouldn't be willing to do. If someone asked for twenty minutes of your time to discuss your favorite hobby, wouldn't you give it to them? Assume people will be pleasant to you, and they will be.

Normally you will want to meet these people at their place of business to get a feel for the environment. At times, however, a conversation over the telephone will provide everything you need. You'll mainly ask questions and listen to their answers. Your questions should revolve around issues left unanswered by your reading. Ask what they like or dislike about their occupation, how they got into it, what their background is. Ask for suggestions regarding job-finding strategies for that field. Ask about salary ranges. (Be tactful about salaries, though—people will not want to reveal how much they make. A good approach is, "With my education and experience, how much do you think I should expect to be offered? I know it's hard to say exactly, so maybe you could just give me a range.") Ask which are the best companies to work for. Finally, ask if they can give you the names of people to talk to.

One of my clients did this type of research in two related fields. She had recently graduated from law school and started her own practice but discovered she did not like the adversarial relationship inherent in the legal system. Two years earlier she and her husband had acted as general contractors while building their own home. That process plus other experiences told her that she really liked the construction and real estate field. After much reading and thought she concluded that she would like to work in a title insurance company or as a right-of-way agent purchasing land or easements for utility companies or the State.

Her first contact was with a right-of-way agent for a nearby city. He was very enthusiastic about his work and gave her a lot of information and encouragement including the names of several organizations, some of which she would never have thought to contact. Next she spoke to a manager of a title insurance company who described what she did and the different ways of reaching that position. She was also very enthusiastic and encouraging. She not only provided the names of all the local title insurance companies but also information about them *and* the name of a key person to contact in each company. By using the manager's name as a reference, she was successful in getting in to see the person with the power to hire her in each company. She found the entire process surprisingly easy and very enjoyable.

One important thing to remember is that once she had decided to pursue those two fields she no longer asked for appointments on the pretext of getting information. Instead, she began requesting ten or fifteen minutes with the person with the power to hire to learn about possible openings. I make this point because in the past some people have abused the opportunity. They pretended to want only information, but they always sought out a person with power to hire and then hit them up for a job. This can leave a bad taste in the mouth of the person who is tricked; people have become a little less willing to help those who genuinely wanted advice and information as a result.

RESUME

Your top-quality resume will open doors and help you land the right job more quickly.

EMPLOYER RESEARCH

Employer research is one of the most important—yet most neglected aspects—of a job search. The research consists of two stages: (1) using the Yellow Pages, professional directories, and other resources to develop a high-priority list of fifty to two hundred employers, and (2) gathering specific information about each organization before an interview, culminating in in-depth studies of organizations which offer you a job.

Stage 1 will normally take three to six hours to complete. Your goal is to quickly develop a list of employers that probably hire people in your field. Later you will prioritize them into groups of twenty using the ABC method. The A group will be your top twenty, the B group your second top twenty, and so on. In most cases you will be prioritizing without a great deal of information to go on, but prioritizing is still very important.

Start with the Yellow Pages or one of the other directories listed in Resources For Employer Research, pages 245 to 253. Many directories list companies by industry using the Standard Industrial Classification (SIC) codes. A guide to the SIC coding system found in each resource will help you find your preferred industries. Once you obtain the proper SIC codes you will be reviewing only those companies in your preferred industries. Some resources also use codes to indicate sales volume, value of assets, and number of employees. Write down the name, address, and phone number of all potential employers on index cards. A card system will make prioritizing your list easier. Copy any other information provided as well.

For each person there are probably two or three ideal resources listed on pages 245 to 253. Before you go to a library, read these pages thoroughly. Place a check by resources that might be useful. When you get to the library explore those resources and choose the ones you want to concentrate on.

Some industries have developed special directories. To locate directories use *The Guide to American Directories* or the *Directory of Directories*. A good example of a directory is *The World Aviation Directory*. It provides names, addresses, and phone numbers for every airline, airport, airplane or parts manufacturer, aviation insurance company, and dealer in the United States. For some people it's the only resource needed.

It will be worth the effort to determine if an association represents your field or industry. Use the *Encyclopedia of Associations* and *National Trade and Professional Associations*. You'll find local associations listed in the Yellow Pages under "Associations." Associations are usually formed to give an industry or profession more political clout as well as to provide a forum for new ideas. They generally publish membership lists and news magazines, hold conventions and meetings, list job openings, and distribute free literature. Associations exist solely to be helpful. If they fail to meet the needs of members, they lose those members and their annual dues. For this reason you'll find most association employees to be very helpful.

Once you have compiled and prioritized your list of fifty to two hundred employers, it's time to do some preliminary research on each of your top-twenty organizations; this begins Stage 2 of Employer Research. For local companies your first step is to visit the nearest major library. Many libraries have a clipping file and house organs (in-house newsletters). Clipping files contain newspaper articles about local companies, with each company having a separate file. If you can't find anything about a company, it may be that the organization is so small that nothing has been written about it. Gathering information about organizations with ten or fewer employees can be difficult.

House organs can be particularly helpful. Published primarily for the benefit of their employees, many companies also send them to customers, suppliers, and libraries for public relations purposes. Most contain a letter from the company president describing results from the recent past or plans for the future. Some provide clues about possible openings by including pictures of employees retiring or being promoted. Feature articles about special employees are also common.

Publicly held companies are required by law to publish annual reports. Actually they are only required to describe their financial status; all the rest of the material is public relations. Very few people actually know how to make sense of the financial material, but there is much more to an annual report. Invariably there is a letter from the president or chairman of the board summarizing the past year and making predictions for the next. Other sections describe recent acquisitions, new products, problems to be faced and overcome, and subsidiaries.

Recruiting brochures can be extremely helpful. Most are designed for recent college graduates but can be useful to anyone. They usually describe the history and background of the company, the training you might receive, company benefits, and the desired backgrounds of employees. Most four-year colleges will have a pretty good selection of recruiting brochures.

The Moody's Manuals provide very good information on large companies; most libraries will have a set. Information includes company history, finances, subsidiaries, products and services, sales, plants and properties, and number of employees.

Other sources of information are magazines and newspapers. Any of the indexes listed on page 254, such as the *Reader's Guide to Periodical Literature*, will lead you to pertinent articles. Many will be feature articles that may give you real insight into the company.

To gain information about your interviewer, try *Who's Who* or the biographical information supplied in *Dun & Bradstreet Reference Book of Corporate Managements* or *Standard and Poor's Vol. 2*, (Register of Directories and Executives).

As valuable as written resources are, information gathered from people is often the most helpful. Talk with people who work for or have worked for your target company, people with competitors or suppliers, and people who work for a customer of the target company. All will have some insight.

You may be saying to yourself, "But I don't know anyone who works for my target companies." That's true, you may not, but I can guarantee that your friends and contacts do. An interesting study by Stanley Milgram (described in *Psychology Today*, May 1967), indicates that nearly all adults have between five hundred and one thousand "contacts." "Contacts" include personal friends, relatives, present and former coworkers, schoolmates, church members, social club members, people you do business with (hair stylist, mechanic, butcher, banker), and even people you barely know. People who collect business cards (a very useful pastime) will probably have more than one thousand contacts. Using two links in the chain (your contacts plus your contacts' contacts) could lead to between 250,000 (500 x 500) and 1,000,000 (1,000 x 1,000) contacts. Add a third link and you get between 125 million and one billion. Pretty extraordinary, isn't it? The article went on to describe experiments in which people used contacts to communicate with a specific person thousands of miles away.

While I'm not going to recommend that you contact your five hundred contacts and ask each of them to contact their five hundred, the above example demonstrates the possibilities. What it boils down to is this: if you want to *badly enough*, you can get direct information about virtually any organization in the country using only one to two links.

Employees and Former Employees

Once you have your list of target organizations, call your contacts and ask them who they know in those organizations. If they don't know anyone, ask them to ask around for you. It's okay to ask for favors. After all, you'd do the same for them. Once you get a name, call the person to learn as much as you can. Be sure to give the name of the person who referred you, or your new contact may be rather cool and reserved. Start by asking about his or her overall view of the company. You need to establish rapport before asking probing questions.

Competitors

Competitors are valuable sources of information, but they may have some obvious biases. When talking to competitors, talk to sales and management people. Employees at lower levels seldom keep up on competitors. The purchasing manager probably belongs to the same association as the purchasing manager in your target company; they may even know each other. Sales people are obviously helpful because it's their business to know about competitors. As you're picking up information, determine if the person seems sincere. If the person shares both positives and negatives about your target organization, instead of just negatives, the information may prove useful.

Suppliers/Customers

Suppliers and customers may be harder to locate than competitors, but a few well-placed phone calls can reveal them. Each will give you a slightly different view of your target organization.

Inside Information

Insiders can give you a great deal of information that is simply unavailable from written resources. Every insider, however, whether employee, former employee, competitor, customer, or supplier has biases, and you must be sensitive enough to recognize them. Everything you hear represents only one viewpoint and needs to be treated as such. This is true of virtually any organization: some love it and some hate it. You'll need to determine whether the person you're talking with has an ax to grind (he may recently have lost out on a promotion), knows enough about the organization (she may really know only about her own department), or is even telling the truth. This is the fun part. You're a detective, evaluating motives and confirming stories.

Interviews are a very important part of employer research.

During most interviews you'll learn a lot about the company and the department you would be working in. Make full use of the opportunity to ask questions. There are, however, some questions which are so sensitive that it is better not to ask them. It's fine to ask about your growth potential, your duties, the interviewer's management style, and the future directions of the company. Questions about relocation policies, company ethics, and salaries should not be asked. Some questions are inappropriate for a first interview but fine in a second. Some topics simply must wait until the job has definitely been offered to you. Sensitivity and discretion will help you discern which questions should be asked and when.

WHY RESEARCH AN ORGANIZATION?

There are four main reasons for researching employers.

1. To determine if it is the right organization for you. Try to discover all the pros and cons you can. Research may reveal a serious problem which might cause you to eliminate the organization, or it may reveal some outstanding opportunities.
2. To impress the interviewer. You'll impress the interviewer simply by explaining in concise terms why you should be hired and by demonstrating that you are full of enthusiasm, experience, and potential. Since so few people bother to research a company, you'll also stand out in a very positive way if you've done your homework and go armed with facts and figures. Don't overwhelm the employer, however; instead, weave your information into the conversation. For example, you might ask, ''Mrs. Brewster, during the last three years Bankshare has grown an average of thirty-five percent each year. Do you expect that to continue?'' A good question; you're a growth-oriented person looking for a growth-oriented company and you're trying to determine if Bankshare's very rapid growth will continue. The question reveals that you have done some research. Some employers will ask, ''What do you know about us?'' Most people will hem, haw, and fail this question miserably, but you will shine. Even when asked this question, don't be overwhelming.
3. To discover problems you can help solve. Discovering problems you have the ability to solve could come before

or during an interview. If it comes before, you'll have time to prepare and perhaps even develop a proposal. If not, listen for clues during the interview. An employer may come right out and describe problems but more likely will merely allude to them. Careful listening can help you match your abilities or experience to the problem area; by all means emphasize those strengths.

4. To identify questions that must be clarified by the employer. An annual report or a magazine article may have mentioned an exciting new product being developed by your target company. If the inteviewer doesn't mention it, you may have to ask if you would have a role in developing, marketing, or selling it. If an inside source told you that a strike could cripple the company, you might ask about the effects of such a strike. If the company has lost money three years in a row, you might ask what the company is doing to reverse the losses.

Interviewing is a continuation of your research. Keep your detective cap on and discover all you can. Ask yourself if you would enjoy working for this person. Will you respect this boss? Do your management philosophies match? Will you like each other? These are all important questions.

Do some research before each interview, even if it's the third or fourth interview with the same company. If you feel really good about the job, your boss, and the company, it's important to discover all you can. Answering questions effectively and asking the right questions could make the difference between being a number-one choice and a number-two choice.

RESEARCH AFTER AN OFFER IS MADE

When you get a job offer, negotiate salary and benefits, and once agreement is reached try this: "Mrs. Torgeson, I'm very glad you had the confidence in me to offer me the position. The salary is about right and I'm really looking forward to working with you. I do have just a few questions that I would like clarified so that I can make the right decision." During the interview process you may have made note of some rather sensitive matters. You tactfully asked some of them, but perhaps the employer evaded them or didn't answer to your satisfaction. You decided not to probe further. After the interview, however, you indicated in your notes that you still needed that question answered. There were other sensitive questions you decided not to ask at all. Now is the time, after the job offer is definite and the salary has been negotiated. Don't be in a hurry to accept the job just because you're excited about it. Take whatever time is needed. Once you are satisfied, ask your boss-to-be when a definite yes or no is needed. It's reasonable to expect a few days for careful consideration. One approach works like this: "Mrs. Torgeson, I'm really excited about the position. Today is Thursday. Would Tuesday be soon enough to give you a definite yes or no?"

You now have time for two important tasks: (1) make a final, all-out effort to discover more about the company from inside sources, and (2) contact those other companies which have expressed some interest in you.

Based on what you've learned about the company, you've basically decided to take the job. Perhaps you would turn it down only if another company made a better offer or if additional research uncovers anything that would cause you to reject the offer. Many people regret their failure to do this final bit of research; I wouldn't want you to be one of them. Throughout your research you learned a lot. During the interviews you learned a great deal more. After the offer was made you asked even more questions, the sensitive ones you had postponed. The answers to those last questions probably cleared away all your doubts and you may have been tempted to accept the job on the spot. Fortunately you didn't. On your way home begin asking yourself if there are still any matters that need more clarification. Determine what sources might answer your questions—if you haven't talked to any competitors yet, this would be a good time. It's also a good time to talk to employees and ex-employees. Ask your contacts if if they know anyone you should talk to.

Things are not always as they appear. The boss who seems so understanding and likable in the interview may be completely different on the job. The company that seems so peaceful may be experiencing severe backbiting and political infighting. Or the company that seems so very stable may be ready for bankruptcy. Organizations often hide serious problems. As a detective it's your job to discover what those problems are.

Maintain a healthy skepticism. Talk it over with your mate, a friend, or a career counselor—anyone who will be more objective about it than you are. It's amazing what a second party can see that you may be blind to.

Suppose the offer was made on Thursday and you agreed to

give your final answer by Tuesday afternoon. Through several insiders you picked up some information plus a few rumors that need to be clarified. On Tuesday morning you might call your boss-to-be and ask for an appointment that afternoon: "Mr. Bradley, this is Paul Johnson. I've been doing a lot of thinking and I have essentially decided to accept the position. I still have a couple questions to ask you and it might be good just to meet with you for a few minutes this afternoon."

With some questions you will simply ask and evaluate the response. If the answer is not complete enough you may have to ask a follow-up question. When asking about any rumors, be tactful.

Mrs. Bascom, I feel certain there's no truth to this one matter, but I did hear it from several sources, so I guess it needs to be clarified. I've heard that the Securities and Exchange Commission is investigating some possible violations. What do you know about that?

✳

Mr. Chou, I'm the type of person who needs to be completely honest with my customers. Some of your competitors and even some customers have told me that they felt your sales staff consistently makes claims for your software packages that can't be backed up. How do you react to that?

After a job is offered, your second task is to contact those other organizations that may have expressed interest in you. Calls would go to the companies that have interviewed you for definite openings. Your call might go like this:

Ms. Esparza, this is Sandy Hogan. We talked last week about your Scheduling Coordinator position. You indicated it could be two weeks before I would be asked back for a second interview, but I thought I'd better call to explain my situation. I've just been offered a really good scheduling position with another company, but based on our conversation I would really rather work for you. What do you suggest I do?

If you aren't being considered for the job, the employer will suggest you take the position already offered. If the person is really interested, another interview may be arranged rather quickly.

Employer research is one of the most important yet most neglected aspects of a job search. By managing your schedule effectively you'll find the time to do your research and you will also reap the benefits—a better job in less time.

CONTACTS

Friends, relatives, acquaintances, and business contacts can all provide useful leads if you approach them in the right way. Before they can help, people must know what you're looking for and what your qualifications are. About twenty-six percent of all jobseekers find positions through such leads.* This number could be increased substantially if people made better use of this method. Include your baker, banker, barber, bellhop, broker, and butcher. Every person who has an interest in your success could be helpful.

1. Start by listing the names of friends, relatives, and contacts in your area (assuming you plan to stay in your present location). Include their employer and title if you can.
2. Develop an A list and a B list. Your A list includes people most likely to hear about an opening of the type you're interested in or who could refer you to other key people. Your B list consists of people you know but are less likely to hear of job openings in your field. You'll still want to contact them but they won't receive the same priority as your A-list people.
3. Mail resumes first to your A-list people with a short handwritten note indicating the type of work you're seeking and stating that you'll call in a few days to explain the resume more fully. The resume is important because most of your friends probably don't know much about your background or qualifications. The note attached to your resume might read like this:

> Janice, I'll be calling you in a few days to tell you about my career goals. I plan to move out of teaching and into sales. I don't expect you to know of any openings right now, but you may hear of some in the coming weeks. I've enclosed my list of preferred companies. If you know anyone, anyone at all, who works there, please let me know. Thanks.
>
> Joyce

---

*Department of Labor, Bureau of Labor Statistics Bulletin 1886 (1975).

4. When you call, or visit in person, explain how they can help. Indicate that you're not asking for a job, but simply ask that they keep their eyes and ears open for leads either within their own organization or others' organizations. Also explain that you don't expect them to set up any appointments for you, but do ask them to pass on leads to follow up on your own. Indicate that you would like to use their name whenever it is appropriate. Ask for any advice they might have for you. Get them involved in your search. After people have given advice, they feel they have a stake in your success.
5. Get referrals. Since you already have your list of preferred employers, enclose that list with your resume. Ask your contacts if they know anyone in those companies. Of course, it's nice if they know some key people, but the name of anyone in the organization can be useful.

Let's assume you're seeking a position as a purchasing assistant. If a contact knows the very person you need to reach in a particular organization—excellent! Learn as much as you can about that individual—likes, dislikes, management style, good points, bad points. If the contact knows someone in a different department, by all means call that person and ask about the purchasing department and its supervisor. If you mention your friend's name, the person will most likely be open with you. If you simply make a cold call and start asking specific questions about departments or department heads, the person will be on the defensive and will seldom give you useful information.

The fact that about twenty-six percent of all people get their jobs through leads supplied by friends, relatives, and business contacts is strong enough reason for using this technique, but there are other advantages. These are also the easiest people to contact and the time consumed is very small, especially if you use the telephone. Use weekends and evening hours to contact friends and relatives. Save your daytime hours for talking to employers.

CALLS

In this phase of the process, it is crucial to meet the person who has the power to hire you. Determining who that person is and getting an appointment requires a well planned strategy.

Determining Who Has the Power to Hire

The person with the power to hire you normally holds a position one or two levels above you in the department or functional area you have focused on. Often this will mean a department head. With very small companies, you might first contact the president or vice president. If that person does not hire people at your level, get a referral to the person who does.

Once you have your list of top-twenty companies, begin identifying the people who do the hiring. Getting their names is easy since nearly every business has a receptionist. Call and ask for the person's name, being sure to get the correct spelling and title. Most receptionists are so busy that they won't bother to ask you why you want to know.

Occasionally the receptionist will not know the proper person, or will hastily connect you with personnel. Don't be startled, just ask your question again with confidence and assertiveness. If the receptionist or personnel clerk asks why you are calling, the most simple response is, ''I have some material to send to your purchasing manager.''

Receptionist: Dearborn Insurance, may I help you?
Steve: Hello, can you give me the name of your Claims Manager?
Receptionist: Yes, that would be John Yaeger.
Steve: Would you spell his last name, please?
Receptionist: Sure, Y A E G E R.
Steve: Thank you very much.

✳

Receptionist: Medico, may I help you?
Sally: Hello, can you give me the name of your EDP Manager?
Receptionist: EDP?
Sally: Yes, Electronic Data Processing. Do you have someone in charge of computer programming?
Receptionist: I think you probably want Bob Benson.
Sally: What is his title?
Receptionist: He's Vice President of Operations, but I think he's in charge of our three programmers.
Sally: OK, thank you very much.

✳

Receptionist: Continental.
Kevin: Can you give me the name of your Purchasing Manager?

225

Receptionist:	Just a moment.
Personnel:	Personnel.
Kevin:	Can you give me the name of your Purchasing Manager?
Personnel:	That would be James Townsend.
Kevin:	Thank you.

✻

Receptionist:	Malco, may I help you?
Holly:	Could you please give me the name of your Advertising Manager?
Receptionist:	Just a moment.
Personnel:	Personnel.
Holly:	Could you please give me the name of your Advertising Manager?
Personnel:	What is this concerning?
Holly:	I have some material to send and I want to make sure it gets to the right person. Could you give me the name of your Advertising Manager?
Personnel:	That would be Janet Lynn.
Holly:	What is her title?
Personnel:	She is Director of Marketing.
Holly:	Thank you.

Occasionally you'll find a firm that is so secretive they won't give out anyone's name. If the organization has a high enough priority for you, there is always a way to find out who you need to talk to. Usually such firms are fairly large. By putting all your contacts together, you should be able to identify someone who works there or who knows about the organization.

Calling the Person with the Power to Hire

Now that you know the names of the appropriate people in your top-twenty companies, start setting up appointments. This part is a little trickier than just getting the names. First, you must often get past the person's secretary. One of the secretary's duties is to protect the boss from unnecessary calls, and some accept this duty with a vengeance. Don't be afraid, you can get through the toughest secretary. Once you get to your potential boss, you must present yourself quickly and ask for an appointment. With a polished opening, you should be able to get interviews sixty to ninety-five percent of the time.

Getting Through Secretaries

Present yourself as a confident businessperson with legitimate business reasons for calling. It is usually best to give your name immediately since the secretary will invariably ask for it. And you'll sound more authoritative. If, after trying all the styles given below, you just can't get past the secretary, try calling very early in the morning or after 5:30 in the afternoon. A busy executive will often answer the phone when the secretary is not there.

Receptionist: Glasgow and Associates.
Polly: I'd like to speak to Marilyn Shelton.
Receptionist: Just a moment, please.
Secretary: Marilyn Shelton's office.
Polly: This is Polly Preston. I'd like to speak with Marilyn Shelton.
Secretary: What is this concerning?
Polly: Don Drummer of Polycorp suggested I speak with her

or

I have some advertising concepts I would like to discuss with her

or

I have some personal matters to discuss with her

or

I sent her a marketing letter and she's expecting my call

or

I have some business matters to discuss with her.
Secretary: Just a moment, I'll ring her office.

If the person is out when you call (or the secretary says so), avoid leaving your phone number. Say that you will be in and out yourself and ask for the best time to call back. It is much better for you to initiate contact. If the employer returns your call, you may be caught unprepared. If you have been calling several people, you may not even recognize the person's name at first.

Secretary: Janet Spurrier's office.
John: This is John Bradley. I'd like to speak with Janet Spurrier.
Secretary: I'm sorry, she's in a meeting now. Can I have her return your call?
John: No, I'll be out most of the day. What do you think would be a good time to reach her?
Secretary: That's hard to say, but probably about 3:30.
John: Thank you.

What Do You Say After Hello?

Your future boss has just answered the phone. You have twenty seconds to sell yourself. A prepared script can give you added confidence and just the right words to make a great first impression. Since it is so easy to say "no," make it easy for the employer to say "yes" when you ask for a brief appointment.

To sell yourself you must quickly summarize your background and present evidence that you are a highly desirable person. Upon concluding your pitch, ask for an interview, but don't call it an interview. Ask to "get together" or have a "brief meeting." You are *not* seeking a traditional job interview. Using a marketing letter (see pages 112-116) can do a lot for preparing this person to give you an appointment.

Practice a few times with low-priority firms. Your voice should convey self-confidence and enthusiasm. Your words should convey potential. Naturally you don't want the employer to know you are reading a script. Practice until you speak in a normal conversational tone.

Some sample approaches:

Mr. Crenshaw, this is Brian Dawlar. I just graduated from the University of Washington with a degree in business, emphasizing marketing. I realize you may not have any openings at this time, but I would appreciate setting up a time when we could meet for ten or fifteen minutes.

✳

Mrs. Garner? Hi, this is Sandra Bennett. I wanted to confirm that you received the letter I sent a few days ago describing my background. Good. I've been teaching for the last six years, but all my sales friends tell me I'd be a natural in sales. I realize you may not have any openings at this time, but I would appreciate arranging, oh, a ten- or fifteen-minute get-together. I'd like to tell you a little more about me and at the same time learn some of the directions Salvo is headed. Would Tuesday morning work for you?

✳

Bob Bradley? This is Jim Thomas. I've been selling radio advertising for the last six years and I'm seriously considering changing stations. Last year I was the top salesperson. In fact, I broke the company record for time sold and dollar volume. I'm not in a rush to leave, but I would like to set a time when we could get together for ten or fifteen minutes.

Each of these scripts can be said in fourteen to twenty seconds. When you've just reached a stranger on the phone, and the most the person has said is "Hello" or "This is Crenshaw," twenty seconds is quite a long time. If your pitch is longer, design it in such a way that half way through, your listener will be forced to make some kind of a short response, allowing you to then finish your pitch.

228

Ideally the person with the power to hire will immediately arrange a time. They may, however, raise some objections.

Employer:	We won't be hiring for at least six months. (How does she know? An employee may quit tomorrow.)
You:	I can understand that. Actually I'm not in a hurry to leave my present job, but I do feel it would be mutually beneficial to chat for ten or fifteen minutes.
Employer:	I'm really tied up for the next three weeks.
You:	That's fine. Let's plan for the following Monday.
Employer:	Probably you should go through personnel and fill out an application.
You:	I'd be glad to at the appropriate time.
Employer:	Right now we're laying off people in your field.
You:	I can appreciate your concern. I know the economy is rough right now. I think that makes it even more important that we get together. My company went through a similar situation a year ago. My money-saving ideas helped turn the company around.
Employer:	I really don't think you have the right experience.
You:	It is a bit unusual, but really, the problems I've dealt with are not much different than the ones you are undoubtedly facing. My new procedures at Silco created a thirty-two percent increase in productivity.

It's unlikely you will face all of these objections from one person, but be prepared for them. Make it easy for the person to say "yes." Asking for only ten minutes is a very reasonable request. Virtually everyone can spare that much time. And because you have much to offer, the interview will prove mutually beneficial. At the very least, the employer will have experienced a pleasant and relaxing ten minutes.

In a normal job market of three to six percent unemployment, I recommend asking for a ten- to fifteen-minute get-together. When unemployment rises above eight percent, employers become inundated with calls and even brief appointments are hard to get. A slightly different strategy is necessary:

1. Speak to the person with power to hire and ask for ten minutes rather than fifteen. Indicate that you realize there may be no openings.
2. If the person responds by saying there are no openings

and therefore doesn't want to meet with you, explain that you understand there are no openings, but that you only want ten minutes to talk about the field.

3. If the person counters by saying there is a freeze on hiring, and it would therefore be a waste of time for both of you, say something like this: "I can sure appreciate the tough economic climate in this area. Since I have you on the phone, let me just take a minute to tell you a little more about myself." Then give a one- to two-minute summary of your strengths and experience.

4. When you finish your summary, ask once more for an appointment. Try one of these:

> Mr. Belquez, I can certainly understand your situation. I am working at this time and what I'd really like to do is meet you and tell you a little more about myself so when openings do develop you'll be able to keep me in mind. I promise I'll take only ten minutes of your time.

❋

> Ms. Baum, that gives you just a sketch of my experience and abilities. It's certainly not uncommon these days for a company to have a hiring freeze, and I can understand your reluctance to take time out of your busy schedule. But it would be very helpful to me if we could meet for just ten minutes.

❋

> Mr. Baker, as you can see, I have a strong background in purchasing. I can guarantee you won't regret taking ten minutes to see me. And I really do mean just ten minutes.

At that point you will have asked three times for an appointment. Don't give up with just two tries; many people relent on the third request. The first two were based on your merit. You're a very capable person and you requested an appointment because most people in management continually have their eyes open for new talent. Make the third request on the basis of a favor. When you appeal to their desire to help others, many people will consent.

5. If you still don't get an appointment, you may still get some valuable information if you hold the person on the phone another two to three minutes. Remember, you worked

hard to get this hiring person on the phone, so don't give up too easily. Consider these: "Mr. Bledsoe, when you do have a position open, what can I do to make sure I'll be considered?" "Mr. Bledsoe, when you have openings in your marketing department, what do you look for in candidates?" "Mr. Bledsoe, I've briefly described my background. Am I the type of person you'd be looking for?"

6. In addition, you could ask about the size of the department, particularly the number of people who do your type of work. Ask about turnover. If no one has left in the last four years, that certainly tells you something. You may want to assign that company a lower priority because of the unlikelihood of an opening. Or you may give it a higher priority, because the low turnover often indicates employee satisfaction. You're the best judge of priority.

7. By this time you probably have convinced the person that you are a highly desirable employee. He may know of something happening in other companies. Do not ask the person if he knows of any openings. Instead, try this: "Mr. Kelsoe, I think you have a pretty good feel for my background. What other companies do you think I should be contacting?" The reason for not asking about specific openings is that referrals are more important to you than knowledge of specific openings. The phrasing of the question will surely cause him to tell you about any openings he knows of. If the person says "Nothing comes to mind right now," he may need some help to jog his memory. Your response might be, "Basically, I'm looking for a progressive firm like yours in the electronics industry. I realize you may not know of specific openings, but your advice on good companies would sure be helpful." If he names some companies, ask for the name of a person to contact in each. Then ask, "Do you mind if I say you suggested I call?" Nearly always you will be given permission. You would simply say "Bob Townsend at Utalco suggested I call you. During the last five years I've been purchasing microcircuits. I realize you may not have any openings, but I would like to set up a time when I could meet with you for about ten minutes."

8. Thank the person for his time. If no appointment was made, indicate that you'll be sending your resume, and that you'll be staying in touch. Send a brief thank-you note with your resume to confirm your appreciation.

Your goal is still to get in and see as many hiring authorities as possible. A personal meeting always creates a much stronger and more lasting impression than just talking by phone. But think of it this way: if you've been unable to make an appointment, virtually no one else is going to, either. When you got the person on the phone you made the most of it and sold yourself. The employer was impressed. Once the person receives your thank-you note, resume, and a follow-up phone call, you'll undoubtedly be one of the first to be informed when a position becomes available.

The primary goal of this strategy is for you to locate job openings in the hidden job market while they still exist. While personal meetings with employers increase your chances, your telephone conversation, resume, thank-you note, and follow-up are the next best things.

Let's look at an additional benefit of this telephone strategy. During high unemployment you may get appointments only twenty to thirty percent of the time, compared to the forty to eighty-five percent rate most experience in better economic conditions. When you don't get an appointment, nine times out of ten it will be because there really are no openings, and when vacancies occur, they are not filled. So it really would have been a waste of your time. While the employer is saving only ten minutes, you'll save the two to three hours it would take to research the organization, drive there, meet the person, and return home.

In your phone calls, use humor whenever possible. My clients report that making the employer laugh has significantly increased their ability to get valuable information, even when they do not get in to see the person.

INTERVIEWS

Meeting a hiring authority in person has about ten times the impact of a resume. A resume, no matter how good it is, is still a piece of paper. You are virtually always more impressive in person than on paper.

Your goal is to meet hiring authorities in person, even if it is for only ten minutes. Whether they have a job opening is immaterial. Lasting impressions are made only from person-to-person contact, not from resumes or even telephone conversations. Something happens when you meet a person. Your name becomes attached to a face, a body, a voice, a personality.

232

In each meeting, create a lasting, positive impression so that when a job opening occurs, you'll be the first person considered. Suppose five weeks ago you spent fifteen minutes with Mrs. Johnson, a key hiring authority in one of your most desired companies. No opening existed at the time, but you did have a pleasant conversation, and as you learned more about her organization you shared some of your accomplishments. Mrs. Johnson told you she was impressed with your background and even mentioned three companies she felt you should look at. Two days later Mrs. Johnson received a nice thank-you note, and she once again remembered you and recalled your potential. She also felt good about herself, because she knew she had been helpful. Three weeks later you called her and had about a one-minute conversation asking if there had been any job developments. Not too surprisingly, there had not.

Two weeks after your call, however, someone informed Mrs. Johnson that he was leaving the company for a better position. What can Mrs. Johnson do? She could have informed personnel immediately and asked them to place an ad. She could also have delved into her file cabinet and the two hundred or so resumes she had accumulated over the last six months.

Instead, she thought of you. She picks up the telephone and calls you for an interview. Your first chat was just that, a nice, pleasant conversation. Your next contact will be a formal interview, and you'll be asked some tough questions. You'll be ready, though.

FOLLOWUP

Followup begins the same day as the interview. Between appointments or when you get home, write a brief typed or handwritten thank-you note. The five minutes it takes to write a thank-you note could be the most valuable time you spend. It will cause an important person to think favorably of you once more. A successful job search includes doing all the little things just right.

Suppose Barbara is making a career change from telephone operator to sales representative. One of fifteen interviewed, she was told that only *three* would be invited back for second interviews. Ten people had sales experience, but despite Barbara's total lack of sales experience, she was ranked *fourth*. She enjoyed the interview and, out of habit, wrote a nice, quick, four-line thank-you note. When the note came in, the sales manager was getting ready to call the three top candidates. In the ten seconds it took to read the note, he began recalling the interview with Barbara. A moment later he was calling Barbara, having decided it wouldn't hurt to interview a fourth person.

A thank-you note is a perfect device. It makes you stand out apart from the vast majority of job seekers who never bother with them. It says that your expression of interest in the company was sincere. Any indication of enthusiasm and interest will be interpreted as evidence that you will work harder and stay with the company longer than others. The reason for taking five minutes to write a thank-you note is simple—it can increase the number of second interviews by twenty percent. People feel good when they know they've been appreciated.

The note can range in length from three sentences to two pages. The note might read like this:

Dear Mr. Mathews,

I really appreciated the time you gave me yesterday. After talking to you I'm more clear than ever that personnel is the right field for me. I'll keep you informed of my progress.

Sincerely,

John Stevens

✳

Dear Mrs. Kelser,

Thank you so much for seeing me yesterday. Our conversation confirmed what others have told me—that Dalco is an exciting company to work for. Of course, when I first called you, I didn't expect you to have any openings. Since our conversation, however, I am convinced that I could be a real asset in the accounting department. My background in auditing and computer programming should make me very valuable.

I will stay in touch to check on any developments.

Sincerely,

John Betterman

✳

Dear Mrs. Madison,

I really enjoyed today's interview and I appreciate the fact that I was invited from among so many candidates. I just wanted to say again that I am quite excited about the prospect of working for Sentry, and especially within your department.

Sincerely,

Roberta Marsh

The first note was in response to an informational interview, the second an interview in which no opening existed, and the third, a formal job interview. Any of these letters could have been longer, but it is usually unnecessary. The only time to write a longer note is when you have a definite purpose. You may want to write a proposal describing a problem you discovered during the interview, along with your proposed solution. If you have forgotten to make a point, a letter is the best opportunity to cover it, even if it takes two pages. An objection may have been raised—if you missed it, didn't handle it adequately, or simply want to attack it from another angle, a letter is the logical answer. Proposals or lengthy letters should usually be typed.

Most of your interviews will be with employers who do not have current openings. Your followup with them can last weeks and even months. Three weeks after your first interview, call to ask if there have been any developments. Don't worry about bothering the person; you'll only talk for about a minute. When you get the person on the phone, introduce yourself, indicate when you met, and briefly describe what you talked about. Do not assume the employer will remember you. He or she may have met forty people in the last three weeks and will probably need a refresher.

Odds are there is still no opening. In closing emphasize your interest in the company and perhaps bring the person up to date on your efforts, particularly if you have contacted any of the people you were referred to.

Bob: Hi, Mr. Benson, this is Bob Phillips. We met about three weeks ago when I came in to talk about microprocessors and the directions Microdata is taking. I just wanted to find out if there have been any new developments in your marketing department.

Benson: Bob, I remember you and I still have your resume, but there haven't been any openings.

Bob: I really appreciated your taking time to see me. The more I hear about Microdata, the more excited I get. I did call Mr. Jensen at Datasoft. He was very helpful. I'll probably talk to you again in four or five weeks. Thanks again.

The only hitch in this strategy is that frequently you will talk to a secretary if the person with power to hire is out or unavailable. You will generally be asked to leave a message and your number so the call can be returned. Instead ask when a good time to call would be. After three or four unsuccessful calls, you might explain that you saw the person three weeks ago and that you just need to talk to him for a minute to ask a couple questions. If the secretary has been brushing you off, that may help. *Always stay on good terms with the secretary*. On the second or third call, ask her name. You may talk to the secretary six or seven times, so you'll want to maintain your composure and sense of humor; try to get to know this person. Make her want to help you.

After your first follow-up call, call every four to five weeks. Try to create and maintain enough interest so that if any openings occur, you'll be notified. Even if they don't call you, you're never more than five weeks away from discovering the opening through one of your calls. In the hidden job market jobs frequently stay open for six to ten weeks.

Another method of followup is to send a note accompanying an article the person may find interesting.

Followup also includes followup with your contacts. Every six weeks you'll need to call them to let them know about your experiences and your progress. If they referred you to someone, tell them what happened. Make them an integral part of your search and make them feel valued. This kind of followup will counter a psychological fact—with every passing week their ears become duller. In the beginning you'll be notified if they hear of a job even half way resembling the one you want, but by seven weeks they're starting to assume you've found another job. By nine weeks they may hear about your perfect job but fail to even think of you.

MORE INTERVIEWS

After talking to key people in most of your top twenty organizations, you have several options. There are advantages to each; the one you choose will depend on a number of factors.

1. *Stop. You've discovered some really outstanding organizations. Maintain your followup until the right opening occurs.* If you've found six to twelve outstanding organizations, and if you're convinced there aren't any others that might interest you, you can stop your search and develop a creative follow-up campaign. Continue to learn as

much as possible about each organization. Look for every opportunity to demonstrate that a position should be created to utilize your unique talents and experiences. Occasionally mailing a really interesting article can be effective.

2. *Repeat the process with your next group of twenty.* This is a logical next step. You've exhausted your top-twenty group and visited or talked to probably ten to twenty hiring authorities. Very likely there were no current openings, but you are confident you will be contacted if openings occur. It makes sense simply to continue what has been working well for you. Progress may seem slow but you're making high-quality contacts.

3. *Mail resumes to the remaining organizations and follow up with phone calls. Arrange interviews only if openings currently exist.* With this strategy try to reach hiring authorities quickly, and sell yourself as much as possible by phone. If no suitable openings exist, ask if they know of openings in other organizations. If after two or three calls you're not able to reach the person, ask the secretary if any openings exist. Talking to employers by phone only does not have the impact of a face-to-face meeting, but it is faster.

4. *Call the personnel department of your remaining organizations and ask if openings exist.* Speed is the main advantage of this strategy. The personnel department is usually accessible. If the personnel manager is unavailable, a personnel clerk will usually know what positions are open. When speaking to someone in personnel, briefly describe your background, and suggest one or more job titles that might be suitable for you.

This strategy has several advantages over just sending a resume. Two negative things can happen when you mail a resume—a rejection or no response at all. In either case, you still don't know what the real situation is, while a quick call can give you a great deal of information. Whether you get a clerk or the personnel manager, ask questions. If you learn that there are no suitable openings, you could confirm that the company does in fact have the types of positions you're interested in. Ask if the company could send any literature to you.

AN IMPORTANT JOB FINDING OPTION

I almost always recommend that job seekers should prioritize their list of potential employers and seek face-to-face meetings with at least the top twenty organizations on their list. There are exceptions, however. In some types of positions, particularly office and clerical jobs, you are actually better off calling personnel, introducing yourself, briefly explaining your background (see page 228 for examples), and asking if any openings currently exist. You should be able to average twelve calls an hour. If you have 120 organizations on your list and call once a week to learn of openings, your total time expended is only ten hours weekly. The strategy should yield two to three interviews weekly.

Don't simply hang up if personnel informs you that no openings are currently available. A conversation might go like this.

Personnel:	Personnel, may I help you?
Carol:	This is Carol Prescott, I have a diploma from Harrington Business College and two years of clerical experience. Do you have any clerical positions available at this time?
Personnel:	No we don't.
Carol:	Do you anticipate adding any office staff in the next month or two?
Personnel:	It's highly doubtful that we'll be adding any positions in the next four months.
Carol:	If someone quit, would the person be replaced?
Personnel:	I'm sure they would.
Carol:	Approximately how many clerical positions do you have?
Personnel:	Counting bookkeepers, probably around thirty.
Carol:	What kind of turnover do you have?
Personnel:	It's nothing unusual, I'm sure it's about average.
Carol:	Thanks a lot for your help, who am I speaking to?
Personnel:	I'm Betty.
Carol:	You've been really helpful. I plan to call once a week and if it's all right, I'll probably just ask for you.

In only two minutes, Carol learned much more than if she had hung up after hearing that no openings existed. She also has a person to talk to in personnel. In a short time, Betty may actually recognize Carol's voice and because Carol is friendly and courteous,

Betty may actually go out of her way to help her. Of course, don't feel you can only talk to one person. If your regular person is unavailable, ask questions of whomever happens to be on the line. This strategy is fast and gets excellent results—but don't use it as a shortcut if you are one of those who should be talking with the person with the power to hire.

SELLING YOURSELF

The strategy of seeking brief interviews should result in appointments forty to eighty-five percent of the time. If you're not getting forty percent, you're probably not using the telephone effectively. (During periods of high unemployment, your success may drop to twenty to thirty percent.) This strategy works because everybody will have fifteen minutes at some time during the next two weeks. You have made a reasonable request. You didn't ask for an entire afternoon or even one hour, you simply asked for ten or fifteen minutes.

You're the one who will make the special effort. You have offered to drive to the business, pay for parking, walk to the building, and wait until the person is available—all for just fifteen minutes of her time. It may take you one to two hours. And the person with the power to hire is going to experience an enjoyable, relaxing time talking with you.

When meeting with a hiring authority, start with the assumption that both of you will gain something. You just might be the highlight of this person's day. If you are knowledgeable and genuinely enthusiastic, this person may gladly give you a half hour or more. People who love their work are glad if they can help others move into their field. They may have another motive for giving you time—genuine interest in you. They may have an opening (but not inform you immediately), or they may be considering creating a position. They may just be smart managers always looking for talent.

During the meeting you have one main goal—make a favorable impression. Do this by describing your strengths and demonstrating your enthusiasm.

Develop a two-minute summary about yourself. It's possible that the employer will spend the entire fifteen minutes talking, without giving you a chance. In such a case, as she stands up to escort you to the door, you should also rise, but as you do, say something like this: "Ms. Gordon, I really appreciate your taking the time to see me today. Perhaps I could take just a minute or two to describe some of my strengths." Even if you had had a chance to touch on some points, a two-minute summary can be very useful. Your final words will be remembered the longest. Developing a two-minute summary will also help you prioritize what you would like to say about yourself during the fifteen minutes.

Some employers may be unsure why you asked for the appointment, and may have agreed only because you asked for just fifteen minutes. Such people may start by asking, "How can I help you?" You'd better be prepared with a response. It might be something like this:

I'm assuming you don't have any immediate openings for a counselor. Basically what I wanted to do was learn a little more about the agency and the direction it's headed, and also tell you about myself, so that when an opening does occur, I would be considered. I thought you might also be aware of what's happening in other local agencies. One of the things I'm curious about is, what do you look for in your counselors?

Try to stay relaxed and make it more of a chat than an interview. Don't be concerned if the employer wants to talk about current events, a mutual friend, or the state of the economy—you'll at least get your two-minute summary in. Whatever you talk about, the person will be assessing you. Even if at the end of the conversation the employer still doesn't know all about your background, don't worry—if you have created the impression that you are a friendly, capable, energetic person, you have done well.

As the fifteen minutes draws to a close you should decide whether you will seek more time with the employer. Remember, you only asked for fifteen minutes. If he seems very interested and shows no signs of looking at his watch, you have three options:

1. At the first opportunity you can stand up and thank the person for graciously giving you some of his valuable time.
2. You can say, "Mr. Barratt, I appreciate the time you've given me. I did ask for just fifteen minutes. Do you have an upcoming appointment?" This will force the person to indicate that he has an appointment or work to do, or that he would like to continue the conversation. If he wants to talk further, you can relax; it is now his responsibility for terminating the conversation.
3. Do nothing, but look for any fidgeting or clock-watching—

dead giveaways that the interview should draw to a close. Perhaps the person does not know how to tactfully close an interview. Don't wear out your welcome.

Using Your Resume During an Interview

Always take several copies of your resume to an interview. If the interviewer already has a copy, don't assume she has read it or remembers any of its contents. Avoid such statements as, ''Well, as you can see in my resume, I...'' She'll start fumbling around with the resume looking for that point and will be distracted from what you're actually saying. Feel free to discuss points that are in the resume, but talk as if the person had never seen your resume, and do not refer to it.

Often the employer will ask for a copy of your resume. Have one handy. Personally, I like to see someone's resume at the beginning. In two minutes I can learn what might require ten to twenty minutes otherwise. If your time has drawn to a close, terminate the interview and say something like this, ''Thanks for taking the time to see me, Mrs. Castor, you've been very helpful. Let me give you a copy of my resume in case anything should develop.'' If nothing else, now the employer will know how to contact you. If you made a favorable impression, she will probably keep your resume in a special folder at her desk. If a position does open up, your resume will be reviewed before the hundreds of mediocre resumes she has seen. Your resume will bring to mind the favorable impression you created while meeting face to face. A top-quality resume continues to work for you for months.

Referrals

At the end of each interview you should seek referrals, unless you were interviewing for a known position. If you impressed the employer, he will be more than ready to do you a small favor. You might try these:

> You: Mr. Sanders, I really appreciate your taking time to see me today. Perhaps you could do one more favor for me. I'd like to leave my resume with you, and if anything would develop within Xytex, or if you hear of anything in another organization, please let me know. Right off hand can you think of anyone that I should contact?

You: Mrs. Bell, I really enjoyed our chat today and I
        appreciate the time you've given me. In my
        research I've identified eight other organizations that
        I'd like to work for and I've gotten the names of the
        people I think I should be contacting. Do you know
        any of these people? (show your list)
Bell: I know Johnson and Coleman.
You: Could you give me just a quick sketch of both of
        them?

Taking Notes

Rarely should you take notes during an interview—it can be very distracting and prevents useful eye contact. You should, however, keep a notepad handy. If the interviewer refers you to someone or suggests an article to read, it's a little embarrassing to ask for pen and paper.

As soon as you get back to your car you should jot down some notes while the interview is still fresh in your mind. Your notes might cover these points:

1. The organization: needs, problems, size, plans, growth, etc.
2. The hiring authority: age, biases, management style, overall personality.
3. The position: hours, travel, unusual aspects, duties, who you answer to.
4. Benefits.
5. Questions that were asked, including objections you may have to overcome.
6. Overall impression.
7. Specific points, such as the date you should call back.
8. Questions you would like to ask in the next interview.

If you had an informal interview, you would probably not know much about benefits or the duties you might perform.

MAKING THE STRATEGY WORK

The people who succeed with this strategy become detectives. Successful detectives never get discouraged. They follow up on each lead until the case is solved. Dozens of leads may dead end, but eventually one pays off. Remember, it only takes one good job offer, and you'll never be able to predict where the lead will come from.

The number-one cause of failure in job hunting is inaction, and the number-one cause of inaction is fear of rejection. Many people are not technically inactive, in fact they may be very busy, but they're inefficient, spinning their wheels and making no headway. And it's a vicious cycle. It usually starts like this. When unemployment rises, people start looking at the want ads. They throw their slightly revised resume around with very little success, but finally an invitation for an interview is offered. Since most people "wing it" in interviews with no research, practice, or forethought, the first few interviews go very poorly and a string of rejections develops. Eventually many people reach what Richard Bolles calls "Desperation Gulch," that feeling of hopelessness and depression that can lead to giving up.

By all means, avoid the vicious cycle: (1) follow the strategy as it has been described; (2) keep busy and use good time management; (3) enjoy several low-stress interviews each week.

I have one more thought to offer you. I'd like to give you a new definition of success. For most job seekers the only success is getting the right job offer. That's all wrong. You can experience success each day and should reward yourself for it by feeling good about yourself. I believe success is having one or more pleasant experiences every day. Success is talking to someone who opens up to you and tells you everything about a field you're interested in. Success is completing your employer list. Success is being a finalist among fifty applicants.

If you have at least one success each day, that ultimate success—a job—will happen as a matter of course. Start your day as if you had a full-time job. If you're used to getting up at 6:30, continue that habit. Put in a solid six- to eight-hour work day. You're different from the rest of your competition. While they're complaining about their rotten luck, you're doing your employer research. While they're sitting next to the telephone waiting for interviews to be arranged for them, you're on the telephone setting up your own appointments. While they're watching soap operas and game shows, you're meeting hiring authorities and getting job leads. While they're hoping for a lucky break, you're creating your own breaks.

Relaxing is one of the most difficult things for an unemployed job seeker to do. Turning your job search into a full-time job is the best medicine. If you're busy with research and appointments, you won't have time for negative thoughts. If you spend six full hours each day on your job search, you've done your job for the day. When you were employed, you didn't worry so much if something didn't get done. You knew you would take care of it the next work day. In a job search you can't do all your work in one day. That's what tomorrow is for. Monday through Friday stay busy between 8:30 a.m. and 4:30 p.m., then call it a day. You've done all you can do. Relax. Enjoy your family. Read a book. Go to the health club.

If you're already feeling good about yourself, keep it up.

Living Testimonies

The following statements demonstrate some of the many ways people find out about their new jobs. These weren't just lucky breaks, the people created these situations.

> I had spoken to someone in each of my top ten companies, but there were no openings. I then developed a new list and was starting to talk to key people. One of the firms had no openings but suggested that I talk to someone in a very young but growing firm that I had never heard of. Sure enough, they were expanding and I got there at just the right time. The training I'm getting is excellent and the income potential is excellent, too.

※

> I was just calling people to get information. I spoke to one person who thought his company was looking for a person with my background. The next day I went in for an interview and got the job.

※

> After I clarified what I really wanted to do, I contacted a former coworker who had moved into the field I was interested in. We talked by phone and later had several meetings. He needed someone to assist him and he knew I had the ability and the background. We're now working together.

※

> A former supervisor went to work for a new company and when an opening occurred, recommended me to his boss. I was hired after several interviews.

RESOURCES FOR EMPLOYER RESEARCH

Employer research takes place in two stages: (1) Obtaining a list of fifty to two-hundred employers, and (2) gathering information about employers prior to the first interview. A survey of professional recruiters indicated knowledge of the company was one of the three most significant factors in successful interviews. "What do you know about us?" is a favorite question of many employers. Fortunately, for most companies over fifty employees, information is available.

STANDARD INDUSTRIAL CLASSIFICATION (SIC)

Many resources list organizations by their Standard Industrial Classification (SIC) code. The Federal Government has assigned codes to several hundred industries and the system is now used almost universally. Every business has one or more SIC codes. I'll discuss particular resources later, but for now remember that resources which arrange organizations by SIC will have a guide to help you identify the industries you are most interested in.

STAGE ONE—EMPLOYER LIST

In stage one, you'll be using various resources to develop your list of fifty to two-hundred employers.

Local Resources

Yellow Pages. The Yellow Pages are valuable because organizations have been categorized by industry, service, or function. Most city libraries will have dozens of Yellow Pages for other cities in your state plus the Yellow Pages for most major cities in the country. The Bell Telephone Companies, General Telephone, and other phone companies have begun publishing what have become known as "Business-to-Business Yellow Pages." These directories concentrate on "listings for businesses that deal with other businesses." These business-to-business directories are useful because they cover large metropolitan areas and provide listings often not found in local Yellow Pages.

Polk's City Directories. This source has been published for 1400 cities in the United States. Most city libraries will have a *Polk's* covering your immediate metropolitan area plus other major cities. The yellow section of *Polk's* will be most useful and is similar in format to the Yellow Pages. *Polk's* is useful because it uses somewhat different categories, and it lists many organizations not found in the Yellow Pages.

Contacts Influential. This comes closest to being a perfect resource. *Contacts Influential* covers specific metropolitan areas, currently including Atlanta, Boulder, Calgary, Chicago, Cleveland, Dallas, Denver, Edmonton, Fort Worth, Kansas City, suburban Maryland, Minneapolis, St. Paul, Oakland, Orange County (California), Phoenix, Portland, San Diego, San Francisco, San Jose, Seattle, St. Louis, St. Paul, St. Petersburg, Tacoma, Tampa Bay, Toronto, Vancouver, British Columbia, northern Virginia, Washington, D.C., and Willamette Valley. Each covers an entire metropolitan area, including suburbs. Concentrate on the SIC section. *Contacts Influential* provides names, addresses, zip codes, phone numbers, key officers, and their titles. With the coded system you can determine the number of employees, and whether it is a local, branch, or headquarter's office.

Because the names of officers are difficult to keep current, do not depend on any resource for absolute accuracy. Call to confirm that that person is still there.

Other Local Resources. People with no desire to leave their current geographical area will get better results with local, rather than national, resources. It would be impossible, of course, to list all local resources, but I can help you find them. The best place to start is in the Business Reference section of your library. In this section you'll find Yellow Pages and *Polk's City Directories*.

After you've scouted out the reference area, talk to the reference librarian and ask about resources. You'll find reference librarians very helpful. Some libraries will have a list of useful resources and directories.

If you are looking for government, nonprofit, or social service agencies, ask the reference librarian for help. United Way generally publishes a booklet describing the agencies it funds. For state, city, or county governments there may be a telephone directory with names of departments, key staff people, and their phone numbers.

Virtually every chamber of commerce publishes information on local companies. Most cost between five and ten dollars but they should also be available at your library.

Don't overlook talking to people with the chamber of commerce or United Way; many can give you a wealth of information about their metropolitan area.

State Directories

Every state publishes a list of manufacturers operating in that state. The alphabetical section gives names, telephone numbers, addresses (including divisions and subsidiaries), key executives, SIC numbers, products manufactured or industrial services, number of employees, locations of branch offices and/or plants, whether they are importers and/or exporters, annual gross sales, and years established. State directories also have SIC and geographical sections. Many are published by private companies, but all are published in conjunction with that state's department of commerce. Arranged by states the directories are: Alabama Directory of Mining and Manufacturing; Alaska Petroleum and Industrial Directory; Directory of Arizona Manufacturers; Arkansas Directory of Manufacturers; California Manufacturers Register; Directory of Colorado Manufacturers; Connecticut State Industrial Directory; Delaware Directory of Commerce and Industry; Principal Employers, Metropolitan Washington D.C.; Directory of Florida Industries; Georgia Manufacturing Directory; Directory of Manufacturers State of Hawaii; Manufacturing Directory of Idaho; Illinois Manufacturers Directory; Indiana Industrial Directory; Directory of Iowa Manufacturers; Directory of Kansas Manufacturers and Products; Kentucky Directory of Manufacturers and Products; Louisiana Directory of Manufacturers; Maine Marketing Directory; Directory of Maryland Manufacturers; Directory of Massachusetts Manufacturers; Minnesota Directory of Manufacturers; Mississippi Manufacturers Directory; Missouri Directory of Manufacturers and Mining; Montana Directory of Manufacturers; Made in New Hampshire; New Jersey State Industrial Directory; Directory of New Mexico Manufacturing and Mining; New York State Industrial Directory; North Carolina Directory of Manufacturing Firms; Directory of North Dakota Manufacturers; Ohio Industrial Directory; Oklahoma Manufacturers Directory; Directory of Oregon Manufacturers; Pennsylvania State Industrial Directory; Puerto Rico Official Industrial Directory; Rhode Island Directory of Manufacturers; Industrial Directory of South Carolina; South Dakota Manufacturers and Processors Directory; Tennessee Directory of Manufacturers; Directory of Texas Manufacturers; Directory of Utah Manufacturers; Directory of Vermont Manufacturers; Virginia Industrial Directory; Washington Manufacturers Register; West Virginia Manufacturing Directory; Classified Directory of Wisconsin Manufacturers; Wyoming Directory of Manufacturing and Mining.

National Resources

Dun and Bradstreet—Million Dollar Directory. This publication lists companies with a net worth of $1,000,000 or more. The alphabetical section includes company names, names of parent companies, addresses, telephone numbers, SIC numbers, sales figures, number of employees, principal officers, and whether companies are involved in importing and exporting. Dun and Bradstreet also has geographic and SIC sections.

Dun and Bradstreet—Middle Market Directory. Same as above except it covers companies with a net worth between $500,000 and $1,000,000.

The College Placement Annual. Contains national companies and lists the college degrees they desire most. Basic information about the company is provided. One section lists college majors and the companies which are seeking those majors.

Standard and Poor's. This directory includes 37 thousand corporations, with names, addresses, zips, telephone numbers, products made, number of employees, and sales volume. Volume 1 has an alphabetical listing, Volume 2 has biographical information on 75 thousand key officers listed alphabetically by last name, and Volume 3 lists corporations by SIC and geographic area.

Mac Rae's Blue Book. Mac Rae's lists 50 thousand firms. It provides addresses, primary products or services, telephone sales offices and distributors, and cities and phone numbers for sales reps or outlets. Volume 1 has an alphabetical listing plus about 100 thousand brand names listed alphabetically with name of company. Volumes 2 through 4 are arranged by product with manufacturers of that product listed below each heading. Volume 5 contains the catalogs of over one hundred companies.

Thomas Register. This directory is like *Mac Rae's*—it was designed primarily to assist purchasing agents locate companies that offer certain products or services. Volumes 1 through 6 list over 50 thousand products and the companies that produce them. Volume 7 indexes these products by the pages they can be found on; it also lists 72 thousand brand names and the companies that own them. Volume 8 is an alphabetical list of United States manufacturers. It provides names, addresses, telephone numbers, dollar values of tangible assets, subsidiaries, and affiliated companies. Volumes 9 through 14 contain the catalogs of over eight hundred companies.

3,000 Leading U. S. Corporations. It lists and provides brief information on the three thousand largest United States manufacturers. Within its SIC section companies are ranked by size rather than alphabetically. Brief financial data are provided.

Walker's Manual of Western Corporations. Companies are listed alphabetically with addresses, phone numbers, products, acquisitions and stock information.

Who Owns Whom. This is useful for tracing subsidiaries, parent companies, affiliations, or divisions.

Directory of Corporate Affiliations. This directory lists four thousand parent companies with addresses and phone numbers. Section 1 gives sales, number of employees, type of business, top officers, divisions, subsidiaries, and affiliates. Section 2 lists 45 thousand divisions, subdivisions, and affiliates alphabetically and gives the parent company. This resource also has a geographical index.

Directory of American Firms Operating in Foreign Countries. Section 1 lists firms alphabetically and the countries each one operates in. Section 2 lists countries and tells which American firms operate in each.

Directory of Foreign Firms Operating in the U. S. This directory lists foreign firms operating in the United States and describes their products.

Industry Directories

Hundreds of directories exist which are helpful to job seekers. As an example, the *World Aviation Directory* lists all airlines, airports, catering services, insurance companies, related government agencies, airplane manufacturers, component manufacturers, repair and maintenance organizations, and flight schools. That may be just about the only resource some people would need.

Several resources are available to help you locate useful directories. Most libraries will have either the *Guide to American Directories* or the *Directory of Directories*. Both list and describe over five thousand directories that are divided into over three hundred categories. They will also tell you what the directories cost and where to order them. Most directories cost between five and twenty-five dollars. After you identify a useful directory, check the card catalog to see if the library has it. Below is a listing of some of the most useful directories.

Administrative
Consultants and Consulting Organizations Directory
Who Audits America
National Trade & Professional Associations of the U. S.
Directory of Management Consultants

Agricultural
   Farm Chemicals Handbook
   Directory of Farmer Cooperatives

Apparel
   Fairchild's Textiles and Apparel Financial Directory
   National Apparel Contractors and Suppliers Directory
   Apparel Industry Magazine Sourcebook
   Davison's Textile Bluebook
   Davison's Knit Goods Trade
   American Apparel Manufacturers Association Directory

Aviation
   Aviation Telephone Directory
   World Aviation Directory
   Aviation Week and Space Technology—Marketing
      Directory Issue

Banking
   American Bank Directory

Broadcasting
   World Radio—TV Handbook
   Broadcasting Yearbook
   Los Angeles Directory of TV Commerical Film Producers
   Broadcasting Engineering's Buyer's Guide
   Video Industry Directory

Conservation and Environment
   Environmental Organizations Directory
   Directory of Public Aquaria of the World
   Directory of Nature Centers and Environmental Educa-
      tion Facilities
   Pollution Equipment News Catalog and Buyers Guide

Construction
   Constructor Directory
   Associated General Contractors Roster of Members

Data Processing
   Official Directory of Data Processing
   National Directory of Computing and Consulting
      Services

Electrical/Electronics
   Telephony's Directory of the Telephone Industry
   Electronic Buyer's Guide and Reference Issue
   Electrical Product Membership Directory
   Who's Who in Electronics

Energy

    Solar Energy Directory

    Electrical World's Directory of Electric Utilities

    Northwest Electric Power Directory

    Directory of Industrial Heating and Combustion
        Equipment

    Energy Systems Product News—Buyers Guide and Direc-
        tory Issue

Engineering

    American Consulting Engineers Council Directory

    Directory of Engineering Firms Engaged in Resource
        Recovery and Solid Waste Management

    Association of Consulting Chemists and Chemical
        Engineers Consulting Services

Fishing

    American Fisheries Directory and Reference Book

    Pacific Packers Report

Food/Food Processing

    Directory of the Wine Industry

    Directory of the Canning, Freezing and Preserving
        Industry

    Directory of Frozen Food Processors

    Beverage Industry Annual Manual

    Food Processing Guide and Directory

    Progressive Grocer's Marketing Guidebook

Food Service

    Thomas Grocery Register

    Vending Times' International Buyers Guide and
        Directory

Glass

    Glass Factory Directory

Health

    Guide to the Health Care Field

    Health Services Directory

    Optical Industry and Systems Purchasing Directory

    Executive Directory of the U. S. Pharmaceutical Industry

    American Surgical Trade Association's Manufacturers
        Directory

    Guide to Scientific Instruments

Hotels

    Hotel—Motel Directory/Facilities Guide of the Hotel Sales
        Management Association

Import/Export

    Directory of United States Importers

    American Register of Importers and Exporters

Marine

    Boat Builders Directory

Marine Engineering/Log Catalog and Buyers Guide
Boat Industry's Marine Buyers Guide
Marine Directory
International Shipping and Shipbuilding Directory

Metal/Metal Manufacturing
Western Machinery and Steel World Buyers Directory
Directory of Iron and Steel Works of the U. S. and Canada
Dun and Bradstreet's Metal Working Directory
National Machine Tool Builders Association Directory
Heat Treating Buyers Guide and Directory
Metal Progress Testing and Inspection Buyers Guide and
Directory

Mining
E and MJ International Directory of Mining and Mineral
Processing Operations
Keystone Coal Industry Mining

Media/Advertising
Graphic Arts Buyers Guide Directory Issue
O'Dwyer's Guide to Corporate Communications
O'Dwyer's Directory of Public Relations Firms
International Directory of Marketing Research Houses
and Services
Standard Directory of Advertising Agencies

Oil
Directory of Oil Well Supply Companies
Worldwide Refining and Gas Processing Directory

Paper
Paper Industry Management Association Directory of
Members

Printing
In-Plant Printer Gold Book

Publishing
Literary Market Place

Research
Research Centers Directory

Retail
Directory of Shopping Centers in the U. S.
Fairchild's Financial Manual of Retail Stores
Sheldon's Retail Trade
Hardware Age Directory

Sales
National Directory of Manufacturers Representatives
Verified Directory of Manufacturers Representatives

Transportation/Shipping
Official Guide of the Railways
Russell's Official National Motor Coach Guide

Truck Broker Directory
Western Material Handling/Packaging/Shipping
Modern Materials Handling
Warehouse Directory

STAGE TWO—OBTAINING INFORMATION
ABOUT THE ORGANIZATION

Once you've landed an appointment or an interview, it's time to shift into high gear and get prepared. A survey of campus recruiters revealed that knowledge of the company was one of three key factors in successful interviews. Armed with knowledge, you can go into interviews with confidence and calmness. Avoid overwhelming the interviewer with your knowledge about products or financial figures, though. Instead, keep your information in reserve and weave it into the conversation when appropriate.

The following resources will provide valuable information.

Moody's. *Moody's Industrial Manual*—Provides financial information, history, subsidiaries, products and services, sales, principal plants and properties, executives, number of empoyees. One to two pages are devoted to most companies.

Moody's OTC (Over the Counter)—Same format as above but covering smaller companies.

Moody's Municipal and Government Manual

Moody's Bank and Finance Manual

Moody's Public Utilities Manual

Moody's Transportation Manual

Clipping File. Many libraries maintain files of news articles and feature articles about local businesses clipped from local papers. While most articles are short news releases, you will also find highly informative feature articles about new developments within target companies.

House Organs. Companies publish house organs (in-house newsletters) as internal public relations vehicles and will have such things as a letter from the president describing past achievements and future goals, pictures of the bowling team and those retiring, and usually a feature article about a person, department, or a new product. House organs are especially helpful. Check with your library to see if a file of house organs is maintained.

Annual Reports. If the company is publicly owned (stock which is publicly traded), it is required by law to publish an annual financial report. Understanding the financial jargon is unnecessary. The past year's failures and achievements will be summarized along with descriptions of new products and future goals.

Recruiting Brochures. Major companies which recruit at college campuses produce recruiting brochures. The brochures describe the history and background of the company, training programs, company benefits, and desired training and characteristics of employees. College placement offices will have many on file and may have some which are free.

Indexes. Besides the *clipping file* you will want to use several indexes to locate articles in magazines or newspapers. Look up companies by name or by industry.

Encyclopedia of Business Information Sources—Lists trade associations, periodicals, directories, bibliographies, and an abstract index of recent articles. An outstanding resource.

Readers Guide to Periodical Literature—Lists articles found in over one hundred periodicals, giving the periodical, date, and title of article.

Business Periodicals Index—The BPI uses business periodicals which are generally not covered in the Readers Guide to Periodical Literature.

F & S Index of Corporations and Industries—Lists articles on industries and companies. Lists trade journals, addresses, and their costs.

Wall Street Journal Index—The first section is alphabetical by company; the second section is alphabetical by subject and people's names.

New York Times Index—Same format

Chicago Tribune Index—Same format

Los Angeles Times Index—Same format

Washington Post Index—Same format

Libraries which carry these indexes will probably also have the newspapers on microfilm.

Your Interviewer. Search the Clipping File and House Organ for articles about your interviewer.

Who's Who In America

Who's Who In The West

You will also find other specialized *Who's Who In . . .* , covering various subjects.

Dun & Bradstreet Reference Book of Corporate Managements—Lists companies alphabetically, then lists executive with name, title, year born, summary of career, education.

Standard and Poor's—Vol. 2, *Register of Directors and Executives.* Same format as Dun's, but executives are listed alphabetically by last name.

INTERVIEWING PRINCIPLES

Effective interviewing is an art which can be learned, and the payoffs can be tremendous. You'll work so hard to get each interview that it would be a shame to go in unprepared. By knowing what to expect in an interview and by preparing for all of the difficult questions which can be asked in an interview, you'll get the job offer where in the past you might have been the second or third choice.

1. An interview is simply an opportunity for two people to meet and determine if an employer-employee relationship will prove beneficial to both parties.
2. Interviewing is a two-way street. You're not begging for a job, you're an equal.
3. The employer is actually on your side. He or she has a problem and has every reason to hope you are the right person to solve it. *Keep the employer on your side.* This requires attentive listening. Try to detect what the real problems are.
4. An objection is not a rejection, it is a request for more information. If the employer states, "You don't have as much experience as we normally want," he is not rejecting you. In fact, he could be totally sold on you but for this one question. Your task is to sell yourself and overcome that objection, but it won't help to argue.
5. Let the employer talk. You listen. The longer the employer talks at the beginning, the more you can learn about the organization and formulate positive responses. Even if the employer talks on and on, don't worry. You'll get your chance.
6. Increase your chance for a second interview by dressing properly, being on time, listening intently, demonstrating potential and enthusiasm, appearing relaxed, providing brief, well thought-out responses, and asking a few intelligent questions.
7. Hiring decisions are based mostly on emotion. Do I like her? Will we get along? Will she accept criticism and be a good team worker? Being liked by the employer is just as important as having the qualifications.
8. Concentrate on giving examples of accomplishments. This demonstrates potential. Stress how you can benefit the organization. Do not give the impression that all you

care about is what the organization can do for you.

9. Be yourself, but also be your best. If you tend to be overly aggressive, consciously tone it down during the interview. If you have strong opinions on everything and like to express them, keep them to yourself. On the other hand, you do not have to agree with the employer on every issue, but when you disagree, be tactful. If you tend to be too quiet and reserved, try to be a little more outgoing and enthusiastic during the interview.

10. Use examples to back up any statements you make. Be prepared for "Are you good with details?" "Are you a hard worker?" "Can you handle difficult people?" You can begin your response with, "Yes, I *am* good with details. For example . . ."

11. Be able to explain any details included in your resume, such as accomplishments or job duties. You can use your resume to predict many of the questions that will be asked. Practice stating your job duties in the most concise way possible.

12. Showing confidence in yourself will create a favorable impression. Such confidence can come only from truly knowing yourself and recognizing your own potential. Your resume will have helped you formulate a positive self-image.

13. Take notes right after the interview. It may be a week or two before a second interview, so don't trust your memory. Write down some of the questions which were asked and details about the job. Note any questions you have.

14. Send a thank-you note that evening. Some employers have never received a thank-you note, yet this simple courtesy frequently can make the difference between selection and rejection.

15. Relax and enjoy your interviews.

OVERCOMING OBJECTIONS

Performing well in interviews requires an ability to recognize the difference between rejections and objections. People who perceive an objection as a rejection either become defensive or simply give up and assume all is lost.

An objection is *not* a rejection. It is simply a request for more information. Good salespeople, like good interviewees, learn to anticipate objections. Cost is a common objection. A salesperson might open with, "This is not the least expensive lawnmower on the market, but a recent survey showed that the average lawnmower lasts eight years, while ours are averaging over twelve years of trouble-free service." This way the objection may be overcome before it is ever expressed.

You also are a salesperson. You want to sell your services to an employer in return for a satisfying job and adequate income. Virtually everyone must overcome several objections during the interviewing process before a job offer is made.

The first step in overcoming objections is predicting what they will be and developing effective responses. Objections will likely occur if you were fired from your last job, you appear to be a job hopper, there is a major gap in your work history, you're changing careers, you don't have a college degree and you're applying for a position that normally requires it, you have three or more years of college education but never received a degree, you're over fifty years of age, or you have too little or too much experience. The list could go on.

When overcoming an objection, don't argue with the employer. If the employer states, "You really don't have enough experience in this field," a good response might be, "I realize there are others with more experience, but I really feel the quality of my experience is the key. There's no question in my mind that I can do an outstanding job for you."

PROJECT ENTHUSIASM AND POTENTIAL

Enthusiasm and potential will land you more job offers than any other qualities. The two are inseparable.

Enthusiasm

Employers seek enthusiastic people who really want to get involved in the job. You should demonstrate genuine enthusiasm— enthusiasm for the job and its duties, enthusiasm for your future boss, enthusiasm for the company, and enthusiasm for any features of the job such as travel, evening work, periodic high pressure situations, and deadlines.

Suppose the field has been narrowed to two equally qualified people. The employer will ask many questions to determine who is the best choice. A common question is, "If we offered you the position, would you accept it?" Notice the difference in the following two responses.

257

Sandra: Yea, I definitely would accept it. The job seems interesting.

Susan: I'm impressed with everything about this job. As I mentioned before, XYZ was one of the ten companies I was most interested in when I contacted you. Now I'm even more impressed with XYZ. I like the philosophy of top management, I like the steady growth of XYZ in the last five years, and I really look forward to working for you. The job itself matches my strengths and interests almost perfectly and the three weeks of travel each year is practically ideal. I'm really looking forward to getting started.

There is little question as to who would be hired.

The best way to appear enthusiastic is to genuinely *be* enthusiastic about the job. If you've considered your long- and short-range goals, and this job would help you attain those goals, it will be easy to demonstrate enthusiasm. Unfortunately, most people never set clear and attainable career goals.

Enthusiasm is not demonstrated in just one response to one question, it must be demonstrated throughout the interview. It starts with listening. Really listening to the interviewer shows respect as well as enthusiasm. Everyone appreciates a good listener. People know you're listening by your body language. Look, but don't stare at the interviewer. Nod to show agreement or understanding. Don't slouch in the chair but sit erect or lean slightly forward. Show enthusiasm by speaking positively about previous jobs or supervisors. Describe how you put all of your energy into a job and describe the results you achieved.

Enthusiasm also comes across through self-confidence. If you are confident you can do the job and you really want it, your enthusiasm will come across spontaneously.

Potential

Potential means your future worth to an organization. Demonstrating enthusiasm without potential will seldom lead to a job offer. The two must go together. Your enthusiasm will give the employer confidence that you want the job, will work hard at it, and will likely stay with the company for several years. But without demonstrated potential you will not receive a job offer.

Although companies often use elaborate personality tests, the best predictor for future success is still past success. If you are the top salesperson at your present company but are interviewing for a new sales position, your past success will give the sales manager the confidence that you will continue to sell well. If you've been fired from four sales positions because of poor results, you'll have your work cut out for you in trying to convince a sales manager that you really do have potential.

Potential is best demonstrated by telling the employer about your accomplishments. Take for example a woman returning to work after twenty years out of the job market. She is applying for Administrative Assistant with a small association that represents pharmacists. Membership has dropped because pharmacists feel they have not been effectively represented. In walks Paula, with no paid work experience and only one year of college, to compete with college graduates with experience working with associations. And she lands the job. The reason—her one-year term as president of the PTA. During that year attendance at meetings increased sixty percent over the previous year, and fund-raising activities brought in twice as much. She organized a banquet that people are still talking about, and she was considered to be the primary lobbying force for new state legislation that benefited her school district. By sharing these accomplishments she proved that she could help turn the pharmacists' association around. That's potential.

Enthusiasm and potential are just as crucial for the experienced person. Your enthusiasm will come through as you explain how much you enjoy your field or work. Potential, of course, will be demonstrated by discussing recent, solid work-related accomplishments.

DESCRIBE ACCOMPLISHMENTS

As we have already seen, sharing accomplishments is the best way to demonstrate potential. If you have several years of work experience, you should write down on paper your fifteen top work-related accomplishments. If you are trying to break into a new field, choose your fifteen top work-related or non-work-related accomplishments that best demonstrate your ability to handle the new job. An accomplishment is anything you've done well and enjoyed doing or received satisfaction from doing.

It is always best to describe accomplishments in terms of dollars or percentages. One of my clients was able to tell employers that in the two years since he had taken over his territory, he had increased the tons of aluminum sold by fifty-four percent, the dollar volume by ninety-six percent, and the profits on his sales by one hundred twenty-four percent. The company had been in that area for forty years. You can see how impressive this would be to an employer.

I'll give you some other examples.

I received a $600 bonus from Boeing for suggesting an idea
that saved $6,000 the first year.

I developed a simplified computer program for a client
which reduced the computer runtime by forty percent and
saved over $17,000.

Dollar figures and percentages are so valuable in accomplishments that you should even estimate them when necessary. The computer programmer in the second example above had to estimate or guesstimate the dollar savings. She knew the runtime was reduced by between thirty-five percent and forty-five percent so she chose forty percent as her figure. She knew how frequently the program was run and she knew the cost of the computer time. The $17 thousand figure was calculated using simple arithmetic.

Not all accomplishments can be quantified, but the majority can. When I'm interviewing people, gathering data for their resumes, I'm frequently told, "There's really no way to estimate it, I just improved it." I will then ask questions from different angles and we'll arrive at a figure to use. See pages 58 to 63 for more on accomplishments. The ideas expressed there for resumes are just as applicable for interviewing.

If you are seeking an entry-level position, you will want to describe accomplishments that are most closely related to the job you're applying for. Accomplishments enable the employer to assume that if you've done well in one field, you can do well again in another field.

Here are some examples.

I haven't missed a day of work in three years.

I became one of the youngest store managers McDonalds
ever had, at the age of seventeen. My boss said she had
never seen anyone learn so fast or who showed as much
maturity as I did.

During the summer after I graduated from high school, I
worked as a stocker in a small grocery store. I got three raises
in three months because the owner said he had never had
anyone who could shelve so fast.

I led my basketball team in assists. I really enjoy being part of
a team.

260

Once you list your accomplishments, practice sharing them. During an interview you must select the most appropriate accomplishment—the one that shows you doing work closely related to the job you're interviewing for, or one that demonstrates highly desirable characteristics.

PROJECT A WINNING PERSONALITY

Either on a conscious or subconscious level, the employer will be evaluating your personality and asking, "Do I like this person? Will we get along and work well together?" When considering two people with equal qualifications, the one with the most pleasing personality will always be hired. A job is similar to marriage—the two of you may in a sense live together for many years. Work will be a lot more enjoyable if you like and respect each other.

Some of the most desirable characteristics are friendliness, cheerfulness, tactfulness, sincerity, maturity, open-mindedness, loyalty, patience, optimism, reliability, flexibility, and emotional stability. There are others, of course, but these are among the most important. During an interview you won't just rattle off claims to each of these characteristics—you will demonstrate each one. In just twenty minutes, a perceptive interviewer can accurately assess you in each area—not by what you say, but by what you are. A famous saying goes like this: "Your actions speak so loudly, I can't hear what you're saying."

Imagine interviewing with a company that just fired an employee because he wouldn't cooperate and insisted on doing his own thing. You might be asked, "In this organization cooperation and teamwork are absolutely essential. Are you a cooperative person?" You might respond, "Yes, I am very cooperative. For example, when I was in the Army I worked with a team dismantling explosives. I really learned to appreciate teamwork and cooperation—our lives depended on it."

PREPARATION

There is no substitute for preparation and practice. Fortunately for you, most people spend little time preparing for interviews. They will get a good night's sleep, polish their shoes, take a shower, and hope for the best. Their attitude is, "Since I don't know what they'll ask, I'll just give it a good shot."

We do, however, know the questions that will be asked. There are approximately 70 commonly asked questions, virtually all others being variations. Then there are the technical questions that can be asked of people in your field. These too, can be predicted. Questions also come from your resume, particularly questions regarding accomplishments.

A complete discussion of the most commonly asked questions follows this introduction on interviewing. In each case the principle behind answering the question is discussed, with an example often included. To prepare your responses, simply jot down the points you want to make. Do not try to develop a word for word response. That would require memorization and is not recommended. If you forget a point during an interview you could become flustered and completely blow the response. Memorizing can also make you seem mechanical. By practicing the responses several times you will feel confident and relaxed. Say your answers slightly different each time so they have a ring of spontaneity.

Thorough preparation will take at least 20 hours. Begin by reading and studying **Sweaty Palms** by Anthony Medley—a 7-9 hour process. Preparing and practicing your responses to the 72 commonly asked questions, the 5-8 technical questions you suspect could be asked, and the 8-10 questions likely to come off your resume, might require 10-15 hours. If you could talk to the people I have personally prepared for interviewing, you would be convinced that such an effort pays big dividends.

BE YOURSELF/BE YOUR BEST

In the following material I will be giving you a lot of techniques. These techniques will prove extremely beneficial, but with techniques there is the danger of becoming mechanical. The overriding advice I will give then is—BE YOURSELF. Act natural, relaxed, and confident and you will do well. My advice is also—BE YOUR BEST. It is important, for example, to show enthusiasm during an interview. Some, however, are not naturally enthusiastic. During the interview that person must consciously turn up the enthusiasm a notch or two—four or five notches would be asking too much and would be self-defeating.

You must also do what seems right for you. I'll be providing many ideas on how to handle certain questions, but your personal judgment is critical to your success.

REVEALING YOURSELF

Employers will "know" about you, whatever you reveal to them. Much of what you reveal about yourself is done unconsciously and by body language. Within a minute the interviewer will know if you are energetic, enthusiastic, confident, prepared, nervous, cheerful, articulate, or reserved. You get only one chance to make a good first impression. By practicing your interviews and knowing what you want to reveal, you will achieve that desired impression.

CONTROLLING THE INTERVIEW

Job seekers are sometimes advised to take control of interviews, but that tactic will inevitably backfire with an experienced interviewer. My advice is: let the interviewer control the questions while you control the content. Controlling the content means that you will be deciding what to say and which examples to give. That is all the "control" you need.

You can greatly influence the questions by having a resume filled with results. You'll be asked to expand on those results, giving you wonderful opportunities to score points.

Develop a game plan and know the points you want to cover and the experiences you want to describe. Then look for the earliest opportunity to "slide" in the points you want to make.

GETTING MORE INFORMATION ABOUT THE JOB

Interviewers typically spend several minutes describing a job and its requirements, but too frequently that task is not adequately handled when out of the blue a really tough question is asked. Without knowledge of where the organization is headed or what challenges will be faced, providing an effective answer will be impossible.

Since it is important to get off to a good start, not knowing enough about the job puts you in a tenuous situation. Without proper information you might emphasize the wrong points.

Let's say that with very little background provided, the interviewer begins by asking about your strengths. Since you have many strengths and want to emphasize the right ones, it is important to have more information. You could respond by stating, "I've got a lot to offer, but in order to cover just the right points, it would help a lot to know more about the position and what your needs are." This will cause the interviewer to realize that he or she failed to cover some key information.

Once the focus is changed to talking more about the job, another question or two can usually be asked to elicit further information so you can tailor your responses. Practice how you will respond when such difficult questions arise early in the interview. Without such practice you will probably lack the confidence to request more information. The success of your interview, however, may depend on it.

LET OTHERS SPEAK FOR YOU

Let others say positive things about you. You can say, "My boss felt some of my most valuable attributes were . . . ." Granted, the person is not there to confirm what you've just said, but if you have successfully established credibility, your statement will be accepted.

CREDIBILITY

Effective interviewing requires credibility. You accomplish this through truthfulness, sincerity, and genuineness. One of the major advantages of truthfulness was stated by Mark Twain, "If I tell the truth I don't need such a good memory." It requires great effort to recall all of the little half-truths told during the interviewing process.

The wonderful benefit to credibility is that once established, whatever you say from that point on tends to be believed. In fact, what you say will be believed unless you give the employer some reason to doubt you. That's why you should do nothing to jeopardize your credibility. A good example is in answering the question, "What is your biggest weakness?" Job finding books written in the 70s frequently recommended that you work out your answer so that your weakness really came across as a strength. One recommended answer ran something like this, "I'd have to say that my greatest weakness is that I work too hard. My wife complains that I'm not around enough and I guess sometimes I work my people too hard too." The employer was supposed to think, "Well, isn't it nice that if this guy is going to have a weakness, it would be something like this." The problem is that it is very difficult to come off sounding sincere. It seems so planned and contrived.

Here's the biggest problem—once you lose your credibility,

264

everything you said before, and everything you say after, will come under greater scrutiny and there will always be an element of doubt. This is not a good way to start a relationship. So, do everything possible to establish credibility, and then do nothing to lose it.

SELLING YOU

During the interview you are selling your personality as much as you are selling your specialized skills. To sell yourself you need to know your personality skills. These skills include such items as being appreciative, cooperative, energetic, and reliable. Employers value such qualities. Even someone seeking a CEO position must sell personality skills.

Your goal during the interview is to reveal as many positive attributes as possible. While your competitors are busy merely "describing" their technical strengths, you will be "selling" your technical strengths along with your personality skills.

There is an old saying that sales are made on emotion and justified with logic. Think about that. On an emotional level you start to like something, but somehow must justify to yourself why you should spend the money on it. Few are even aware that this process is taking place, but it is very real. Think of every TV commercial you've ever seen—are they playing to logic—or emotion?

Hiring decisions are identical. Your challenge is to get the employer to like you and to begin "leaning" your way. You do this by projecting enthusiasm, potential, and a winning personality. On an emotional level the employer begins to like you and feel comfortable with you. He senses your potential. Once you have hooked the employer emotionally, he will always find a way to justify hiring you.

To better understand the importance of personality skills, it is best to dive right in and rate yourself on these 42 key skills. Rate yourself on a scale of 1-10 where 10 is excellent and 1 is poor. Be sure to give yourself a range—not all 8s, 9s, and 10s. Give yourself an almost instantaneous rating—don't analyze yourself.

Appreciative	Goal Oriented
Assertive	Growth Oriented
Cheerful	Honesty/Integrity
Compassionate	Insightful
Considerate	Joyful
Cooperative	Loyal

Curious/Inquisitive	Open-minded
Decision Making	Optimistic
Decisive	Patient
Discreet	Persistent
Easy-going	Practical
Effective Under Stress	Real
Efficient/Productive	Reliable
Emotionally Stable	Responsible
Energetic/Stamina	Resourceful
Enthusiastic	Risk Taking
Flexible	Self-confident
Forgiving	Sense of Humor
Frank	Sincere
Friendly/Nice	Sound Judgment
Generous	Thorough

Now pick out your top ten personality skills and write a short paragraph describing how you are that way. This is a quick exercise, you're not trying for polished writing. Writing about some of your personality skills will prepare you for interviews. There is no substitute for taking time to think about them. They might read like this:

Although some may say I seldom get excited, I do have a high degree of *enthusiasm* in many areas. It is not a gushy enthusiasm, but a strong, deep enthusiasm that comes from conviction.

I am very *efficient*. This quality has been my worst enemy where I am now working. A difficult, demanding job appears so easy because I am efficient. No one fully recognizes my worth.

I was *diplomatic* when I had to discuss accounting irregularities with the client's accountants.

Because they are so critical in interviews, you need to learn how to sell personality skills. There are four primary ways: 1) State the skill and then give an example to back it up, 2) State the skill and describe how you use it, 3) While selling a skill using a specific experience, describe the experience so vividly that some of your personality skills are clearly evidenced, and 4) Be it. I will explain these points in greater detail.

State the skill and give an example. During an interview you might be asked to describe your strengths. You could respond by saying, "I'd have to say that one of my strengths is my ability to work effectively under stress. A good example would be when I was working on the Otis account. Out of nowhere our client told us that they needed a new ad campaign for a product that was not doing well in the market. To tie it in with other promotions they were doing we had only two weeks to get it out. Normally it would have been a two month project. My staff and I practically lived at the office but we got it out. We put together some really good stuff." If warranted you could expand on this and take two or three minutes to detail the project.

State the skill and describe how you use it. Sometimes an example is just not appropriate. Instead of giving an example you might say, "I have a reputation for being reliable. People at work know that if a tough project has to get out on schedule, it had better be given to me. When I agree to take on a project my boss knows it's as good as done. I'll get it done no matter what it takes."

Describe an experience so vividly that other skills are evident. You may have indicated that one of your strengths is your high energy level and offered an example. When described vividly, even a half-way perceptive person will pick up other positive qualities without your having to label them.

Be it. Don't say it, demonstrate it. Energy is demonstrated. The way you walk and talk, your body language, facial expressions, and your voice inflection, all demonstrate your energy level. I can tell a person's energy level within the first minute we are together. Cheerfulness, insightfulness, joyfulness, open-mindedness, optimism, self-confidence, enthusiasm, sense of humor, and sincerity can all be demonstrated.

Practice telling your stories. Only by doing so can you really hone them down to their most important points. Describe the experiences so vividly that the interviewer forms a mental image. Mental images can last for weeks or months in an employer's mind, mere thoughts may last five minutes or five days.

SAFE ANSWERS

As you read my suggestions you may pick up the idea that I often recommend "safe" answers. There is, in fact, a strong case to be made for safe answers, but always within the context of truthfulness. It is important to give the interviewer a sense of your openness and you certainly need to achieve credibility. But all of this also requires discretion.

Your challenge is to receive a job offer. You want the opportunity to accept it or reject it and you do not want to give the interviewer any excuses for rejecting you. So discretion is the key. If you are asked why you want to leave your present job, you may have six reasons. Discretion tells you to only mention three of them. The interviewer may ask about your greatest weakness or the greatest job related mistake you ever made. By all means share a genuine weakness and reveal a real mistake, but it need not be your greatest weakness or your greatest mistake. Revealing either might hurt your chances for a job offer.

This is a tricky topic to cover because I believe in the importance of honesty. With all of this in mind, I have accepted the fact that there are times when we must choose not to reveal something. Whatever you say should be true, but there are certainly times when you may withhold additional information. Use this as a principle and then begin thinking how you will respond to some of the really tough questions.

The honesty issue and the safe issue are not identical so let's return to safe answers. Controversy will virtually never benefit you and should be avoided. An issue might come up during an interview that you would just love to go after and give all of your opinions on. Don't do it. In fact the interviewer may even be baiting you, just to see how you will react.

I frequently suggest that you base your answers on what you have already learned about the job and your prospective boss. If you have 20 strengths that you are prepared to discuss during an interview, you might quickly realize that four of them would simply not sell you in this particular job with this particular supervisor. Naturally you would choose not to mention those four, but would sell the other 16 at every opportunity. That is safe and prudent.

You may be a person who relishes independence on the job. Yet when asked what job-related needs you have, you might not mention it because you have sensed that this employer likes to maintain close contact with employees—not watching over their shoulders mind you, but a close watch nevertheless.

Someone might suggest that it's better to clear the air right away, telling it like it is, letting the chips fall where they may. I call this the let-it-all-hang-out syndrome. It has a logic, but it does not yield the desired result—a job. It is justified by the belief that "if they don't like me just the way I am, then I don't want to work there anyway." Get the offer, then decide if you want to work there.

SELL YOURSELF AT EVERY OPPORTUNITY

Selling yourself at every opportunity is a key premise to successful interviewing. View the process as a balance scale with every effective answer adding weight to your side. If your competitors have more experience than you, they enter the interviewing process with greater weight on their side of the scale. You, therefore, must seize every opportunity and sell yourself as best you can. By placing just a little extra weight on your side with each question, you can overcome major disadvantages. Eventually the scale will tip in your favor and the interviewer will ''know'' that you are the right person.

EXCITE AN EMPLOYER

You can genuinely get an employer excited about you. You do so by achieving any one of the following: Show the employer how you can 1) **make** money for the company, 2) **save** money for the company 3) **solve** problems the employer is facing, 4) **reduce** the level of stress and pressure the employer is under.

The concept of making money, saving money, and solving problems is fairly obvious, and is best achieved by describing actual examples. Less obvious, but just as valuable, is demonstrating that you can reduce the stress and pressure your prospective boss is facing. Start by selling your reliability, responsibility, and resourcefulness. By having confidence that additional responsibilities can be delegated to someone of your caliber, your prospective boss will actually visualize a life of less pressure. That is highly appealing.

GO FOR IT!

One principle in interviewing is to always go for it. When the job you are interviewing for is fully described, and it seems to be less than what you really want, go for the offer. People often consciously or unconsciously sabotage their efforts and as a result, don't get asked back for a second interview. My belief is, you never know whether you want the job until an offer is made, there is money on the table, benefits have been fully covered, and you have had a chance to negotiate in the things you want, and to negotiate out the things you do not want. People have negotiated for amazing things—and gotten them—but only because they had sold themselves so well that the employers were willing to do almost anything to bring them on board.

By "sabotaging" I mean failing to do your best. Consciously or unconsciously, your answers are not as sharp, not as well thought out, the zip in your voice is missing. The interviewer picks it up immediately.

I realize there are times when you immediately know the job is not for you. Resist the temptation to tune out. Perhaps the interviewer will also realize **this** job is not the right one for you and will offer you a different job instead.

You might indicate at the end of the interview that the job is not a good match. If, however, you are highly interested in the company or would especially like to work for this person, say so. There may be nothing else available right now, but the perfect job could materialize during the next six months and you might be the prime candidate. Or, if the person is impressed, he may refer you to someone else in the company who could use your talents. None of these positive things can happen if you tune out and fail to respond as well as you are capable of.

SHOW WHAT YOU CAN DO FOR THEM

One of the biggest turnoffs for employers is the candidate who seems self-centered and cares only about what the company can do for him. Employment is certainly a two-way street and there must be give and take, but during the interview the emphasis must be on how you can benefit the organization.

To paraphrase John Kennedy's famous challenge, "Ask not what your company can do for you, but ask what you can do for your company." After the offer is made there is plenty of time to talk money and other things. Until then, stress what you can do for the organization.

ANSWERING AMBIGUOUS QUESTIONS

Employers often ask questions that could be interpreted in more than one way. Examples could be, "What is the biggest mistake you ever made?" or "What was the biggest crisis you ever experienced?" In both, it is unclear whether the employer wants job-related experiences or personal experiences. My belief is that it is generally unwise to ask for clarification. Simply make a quick decision—then go for it. Take a direction that is easier for you, safer, or will show you in a better light. Consider the question about your biggest mistake. Sometimes it is simply easier and wiser to mention a personal experience. Of course the employer can always come back and ask the question again more specifically, but at least you gave an honest answer. Usually, if it was a quality answer, the person will be satisfied and will go on to the next question.

One reason for not asking for clarification is that it breaks the continuity of the interview and can seem awkward. You may seem too cautious, and afraid to take any risks. I am not saying never ask for clarification. At times you must. The question may be of such importance, and the ambiguity so great, that you dare not take a wrong direction. By all means ask for clarification.

QUESTIONS TO BE PREPARED FOR

Below are seventy-two of the most frequently asked questions. Prepare a brief response for each one and practice aloud in front of a mirror. Write each question on a sheet of paper and then list the points you would like to make. Don't write it out word for word and then try to memorize the answers. In an interview you may forget parts and stumble. Besides, they would sound "canned" instead of spontaneous.

I see a lot of people who merely do a passable job in interviews, and the cause is almost always lack of preparation. Since nearly every conceivable question can be anticipated, you can have a real edge over others by being ready for them.

1. Tell me about yourself.
2. What is your greatest strength?
3. What can you offer us that someone else can't?
4. What are your three most important career accomplishments?
5. What is your greatest weakness?
6. What kind of recommendations will you get from previous employers?
7. What are your career goals?
8. Describe your perfect job.
9. What is most important to you in a job?
10. Why do you want to change careers?
11. Why do you want to get into this field?
12. What do you really want to do in life?
13. What position do you expect to hold in five years?
14. Why would you like to work for us?

15. Why do you want to leave your present employer?
16. How long have you been out of work?
17. Why did you leave?
18. What actions would you take if you came on board?
19. How long will it take before you make a positive contribution to our organization?
20. What is your opinion of your organization?
21. How long would you stay if we offered you this position?
22. What do you like least about this position? Most?
23. What personal, non-job-related goals have you set for yourself?
24. What do you know about our company?
25. Are you willing to relocate?
26. Can you supervise people?
27. Can you work well under stress?
28. Do you prefer to work individually or as part of a team?
29. Tell me about your duties at your present job.
30. What frustrates you about your job?
31. Explain the reasons for leaving each company.
32. Describe your relationship with your last three supervisors.
33. Are you willing to travel overnight?
34. How do you feel about overtime?
35. What jobs have you enjoyed most? Least? Why?
36. What are your supervisor's strengths and weaknesses?
37. What have you learned from your mistakes? What were some of them?
38. What do you think determines a person's progress with a good company?
39. How would you describe yourself?
40. Why did you pick your major?
41. What kind of grades did you have?
42. What courses did you like most? Least? Why?
43. How has your schooling prepared you for this job?
44. Do you feel you did the best work at school that you were capable of doing?
45. Why should I hire you?
46. Who has exercised the greatest influence on you? How?
47. What duties have you enjoyed most? Least? Why?
48. What kind of supervisors do you like most? Least? Why?
49. Have you ever been fired or asked to resign?
50. Why have you changed jobs so frequently?
51. Describe the biggest crisis in your career.

52. Why were you out of work so long? What were you doing?
53. What public figures do you admire most and why?
54. What are your primary outside activities?
55. Would you have any concern if we did a full background check on you? What would we find?
56. What qualities do you most admire in other people?
57. Tell me about the last incident that made you angry. How did you handle it?
58. How has your supervisor helped you grow?
59. What did your supervisor rate you highest on during your last review? Lowest?
60. What are the things that motivate you?
61. How do you handle people that you really don't get along with?
62. Describe your management philosophy and management style.
63. What is the biggest mistake you ever made?
64. How many people have you hired? How do you go about it? How successful have the people been?
65. How many people have you fired? How did you handle it?
66. How would your subordinates describe you as a supervisor?
67. Some managers watch their employees very closely while others use a loose rein. How do you manage?
68. How have you improved as a supervisor over the years?
69. What kind of supervisor gets the best results out of you?
70. What have you done to increase your personal development?
71. How do you feel about your career progress?
72. What is unique about you?

In the following material I have done my best to give you the principles behind answering each of these commonly asked questions. I have concentrated on principles rather than trying to cover each one exhaustively. In some instances I have given examples of what could be said. When examples have been provided, it is not with the belief that these short responses are adequate to answer the entire question. Your responses will almost assuredly be longer. Use this material as a guide and then develop your own responses.

1. Tell me about yourself. Most people hate this question, but by the time you get through preparing your response, I hope you will look forward to it being asked in interviews. It is a wonderful opportunity to sell yourself. The employer is not asking whether you had a happy childhood or whether your mother loved you. Do not try to summarize your entire life in five minutes. This question is commonly asked at the beginning of an interview as a bridge from small talk to the interview itself. The two of you may have been talking about the weather, but now it is time to get into it. It would not be polite, however, to immediately dive into a question like, "What was the biggest mistake you ever made?"

It is appropriate to briefly describe your education or your work history. Even though the employer probably has your resume at hand, making note of some interesting aspects of each job can be a nice touch. Expand briefly on some of your results. This can then increase the likelihood that the employer will pick one of your results that is of particular interest, and ask you to expand on it further. That is exactly what you want because you score points every time you discuss results. After bringing the employer up to the present, and if you feel that you have maintained her interest, feel free to then mention what you feel is one of your top strengths. You might summarize by saying, "Basically I'm an analytical person. For example, at Dependable Services, no one really knew how much our services were costing the company. I had a little cost accounting in college, so I figured out the actual costs, taking depreciation of our equipment into consideration. I discovered that one of our services actually cost us seven percent more than we charged for it. We raised our fees immediately. That alone earned an additional $17,000."

2. What is your greatest strength? The question asks for your number-one strength, skill, or asset and requires you to analyze yourself. Begin with a brief statement and provide a clear example. A manager might respond, "I would say it is my ability to train people, motivate them, and get maximum output from each one. For example, XYZ had a severe turnover problem of about thirty-five percent annually of its first-line supervisors. Even without the benefit of a pay increase, which they deserved, I reduced the turnover to eight percent in just six months and to five percent by the end of the year. My analysis indicated that our foremen were receiving inadequate training when they were promoted to supervisors. They weren't sure how they fit in or even what was expected of them. Most were unsure of their authority and how to use it. Many quit out of frustration. With the help of the Human Resources Department, I developed a training program which is still used. Productivity in the plant rose substantially."

3. What can you offer us that someone else can't? Since you can't possibly know what backgrounds the other candidates have, you must respond by describing your known strengths. If you feel certain that you have some valuable or unique experience, you would certainly want to use that as an example.

4. What are your three most important career accomplishments? Choose accomplishments that are related to the job you are interviewing for, and ones which your interviewer can relate to. Avoid unnecessary detail. A question like this gives you a fantastic opportunity to sell yourself. Take full advantage of it.

5. What is your greatest weakness? When asked this difficult question, it is best to state a genuine weakness, but one which will not be required for the job you are seeking. "I'm not good at working with repetitive details. I learn methods very quickly, but if I do the same thing over and over, my mind starts to wander. I guess I need variety. I'm very good with details, however, when I'm working on a project. For example, I handled all the details for a large convention. Our president said it was the best organized convention he had ever attended." When using this response, make sure it sounds reasonable. If you were a chemist, you wouldn't state that your greatest weakness is that you're a lousy typist.

You can also answer by stating a weakness that others perceive and then state your opinion. "Some people tell me I'm not aggressive enough when I sell. Sometimes I agree with them, but then I remind myself that my sales are as high or higher than theirs. I think I've found the sales style that is right for me."

Or you could state a weakness and then explain how you have overcome it. "I don't like to fire people. I've compensated for that by holding extensive interviews with the top candidates and performing thorough background checks. That way I hire only those with the greatest potential. If I don't find what I want, I won't hire second best. I'll keep looking until I find the right person. Then I develop a complete training program. I haven't had to fire anyone in three years. Everyone I've hired has been promoted, and I believe each of them will be promoted several more times."

6. What kind of recommendations will you get from previous employers? You should know the answer to this question. Companies today are very hesitant to make negative statements about former employees because of possible lawsuits, yet some will. If you have been fired from one of your last three jobs, you would be wise to contact your former boss or the personnel department and ask what they will say. If the termination was justified but you have since changed your ways, explain that to your former boss. Explain, too, how the firing was actually a blessing in disguise because you really learned from the experience.

If you know you will receive good recommendations you might simply say, "I'm certain each of my former bosses will have only positive things to say about me. We worked well together and I learned a lot from each one." You could also expand and describe some specific points the supervisors might make. In other words, let your supervisors sell you even though they are not present.

You may have had excellent relations with all but one former employer, in which case you might state, "I'm confident I'll get high marks from all of them except possibly Simmons Company. I feel I made some very positive contributions there. I decreased staff turnover, and I also increased the hiring of women and minorities in my department. That was appreciated by personnel, but I know it wasn't appreciated by my boss. I really don't know what she will say about me."

7. What are your career goals? This question tests whether your career goals match what the organization has to offer and whether you have carefully determined your goals. Sound clear and definite about your goals, but express yourself based on what you know about the organization. Mention only those goals that you feel the organization can help you attain. Express them in terms of the experience you hope to receive and the expertise you hope to develop. You could use the opportunity to describe your present level of expertise and then how you want to develop yourself. You want to leave the impression that you are a growth-oriented person with realistic expectations regarding promotion opportunities.

8. Describe your perfect job. Be careful. This is not the place to describe your dream job. Select those *parts* of your dream job, however, that you think could be fulfilled in the job you are interviewing for. If you dream of a job that would take you to Europe twice a year but this job offers no chance of that, don't mention your desire to travel. The greatest danger here is in becoming too specific. If you mention things that cannot be fulfilled in the job, the employer may assume you would soon become dissatisfied.

9. What is most important to you in a job? What do you value in a job—challenge, good working conditions, friendly coworkers, a boss you respect? Mention one or two items and explain why it is important. If money is number one, list at least one other aspect so that the interviewer won't think that it's the only thing that matters.

10. Why do you want to change careers? I define career change as a change of fields, such that the skills and knowledge required to adequately perform the new occupation appear on *the surface* to be significantly different from what was required in the former occupation. The key phrase is "on the surface." Most would agree that moving from teacher to sales representative is a career change, but when you get below the surface, you will see the similarities. Both motivate—one to buy, the other to learn. Both must be able to simplify and explain difficult concepts. Of course the teacher must develop product knowledge and learn closing techniques, but teachers frequently make excellent salespeople.

Here's my point. In most cases, refuse to accept the label of career change. Here's an example. "I really don't feel I'm changing careers. Basically I'll be using the same skills I've developed during the last eight years of my career. My knowledge base will be somewhat different, but I took several college courses in this area, and during the last three years I've been subscribing to three trade journals and devouring every article in this specialty."

This is not just a question of semantics. The employer has stated that she believes you are making a career change. In essence, that's an objection. The employer is actually saying, "You don't have a track record, so how can I judge your ability to perform this job?" Unless you can overcome the objection, no job offer will be made. Respond by saying, "I really don't feel I'm changing careers." Avoid defensiveness.

11. Why do you want to get into this field? This is different than "Why do you want to change careers?" The interviewer is looking for evidence that you really know what you're getting into. People getting into personnel work often respond, "I enjoy helping people." That is just about the last response a personnel manager wants to hear because it indicates a misunderstanding of personnel work. In answering this question let the interviewer know that you are aware of drawbacks, then state the positive aspects.

12. What do you really want to do in life? Sometimes this is a filler question. Most interviewers have received no training in the art of interviewing and many have little experience. Sometimes an interviewer inserts a question like this so he can think of the next question. Still, you want to be prepared so that your every response will demonstrate enthusiasm and potential. This could be a time to share one of your dreams. Perhaps you want to enjoy a cruise around the world someday. Or you could select a job-related dream. Almost anything will be positive as long as you are genuinely enthusiastic about it.

13. What position do you expect to hold in five years? A question like this tests how realistic you are. If you say you want to be president in five years when you are five levels below that and there are four hundred people ahead of you, that is not a realistic response. It's okay to have such a goal, but don't express it. Employers seek promotable people but tend to be suspicious of the person who expects to turn the company upside down. If your interviewer will be your boss or your boss' boss, you might say, "I would like to move up the ladder with you. I realize you have other very capable people in this department, but through my productivity and accomplishments I will seek to be the person who moves into your position when you are promoted. In five years I'd like to move up two or three notches."

14. Why would you like to work for us? If this question is asked at or near the beginning of the first interview, you have an opportunity to describe what you know about the organization. If the question is asked after the interviewer has described the job and the company in detail, you could mention positive points that you had discovered on your own as well as some mentioned by the interviewer. This might include the reputation of the company or department, its rapid growth, your personal attraction to the interviewer as a boss, or the idealness of the job itself.

15. Why do you want to leave your present employer? The four most acceptable reasons are the desire for more money, more responsibility, more challenge, or more job satisfaction. Less acceptable or unacceptable reasons might be a personality conflict with your boss, not wishing to relocate, or having to work too much overtime. These reasons may be real, but they cast serious suspicion on you as a worker. Be prepared to offer two or three reasons. Most employers realize that changes are seldom made for one reason alone.

Every employer understands someone wanting more money. A good response might be, "Quite frankly, with my level of expertise, I should be earning more. Of course I realize my company is not going to pay me more than my boss earns, so I've decided to look elsewhere. It's a fine company and I've had some outstanding experiences there. I hate to leave the company and I would do so only for the right position with a really outstanding company. That's why I contacted you. I've been studying Prodata and I'm convinced that this division is one of the best managed anywhere."

Top-quality people seek greater challenges and more responsibility; some companies allow faster growth than others. Companies that promote primarily by seniority and those with slow growth make promotions more difficult. "Western Gear is an outstanding company and I've learned a lot, but right now it's in a slow growth pattern. My boss has told me I'll have his spot when he moves up, but both of us realize that could take four or five years. I know if I wait I'll get promoted, but right now I know I'm capable of handling much more responsibility. I'm basically a very patient person, but I also want to use my abilities to the fullest. Our president wrote a letter of commendation for the research my staff and I did on locating and purchasing the land for our next plant. The site is perfect and we got it for $165 thousand less than had been expected. I negotiated the final contract and I really did my homework. The only reason I negotiated it was that my boss was tied up with another deal. I may not get another chance like that for a couple of years."

16. How long have you been out of work? If it's been several months, you need to develop a response that will cover the time. For example, "I left Wilson Manufacturing six months ago. The first month was spent finishing the basement of my home to get it ready to sell, and then it took two months to actually sell. Once the house was sold my wife and I took the first real vacation we've had in years. We moved from Portland to Seattle just two months ago, which is when I started my job search."

17. Why did you leave? This question often follows "How long have you been out of work?" Here you must overcome another objection, since it often seems safer to hire someone who has a job. Even when a person has been laid off during a recession, the question in the interviewer's mind is, "Most people in her company are still there, why was she laid off?" The concern is that perhaps you sound impressive, but are not able to produce under pressure. Remember—an objection is not a rejection; it is a request for more information.

If you left voluntarily, make that clear and then explain the reason. A resignation due to a personality conflict must be handled carefully. In principle, your explanation should sound like a reasonable, justifiable, logical decision such that the interviewer will say in her own mind, "I would have done the same thing." You might say, "I had been at Sears for nearly two years when I decided I really didn't like retail sales. During the next six months I tried to develop a job search, but I was working so much overtime that I just wasn't able to get away for interviews. I had saved up several thousand dollars and decided I would be better off making job hunting a full-time job."

If you were fired, terminated, or laid off, you must handle this question very carefully. Do not become defensive and do not start criticizing your former boss. A good answer will require a carefully considered response. It is wise to know what your former employer will say about it. You might say, "Basically I wasn't the best person for the job. They really needed someone with a stronger math background than I have. I made some real contributions in other areas, and I really worked hard, but eventually my boss felt they should get someone else who could handle all areas of the job. I left on a very friendly basis and they gave me a nice severance package. I learned a lot from the experience and that's why I'm particularly interested in this position—I'm convinced I have all of the qualifications and know I would do an outstanding job."

18. What actions would you take if you came on board? This question is usually asked to determine if you have preset ideas on what should be done. The person with all the answers after one or two interviews is usually not trusted. The people interviewing you consider themselves capable, yet if they have been studying a problem for months and don't have the answers, they don't expect you to have the answers either. Perhaps you really do have some solutions, but don't sound cocky: "Mr. Egelson, I believe I would first review all the reports your staff has put together. I think I would also meet with some of the key people to get their feelings. From what I know so far, however, it sounds very similar to a situation we had at Smith and Smith. I didn't come up with any magical solutions, but in six months we nearly had things turned around. We brought in a very fine consulting firm for a study of our operations. I adopted several of their recommendations, and although we initially experienced resistance among our supervisors, the payoffs came in almost immediately. At this stage, of course, I can't be sure that the same conditions exist. I feel it would take about three months of study before I could make realistic recommendations." You'll be respected more if you admit it will take three months of study than to say you will have a complete set of recommendations by next week.

This question also tests your thought process. Knowing the steps you would take to solve a problem reveals more about your character and your expertise than the actual recommendations you might make.

19. How long will it take before you make a positive contribu-

tion to our organization? This question tests your self-confidence. A good response might be, ''After a brief orientation to your methods I think I can contribute almost immediately. The duties you've outlined are very similar to the ones I've been performing at Jersey Central.'' The interviewer will be looking for a realistic, self-confident response.

20. What is your opinion of your present (or past) employer? The interviewer does not require that you speak only in glowing terms about your employer, but it is important to mix any negatives with positives. No organization is all bad or all good. If you really like your present organization, your response will be easy. If you hate it, be careful. Start by saying something positive, followed by one or two negatives, and finish with a positive. The interviewer may have an opinion about your organization and want to see if it matches yours. The best way to handle this question is to avoid both extremes. If you only mention negatives, the interviewer may assume that you are a negative person and are difficult to satisfy.

21. How long would you stay if we offered you this position? This is an impossible question to answer. No one really knows how long he will stay. The best way to handle it is to lay out the conditions for your staying. ''I hope to stay indefinitely. Everything I know about the company tells me this is an ideal fit. The philosophy of top management matches mine and I like everything I've seen so far. Advancement and pay are certainly important to me. As long as my responsibilities and income grow with my proven worth, I'll be satisfied to stay indefinitely.''

If you have a history of job-hopping, you must develop a convincing statement that those days have ended. ''As you can see by my work history I've moved around, but now stability and security are a lot more important to me.''

22. What do you like least about this position? Most? The interviewer is trying to get below the surface and force you to make some definite statements. This is a hard one to prepare for because you usually will not know enough about the job prior to the interview. In principle you should choose a minor duty to like least and a major duty to like most.

23. What personal, non-job-related goals have you set for yourself? If you take time to consider your goals in life, both job- and nonwork-related, the answer will be easy. The interviewer will probably be determining if you are a thoughtful, ''together'' person. Goals related to your family are always acceptable and often preferred because they demonstrate stability. Anything related to personal growth is very acceptable—taking night classes, learning a foreign language, building your own home, or jogging.

24. *What do you know about our company?* The employer asks this question to determine your interest, enthusiasm, and initiative. There's no faking this question—either you've done your homework or you haven't.

25. *Are you willing to relocate?* The only response is, "Yes, I'm prepared to make a move." If you answer "no," the interview is over. At this stage no harm is done by saying "yes;" you've merely kept the interview alive. Actually what you're saying secretly to yourself is, "Yes, I'd relocate for a really fantastic opportunity." Of course by the time the job is offered, you should know whether you would actually be willing to relocate.

26. *Can you supervise people?* A positive statement followed by an example works well. "Yes, I supervise people very well; for example, at Somestates Insurance I supervised eight claims adjusters. Through my personal training I was able to teach more effective negotiating techniques. As a result our average personal injury settlement was reduced seven percent last year." Relate one or more good examples, always keeping them short and to the point. When appropriate you might discuss your philosophy and techniques of supervision.

27. *Can you work well under stress?* You don't have to say that you like stress, but you should provide an example or two demonstrating that you work effectively under stress. Most stress comes from deadlines and long hours. Perhaps the question is asked since in the past people have quit because they could not tolerate the stress. You should know in advance whether this field or industry typically requires long hours or faces lots of deadlines.

28. *Do you prefer to work individually or as part of a team?* The best response depends on what you know about the job. If the organization is looking for a decisive person, you would emphasize the individualistic part of you. If most work is done by committees and task forces, emphasize the teamwork side of you. If you are not sure of the best response, describe how you enjoy both aspects.

29. *Tell me about your duties at your present job.* The employer has once again given you the opportunity to sell yourself, yet many people miss this opportunity. This is a time to be selective. Mention only those duties that will help sell you. Sometimes this even means overlooking a major duty simply because that duty would not be related to the job you're interviewing for. As you describe your duties also describe an accomplishment related to

each. Remember, each accomplishment need not be earthshaking, it merely should be valid and solid.

Conciseness is crucial. Because people know their duties so well, many often go on and on, adding unnecessary details that bore the interviewer. Conciseness will come only through practice. First you should list all of your duties for each of your last three jobs. Based on what you know of the job you will be interviewing for, select those duties that you would like to discuss, then practice sharing them concisely and with enthusiasm. While emphasizing the word *conciseness*, I don't mean a thirty-second response. Your response to this question will probably last from two to six minutes. You need to cover your duties adequately, and that will take time.

30. What frustrates you about your job? Give concrete examples when answering this question. If you feel strongly about a particular frustration and would refuse future job offers if you would continue to face that frustration, you could describe that frustration in very bold terms. For example, "When I started in quality control, Acme was producing very high quality drill bits and we applied stringent tests before they passed inspection. Our new plant superintendent, however, gets his annual bonus based on production, and he has forced me during the last year or so to approve shipments that simply will not produce the results that our reputation was built on. That's why I'm especially interested in Best Tools. All of our tests on competitors show that you consistently produce the best drill bits and at a competitive price."

If you don't feel so strongly about any of your frustrations, or you wouldn't let them stand in the way of accepting a job, you'll want to choose more minor frustrations. Another quality inspector might say, "There really aren't any major frustrations. I was frustrated a few times when I wasn't allowed to buy new testing equipment when I felt we could use it, but we got by." In principle your response should sound justifiable, such that your interviewer will say, "I'd be frustrated, too."

31. Explain the reasons for leaving each company. Generally there are several reasons for leaving a company. Select the most appropriate and acceptable reason for each move. Do not use such negative statements as "I had a personality conflict with my boss" or "It was a lousy company to work for." Learn how to soften your statements. Your answers may require some elaboration since the reasons for leaving are often complex. Remember, if you had four or five reasons for leaving, select one or two that will cause the employer to understand and accept your reasons.

32. Describe your relationship with your last three supervisors.

Accentuate the positive. Even if you had a hot and cold relationship with a supervisor, stress the things which you know your boss most highly valued. You will come across much more credible if you do so. Obviously this answer is easy if you really did have a great relationship, but such is not always the case. If the relationship was less than sterling, you don't have to pretend it was wonderful, but again accentuate the positive. It is acceptable to say, "We didn't agree on everything, but we both respected the other a great deal. We learned how to work around those differences. Once decisions were made, I would back her completely, and she valued that." A statement like this shows maturity on the interviewee's part. After all, you are talking to someone who has probably had four or more bosses. I can guarantee you that not all of them were wonderful. If you try to paint a picture that your relationship with each was ideal, you will forfeit credibility.

33. *Are you willing to travel overnight?* The question can be worded as generally as this or it could be, "This job involves at least four nights on the road each month. Is that acceptable to you?" Even before the interview you should have an idea of whether the job you are seeking typically involves overnight travel. Even if the indicated travel is more than anticipated, respond with, "That's no problem." That will simply keep the interview alive. Later you must sort it out and determine if you are willing to do it. If it is more than you want, but you believe there are ways to reduce the travel, keep selling yourself. Get the offer and then negotiate the travel issue.

34. *How do you feel about overtime?* If you have had jobs that required overtime, simply describe how you handled it. If you have not had a job which required much overtime, you might respond, "I'm the type of person who will do whatever it takes to get the job done right." Before accepting the job you need to know if you will be involved with constant overtime or only occasionally.

35. *What jobs have you enjoyed most? Least? Why?* Preparation for this question requires that you think through and recall each of your positions. Relive them. What brought you satisfaction? What was frustrating? If you have been out of college several years, do not bring up summer or part-time jobs—they are expected to be unrewarding and frustrating. You need not admit that you hated any of the positions. You were only asked what you enjoyed least.

36. *What are your supervisor's strengths? Weaknesses?* This question could be asked of any previous supervisor. Concentrate on strengths. Play down weaknesses even if they were many, and select a fairly minor weakness to discuss.

37. What have you learned from your past mistakes? What were some of them? All of us have made mistakes and there were lessons to be learned from each one. Share some of them, but not necessarily the really big ones. Determine if you will discuss personal mistakes or business-related mistakes. Share ones that you were able to recover from. Use the opportunity to show how you have matured and grown from the experiences.

38. What do you think determines a person's progress with a good company? A survey by Korn-Ferry, the international executive search firm, indicated that senior executives believed that hard work, high integrity, intelligence, and excellent human relations skills got them where they are today. Your answer should reflect those main points, with such additional responses as the ability to get results and the ability to sell ideas.

39. How would you describe yourself? Pick only positive attributes and then describe how you typically demonstrate those attributes, or give a specific example that backs it up. Emphasize personality skills.

40. Why did you pick your major? This question will typically only be asked of those who graduated in the last five years. Try to recall your reasons and then give only the most positive ones. This question gives the opportunity to demonstrate your forethought and planning ability. Indicate that the decision was made only after considerable thought. If you are not using your major—you were a psych major now looking to get into banking—indicate the strengths you were able to develop as a result of your major.

41. What kind of grades did you have? If they were mediocre, you need to prepare for this one. If you worked 20-30 hours per week you might say, "I was a good student and worked hard in my classes. I'm confident that if I hadn't worked 25 hours per week during school that I would have raised my GPA half a point or so." If you just were not a good student you might say, "I've never been a great student, but I do retain well and I use a lot of common sense. That's always been my strength."

42. What courses did you like most? Least? Why? Mention as liking, any courses that are directly related to the job you are interviewing for. Otherwise simply choose courses which excited you and explain why. Business majors can say they least enjoyed science courses and can even admit they disliked accounting.

43. How has your schooling prepared you for this job? If your education is directly related to the job you are interviewing for, emphasize that you received a strong foundation that can now be built on. If you are a liberal arts major, emphasize your broad education, your written and verbal communciations skills, and your analytical ability. If you are seeking a job in private enterprise, discuss any business related courses you took, such as macroeconomics.

44. Do you feel you did the best work at school that you were capable of doing? If you truly worked hard at your studies, you might say, "I worked very hard and really took my studies seriously. I graduated with a 3.2 GPA (or with honors). Even in some of the classes where I didn't do so well grade-wise, I feel I really got something from them." Or, you might say, "I worked hard and got good grades, but I also wanted to balance my education. I was active in (student government, debate, sports, dorm counseling, etc.)." If you were a lousy student you could admit to a lack of focus at the time, adding that you are now very focused.

45. Why should I hire you? This is often asked at the end of an interview and allows you to summarize your strengths. You can discuss points that you have already covered since this is a summary, and you could bring in new points as well. Sell yourself. This may be one of your best opportunities. Be prepared to take up to four minutes. Try to focus on everything you have learned about the job, your future boss, and the needs of the company. With such limited time, you must cover only those points which will have the greatest impact. That impact often comes by describing a combination of personality skills, transferable skills, and technical skills.

46. Who has exercised the greatest influence on you? How? This question is designed to discover what type of person you are and to reveal a side of you that would rarely be seen otherwise. Parents, relatives, coaches, and teachers are most commonly cited. This is an opportunity to describe what they taught you. Emphasize that these qualities are deeply ingrained in you.

47. What duties have you enjoyed most? Least? Why? Select your most liked and least liked duties based on what you have learned about the job at that point in the interview. In general, pick major duties to like and minor duties to dislike. A disliked duty might be one you have done in the past but would not be doing at all in the job being interviewed for.

48. What kind of supervisors do you like most? Least? Why? To prepare for this one list all of the qualities you truly like and dislike in a supervisor. When the question is asked, select those that are most appropriate. For your preferred characteristics, select two or more that your future boss appears to have. For dislikes, select qualities that appear not to be true of this person. Be careful with a statement like, "I don't like a supervisor who won't give me enough independence." You may come across as a maverick. Learn to couch your words. Don't just make a statement—explain what you mean. Instead of the above, you might say, "It's frustrating working for someone who can't delegate effectively." See the difference? No one appreciates someone who does not delegate well. You would then go on to describe yourself as one who is highly reliable and self-directing, capable of taking on major challenges.

49. Have you ever been fired or asked to resign? This is perhaps the most difficult of all questions. Fortunately, many managers have at some time in their career been fired, or sought new employment while under pressure to do so. Studies indicate that about 80% of firings are over personality issues rather than competence: Good chemistry becomes bad chemistry, company needs change but the employee cannot adapt, new managers come in with different values and expectations. Being fired is not the kiss of death to a career.

Your goal is to develop a response that demonstrates maturity. If you can handle this question with dignity and maturity you will raise your esteem in the eyes of the interviewer. Cause the interviewer to realize that regardless of the reasons for the termination, you are a person with a great deal of potential. Speak in such a way that the interviewer neither questions your competency nor integrity. For this reason you must never "attack" your former boss or company. Everything you say must be said without the hint of defensiveness or rancor.

Another goal is to go into interviews calmly and with confidence, with no fear of this question being asked. I have worked with clients who dreaded this question and the nervousness would show. We worked on the response and the delivery until it became merely another question.

If you were recently fired, one approach is to tackle it head on. Admit that you were fired, and then without any defensiveness, explain the reasons. Feel free to explain what your contributions and strengths were. If you feel it was unfair, say so, but do not call your boss names and do not raise your voice or lose your temper. While not blaming yourself for the outcome, you could mention things that, looking back now, you wish you had done differently. Concentrate on describing the situation and explaining that under those conditions a termination occurred. The key to this approach is explaining things in a totally nondefensive manner. Because of the understandable concern of the employer, your task is to convince the person that this was a one time occurrence which will in no way affect future performance.

It is perfectly acceptable to indicate that you were an excellent employee who received excellent reviews. You might indicate that you got caught in a political squeeze. In such a case state that you understand that this is simply part of business. Sometimes you can say you supported the wrong person during a power struggle. Frequently if the boss is fired, the subordinate is not far behind.

You may want to admit that had you been more astute, you would have quit months earlier. You might mention that two years prior to the termination the job had taken a turn for the worse— morale in the office went down, the number of employees was reduced while workload increased dramatically, new management came in with totally different methods and expectations, or your boss was under intense pressure from top management. Looking back you should have started looking for another job, but out of loyalty to the company and a desire to make things work, you stayed too long.

During your answer you can admit that you and your boss differed in management style and philosophy of management. You could say, "She's a very good manager, we just had different ways of getting the job done."

If your position has not been filled since you left, that could give you an out. You could explain that the company was having difficulties and that you were laid off.

By the way, it is always more positive if you can say you were laid off rather than terminated or fired. It may be beneficial to work such an arrangement out with your former boss or human resources.

Generally your past employer has no desire to hurt your career. In that case, discuss your situation with your former boss and reach an agreement on what both of you will say when asked. Agreement is essential. Your former boss needs to know what you will be saying so she can back you up. In these days when people are suing their former employers for defamation of character, your company has every reason to want to help you.

If you were fired from a job several years ago, you should contact your former boss. You might explain that getting fired was the best thing that ever happened because it shook you up and you got your act together. You would go on to explain that you have been successful since that time. You might then suggest some things the former boss could say if contacted by a prospective company. The former boss will probably be glad to hear from you and will be more than happy to assist you. Surprisingly, the negative things which caused the termination are often forgotten, with only positive qualities now being remembered.

Even if you still hate your former boss, the two of you need to talk. I have had clients who strongly resisted this and absolutely never wanted to see or talk to that person again. Once accomplished, however, I have never seen anyone regret having done it, even when the outcome was less than total success.

Now I'm going to make a bold statement: If you've been fired, you must know what your former boss is saying about you! This issue is often taken care of in your discussion with your former boss, and can be confirmed by having the person write a letter of recommendation for you. When someone has *written* nice things about you, it is much harder to *say* bad things about you. If there are any hints of half-hearted recommendation, have the person write it again. One client had her boss revise the letter three times before she was satisfied. You are not powerless. While requesting tactfully, she virtually forced him to write a better letter. Having the discussion, with a letter, may be enough, but often it isn't.

Sometimes you just won't trust your former boss. If you have any doubts about what is being said concerning you, obtain the help of someone who can find out. An executive recruiter or employment agency counselor could be perfect, but a friend or anyone who does hiring could do it just as well. The person should not only write down what is said, but also indicate the tone of voice.

I've had many clients who were fired from positions. One person particularly comes to mind. He had been fired from an executive position and quickly began getting interviews throughout the country. Due to his past successes he was highly marketable. He was flown down for interviews in several major cities. After what seemed to be highly successful interviews, he was rejected in each case. Early on in our work I had suggested that he find out what his former boss was saying. Unfortunately I assumed that had been done. After three months, and interviews for seven high level positions, he discovered that he was receiving highly negative ''recommendations.'' He confronted the person and ultimately it was agreed that a more favorable person would provide recommendations. He then quickly found another job. Numerous golden opportunities, however, had been lost because he failed to know what was being said about him.

Former bosses often give bad references by ''how'' they say things rather than ''what'' they say. The words can all be right but the tone of voice can give a completely different message. Imagine someone saying, ''Yes, he was a very good employee.'' Imagine enthusiasm coming through in the voice. Then imagine the same words with a couple pauses and a complete lack of enthusiasm. Same words—two totally different impressions.

If you know your boss is going to be a bad reference, seek out someone else in the company. If the boss who fired you was not always your boss, you could list a previous boss, even if that person is no longer with the company. Sometimes your boss' boss will do an excellent job since he is not hindered by all of the emotional issues of your boss. Of course, whoever you use, that person must know what you are doing and must agree to assist you.

Because of defamation of character lawsuits many companies will not allow managers to give references. In those cases people trying to check references will be referred to the personnel department where only job titles and the dates of employment will be confirmed. If your company has a strict policy of giving out only dates of employment, your task is made easier and you won't have to be concerned about what your boss might say.

If you were fired from a job years ago and there is no way for a company to discover that, you must decide whether you will reveal the firing or not.

I've tried to give you some principles in answering this difficult question. If your situation is particularly sticky, and you just can't come up with a good response, I would recommend the advice of a career specialist. Expect to pay $40-80 per hour. If you come up with a good response the money will have been well spent. If you are unable to get a referral to someone, you will typically find such counselors in the Yellow Pages under Career or Vocational Guidance. Ask whether they have enough experience in this area to be helpful. If you have used an executive recruiter in the past that person may be able to help.

50. Why have you changed jobs so frequently? Something in your work background has given the appearance of your being a job hopper. If, at the end of your response, the interviewer still views you as unstable and unlikely to stay long enough to really contribute, you probably will not get the offer. If you have worked for three different companies in the last six years, you have not been the epitome of stability. Recognize that and determine to change it. Besides, research shows that people who stay longer with companies earn more than people who change frequently.

You might begin by stating that there have been good reasons for leaving each position (there's no need to detail the reasons unless specifically asked) and that long-term employment is certainly your goal. Sometimes a person has spent 15 years with one company and then has a string of three one-year jobs. Emphasize the long-term position and indicate that that is the true you. If there are only three or four changes to account for, you might do so briefly.

If you have not been stable, you might point out that you are now married, own a home, or any other point that might convince a person that stability has entered your life.

51. Describe the biggest crisis in your life. Describe a genuine crisis or difficult situation, not necessarily the biggest. As the question is worded, it is your decision whether to mention a personal crisis or a work-related crisis, but be prepared to describe either. Select an example that will demonstrate positive qualities and one in which you ultimately came out on top. Tell it vividly yet concisely to reveal the most qualities possible. This is an opportunity to sell such qualities as maturity, perseverance, emotional stability, effectiveness under stress, and sound judgment.

52. Why were you out of work so long? What were you doing? This question is usually only asked of those who have been out of work for over six months. The concern is that while you seem capable, other employers have apparently discovered something negative enough so as not to hire you. Prepare for this question by listing on paper what you were doing at each period. Did you take a long vacation or drop out for a while?

One approach is to show that you really have not been looking for long. Numerous things can account for your situation: you were waiting on a job which was promised you but never came through, you took care of a sick relative, you were managing the estate of a relative, or you took a long vacation. You may have worked briefly for a friend who needed help, decided to work on a temporary basis for awhile, or you took a break from work to recover from your last job. You may have spent considerable time deciding what you really wanted to do and just recently made that determination. You might mention only one item that kept you from your job search or there may have been more. Plausibility is the key. Explaining the reason for a long period of unemployment, using an example like one of these, is called damage control. In other words, they won't help sell you, they simply reduce the concern an employer may have.

You may in fact have been looking steadily for the past six or nine months. Sell the fact that you have been working hard at the job search, after all, you work hard at everything you do. You might indicate you have been quite selective and that this is one of the few jobs that have really been attractive. If you have had offers but turned them down you might mention those also.

If you have been looking for over a year without success you should seek out the help of a professional career counselor who can help evaluate any weaknesses in your search and can get you back on track.

Even if you are having trouble paying the rent, do not allow any sense of desperation to show through. You are a confident person merely waiting for the right opportunity.

In this situation women actually have an advantage. If women have long gaps in employment it is assumed that child rearing was involved. Of course that is not always the case, but it is usually assumed. When that is the case merely explain it and do not sound in the least defensive about it. There is no need to defend the choice of staying home with children, even if a fast climbing career was temporarily put on hold as a result.

53. What public figure do you admire most? Why? Do not spend a lot of time on this one, just do not get caught by surprise. Come up with two or three people, think through what you like about them, and file it away. Generally they should be people who are widely admired and not overly controversial. If you are talking to a GM executive it might be unwise to mention Ralph Nader. Mentioning Jane Fonda to someone who remembers her foray into North Vietnam during the war, would not be a good idea. Lee Iaccoca is fairly safe. Political figures are fairly risky, but can be done effectively. In the late 70s I had a client who indicated he admired both Menachem Begin and Anwar Sadat for the courage they showed during the Middle East peace negotiations. Another person did a good job with Richard Nixon. He said he did not like everything Nixon ever did, but he admired him for the way he opened up contact with mainland China. You could choose a local figure who is well known. Usually the question indicates a living person so forget Honest Abe. Your reasons for admiring the person are more important than the specific person.

54. What are your primary outside activities? All of your activities reveal things about you so choose your answers carefully. If you mention one thing you might balance it with another. As an example, mentioning family activities shows certain positive qualities, but might be balanced with mentioning that you enjoy reading trade journals in your field. Physical activities are always positive but think twice before mentioning skydiving or hang gliding. In your mind they may seem very safe, but the perception of others may make these activities seem like unnecessary risks. If you have numerous activities, why mention that you dive off bridges, held only by a bunji rope?

55. *Would you have any concern if we did a full background check on you?* The immediate response should be a simple, "Not at all." If damaging information would be discovered, however, this might be the time to share it so you can put it in the best light. This is not the time, however, to bare your soul and confess everything you ever did. Use discretion.

56. *What qualities do you most admire in other people?* Pick four or five and explain why you so highly value them. All of this tells the employer more about you and your character.

57. *Tell me about the last incident that made you angry. How did you handle it?* Pick an example that would have gotten anyone angry. Describing how you reacted is particularly important. Make sure your reaction was a mature, not a childish one. If it was a somewhat childish reaction, tell it in a humorous way so both of you can laugh about it.

58. *How has your supervisor helped you grow?* Whether you have a great supervisor or a lousy one, every supervisor will add to your personal growth in some way. If the person has no human relations skills, emphasize how the person has imparted greater knowledge to you.

59. *What did your supervisor rate you highest on during your last review? Lowest?* Emphasize the positive and give a complete explanation as to why your supervisor valued that quality. Undoubtedly there are four or five things that you were rated highly on, therefore pick the one or two items that will score the most points with this particular interviewer. Of those things you were rated lower in, you might say, "Overall I was rated quite high in everything. I suppose if there was anything that my boss wanted me to work on it would be to work on my presentation skills. I'm now enrolled in Toastmasters and really enjoying it." When possible emphasize a technical skill that your boss simply wants you to work on, as opposed to a personality characteristic. That is always more acceptable than saying "My boss wants me to work on my tendency to be rude to customers." I may be exaggerating slightly to make a point.

60. *What are the things that motivate you?* Challenge, creativity, success, opportunity, and personal growth, are the ones most frequently mentioned. You can also mention specific skills that you are motivated to use—troubleshooting, problem solving, planning, implementing, speaking, writing, helping people, etc.

61. *How do you handle people that you really don't get along with?* If you are one of those fortunate types who get along with

almost anyone, tell the interviewer so. However you answer the question, indicate that you work hard to get along with others. Think through how you really do respond to difficult people. The interviewer is using this question as an opportunity to learn about your human relations skills. As a follow-up question the interviewer could ask you to describe an actual instance.

62. *Describe your management philosophy and management style.* This takes thought, and perhaps you have never defined your management philosophy or style. This question is common enough that you need to be prepared.

63. *What is the biggest mistake you ever made?* If asked in this way you must decide whether to mention a personal mistake or a job-related mistake. A personal mistake could be that you wish you had selected a different college major or not dropped out of college. Personal mistakes are a little safer to discuss than job-related mistakes, but be prepared to discuss either. As a rule, pick something that happened two or more years ago. That way you will be more objective and will be better able to discuss what you learned from it.

If there is an obvious and glaring mistake in your background that the employer will be aware of, this might be the chance to deal with it. If you have two years of college but never finished, that might be the mistake to discuss since you are merely answering a question that the interviewer is already curious about.

Reveal a mistake, but don't feel obligated to reveal the absolute biggest mistake in your life. If you reveal a really major mistake to me I wouldn't hire you because you demonstrated a lack of discretion.

64. *How many people have you hired? How do you go about it? How successful have the people been?* The interviewer is trying to learn "how" you operate. Describe your methods, but your emphasis should be on your results. If you have hired five or more people it is highly unlikely that each of them has gone on to great success. You do not need to claim perfect insight or judgment. You do want to get across the idea that you are very careful in your hiring decisions, that you are a good judge of character, and that you provide adequate training so that employees achieve their full potential.

65. *How many people have you fired? How did you handle it?* Here the interviewer is generally trying to determine how decisive you are, and how "cleanly" you can fire people. Terminations are the ultimate test of decisiveness. Typically, employers agonize over it even when it is clear that the employee is ineffective and cannot be salvaged. As you describe your termination process, demon-

strate that you were decisive as well as humane.

66. *How would your subordinates describe you as a supervisor?* Indicate that you work hard to gain their respect, but that being liked by everyone is not your main concern. "They would say that they enjoy working for me. I'm fairly tough as a manager, but I'm fair. I give them room for independence and I seek self-starters. They would say I'm an excellent trainer. I'm patient but they know I can get pretty upset when I see the same mistakes occurring." Here is a chance to share some of your philosophy of management as you answer the question. Use this question to demonstrate that you gain maximum output from your employees.

67. *Some managers watch their employees very closely, while others use a loose rein. How do you manage?* Obviously you should watch your employees neither too closely nor too loosely. Employees should be monitored carefully when new to the job and until they have demonstrated the ability to do the job with little assistance from you. Use this as an opportunity to emphasize results you have achieved through those working for you.

68. *How have you improved as a supervisor over the years?* The interviewer is assuming you have improved as a supervisor, which means you can admit to past mistakes. Management is learned through experience, not textbooks, so it is safe to admit that you were far from perfect in the past. You might admit that early in your management experience you had difficulty delegating, or that sometimes you were too demanding. This is a good time to reflect and see how you have genuinely improved over the years, and then be prepared to share it.

69. *What kind of supervisor gets the best results out of you?* Base your answer on what you've learned about your prospective boss. If you know this person keeps a tight rein on employees, you would not mention your strong need for independence. Think through and identify several qualities that really help motivate you and be prepared to share two or three. It could be a supervisor who is fair, open-minded, and has high integrity, or one who leads by example and motivates people.

70. *What have you done to increase your personal development?* The employer is trying to determine if you are a growth oriented person. You might mention courses, seminars, or self-study you have undertaken. Whether you did it on your own time or company time does not matter. The things you mention need not all be work related unless the question was worded that way. You may have started studying a foreign language, taken up karate, or joined Toastmasters. Be prepared to discuss why you started these

things and how they have helped you.

71. How do you feel about your career progress? If you are not feeling good about your progress you could mention that that is one of the reasons for job hunting—career progress in your current company is blocked. Indicate that you have done the right things and have received excellent reviews, but that lack of company growth, or some other factor, is preventing you from moving ahead as you would like. Indicate that you know patience is important, and balance it with your strong ambition to take on more responsibility.

If you've made rapid progress, you should acknowledge it and supply the reasons—your results and accomplishments for example. Be positive about your past progress and indicate you feel you are capable of continued strong growth. Be sensitive to your interviewer's situation, however. If she has not been promoted for some time, you might want to tone down your own success, so as not to appear to be a threat. Of course you would also have to determine if your prospective boss' lack of progress could block yours.

72. What is unique about you? The interviewer is not asking what is absolutely unique about you. In other words, none of us is totally unique. After all, you might be great at analytical thinking, but you are certainly not the only one who has that talent. In essence the interviewer is asking what is special about you. So, once again, reach into your mental check list and pull out some of your strengths.

ATTITUDES

I've covered the areas of overcoming objections and projecting enthusiasm, potential and a winning personality. I've also given examples and provided principles for handling difficult interview questions. Now I'd like to cover four attitudes that can destroy your interviewing effectiveness. These attitudes are modesty, being apologetic or defensive, providing inappropriate information, and expressing antibusiness feelings.

Modesty

One of the most common mistakes in interviews is being too modest. If you don't say positive things about yourself in an interview, who will?

"Sally, what is your major accomplishment at your present job?"

"Gee, I really haven't done anything out of the ordinary, you know what I mean, nothing outstanding. I just try to do my best."

Sally may have just lost a job offer. She has some genuine accomplishments but she was afraid of bragging, and she was also afraid the interviewer would consider her accomplishments insignificant. Let me assure you, genuine accomplishments, no matter how small, are virtually never considered insignificant.

The best way to avoid bragging is to let the experience speak for itself. Here's a response to the question, "How good a salesperson are you?" "I feel I'm an excellent salesperson. I've been in the top five in sales each of the last five years. Historically my territory always had one of the worst sales volumes, but I proved that the territory wasn't being worked right. My customers view me more as a consultant than a salesperson. I'll demonstrate new applications for our products and I'll get in there and solve their problems and work with their engineers."

Was he bragging or is he just a good salesperson with confidence? Look for opportunities to say positive things about yourself. Practice if you're prone to excessive modesty.

Apologetic/Defensive

Many job applicants come across as too apologetic or too defensive. This usually occurs because they feel insecure and believe their background is weak in certain areas. Consider the answers to this question, "Ted, we're looking for someone with six years of computer programming and systems analysis."

An apologetic response:

"I'm sorry, I only have four years of experience. I wish I had gone to school earlier in my career, then I'd have the six years. I really blew it."

A defensive response:

"Well, I don't have six years of experience, I have four years. Every place I go they want more experience than I have. What's wrong with four years?"

Whether apologetic or defensive, Ted's lack of confidence comes through loud and clear. If the applicant lacks self-confidence, how can the interviewer be expected to have confidence in his or her ability?

Now consider Ted's response after he's had some interview coaching:

"Mr. Jenkins, as you can see from my resume, I've had four years of experience. Because of the variety of my experience, however, it's equal to what most people accomplish in seven or eight years. During these last four years I've taken on every challenge I could so I'd be ready for this type of responsibility. There's no question in my mind that I'll do an excellent job."

Ted has learned the art of overcoming objections. The interviewer was probably impressed with Ted already when the question was asked. The job description specified six years of experience, but the interviewer realized it was not just a matter of years, but of quality of experience. He was testing Ted, and Ted passed.

Inappropriate Information

Adding inappropriate information to an interview can be disastrous. Let's assume an interview has just started and the two people are still involved in small talk.

Interviewer: Did you see the latest Gallup Poll? It indicated the number-one goal of college students today is to get a good job and make a lot of money. Things sure have changed since the 60s, haven't they?

Sandy: I think they've sold out. Everything now is "what's in it for me?" When I was in school people cared and they took action. Look at what we did with the marches on Washington and at the 1968 Democratic Convention.

Job interviews are not the place to discuss religion or politics. Both are emotional issues. The only way you can win in such discussions is if your views coincide with the interviewer's. It's seldom worth a chance. In principle, any statements that do not help to sell you should be left out.

Another form of inappropriate information is your opinions. Have you known people who are so opinionated that they constantly insist on telling you what they think, whether you want to know or not? Listen to this: "Mr. Bertram, it's probably none of my business, but have you noticed how old fashioned your logo looks?" Do you think this person scored any points?

Antibusiness

Especially during the 60s and early 70s, many college graduates went into interviews expressing a strong distaste for big business and capitalism. Business people do not feel the need to defend the profit motive, neither do they want to enter a debate regarding investments in South Africa or their record on pollution control. Raising these and other issues merely raises questions about you.

If you have strong views on various issues, there is a solution. Research the company prior to the interview and determine how well it matches your values. If you don't research the company prior to the first interview, however, attend the interview but don't raise the controversial issues. If you like the organization and you're called in for a second interview, then do your research or contact someone who knows about the organization. If you still don't have your answer, wait until the job is offered, negotiate your salary, and then ask your questions in a calm, objective fashion. If the company passes your test, you have an excellent employer; if the company fails your test, you got some excellent interviewing experience and proved that you can sell yourself.

WHEN YOU DON'T SUCCEED

No matter how well one prepares, and no matter how effective one is in the interview, no one gets every job interviewed for. Often clients come to see me and ask, ''Why didn't I get the job? I would have been perfect.'' Other than failure to fully sell your potential, there are four primary reasons why a person might not get hired.

1. **More Experience/Right Experience**—Job seekers are often told that someone with more experience or just the perfect combination of experience was hired. Effectively selling potential will not always get the job, and you cannot always have the ideal background. Sometimes the job responsibilities are so technical or require such specialization, that a three-eyed obnoxious slob—with the right background—would still get the offer. The employer may be in such a bind that there is no time for training.

2. **Biases**—Every interviewer has biases, some held consciously, others unconsciously. By being perceptive you can pick up some of those biases, but you cannot detect all of them. Most of us are not proud of our biases and will go to great lengths to hide them. Interviewers are no different. Some biases are plain old-fashioned discrimination, others are more minor, but just as insidious. The 26-year-old manager may not feel comfortable with someone three or four years older and hires people the same age or younger. A fifty-year-old manager prefers secretaries who are ''more mature'' and

will not hire anyone under 40. A conservative businessman still cannot stand someone with a beard or hair extending over a shirt collar.

Some biases can be predicted and action taken. For example, a man can trim or remove the shaggy beard, shorten the hair, dress up for the occasion, and so forth. Once you are hired and have proven your worth, the very thing that would have prevented getting an offer, may now be accepted without difficulty.

Unfortunately some biases cannot be detected. If a person has a bias against taller people, or those with college degrees, there's little you can do. Fortunately most biases are not knockouts, but they can have an impact on your chances. And of course, religious, ethnic, racial, and age discrimination still thrive in this country.

3. **Inside Track**—Sometimes the hiring decision has been made before the interviewing even begins. There is a favorite. It could be a person within the company who is a "known quantity" and has the inside track. Other times it is a friend or former colleague. It could be the owner's nephew. Or, it could simply be a person who four months ago managed to get in for a fifteen minute get acquainted appointment.

Some government jobs are filled with favorites. Those who are aware of this practice often call their friends in the department with the opening and ask if the job has been "wired." When the answer is yes they do not bother to apply. Because of civil service, several people must be interviewed, but department heads always have ways to make sure their favorites survive the screening process. Sometimes they even design the job description so that their favorite is the only one perfectly qualified.

4. **Feeling Threatened**—Sometimes the person interviewing feels threatened by a highly talented, knowledgeable applicant and will not hire that person. A good manager welcomes talent and is never afraid of it, knowing that his replacement must be trained if he is to receive a promotion. The insecure manager, however, is fearful and often hires lower caliber people. The principle of interviewing is to always sell yourself to the limit. The one exception would be if you detect that the manager is insecure. Don't undersell yourself, but you can tone it down a bit. Once you get the offer you must determine if you should accept. In a large company you might be able to move up by making a lateral move to another department. In a smaller company that may not be possible.

What Do You Do Now—Now that you know some of the

reasons why you did not get that job you really wanted, what should you do with this knowledge? The worst thing you can do is wallow in self-pity and complain of prejudice and discrimination. Instead, assume that someone with the perfect background came along and that no matter what you could have done or said, that person was going to get the job. If the job that got away was the one you really wanted, it's okay to feel down—for an hour, or even half a day. Then let go of it and move on. Cry, get angry, be sad, then let go. There is something better out there for you—go for it.

INCREASE YOUR REPERTOIRE

The more skills you have to discuss in an interview the better off you'll be. Here is an exercise that will help. Rate yourself on a scale of one to ten for each skill; ten being very high, one being very low. Your ratings should be almost instant, without taking time to analyze them. Since there are over 390 skills, it is important to do it quickly. As you finish rating the skills in each skill cluster, give yourself an overall rating for that cluster in the space to the left of each skill cluster title. For interviews, concentrate on your top twelve skill clusters and your top 5-9 skills within each skill cluster. This will give you quite a repertoire. Then determine how you might discuss them in an interview.

You have used virtually all of these skills. Some you have used on jobs, others were used in school, in hobbies, in volunteer activities, or just in everyday living.

TRANSFERABLE SKILLS

___Human Relations Skills
Sensitivity to others
Treating people fairly
Listening intently
Communicating warmth
Establishing rapport
Understanding human
  behavior
Empathy
Tactfulness
Cooperative team member
Avoiding stereotyping people
Feeling comfortable with differ-
  ent kinds of people
Fun person to work with

Treating others as equals
Dealing effectively with conflict
Helping clarify misunder-
  standings
Creating an environment con-
  ducive to social interaction

___Helping Skills
Helping people
Patient with difficult people
Responsive to people's feelings
  and needs
Counseling/Empowering/
  Encouraging people

Assisting people in making decisions

Enhancing people's self-esteem

Working effectively with those often ignored or considered undesirable

Letting people know you really care about them

People sense you feel what they're feeling

Helping people help themselves

Encouraging others to expand and grow

Facilitating self-assessment and personal development

Training/Instructing Skills

Instilling the love of a subject

Perceptively answering questions

Explaining difficult ideas and concepts

Creating a stimulating learning environment

Enabling self-discovery

Encouraging creativity

Effectively using behavior modification

Teaching at the student's or group's level

Training people at work

Developing training materials that enhance and speed up learning

Keeping classes interesting

Presenting interesting lectures

Creating the sense of being part of a caring group

Assessing learning styles of individuals and tailoring training

Presenting written or spoken information in a logical step-by-step fashion that builds a solid foundation for future learning

Sensing when people aren't "getting" it

Being able to rephrase points so people do "get" it

Quickly establishing rapport with a group

Developing and effectively using audio-visual aids

Maintaining productive group discussions

Leadership Skills

Leader

Motivating/Inspiring people

Getting elected/Getting selected as a group leader

People believe in you/trust you

Causing change

Stirring people up

Making difficult decisions

People are motivated to follow your lead and recommendations

Fighting the establishment or unfair policies

Accepting responsibility for failures

Decisive in crisis situations

Sound judgment in emergencies

Settling disagreements

Open to other people's ideas

A person of vision

Getting others to share your vision

Recognizing the need for change and willing to undertake it

Perceived as a person with high integrity

Recognizing windows of opportunity

Recognized as one worthy of taking the lead

Sensing when to compromise and when to fight

Reputation for being highly reliable and taking on new responsibilities

Giving credit to others

Managing Skills

Seeing the big picture
Completing projects on time
Setting priorities
Breaking through red tape
Organizing projects and programs
Managing projects
Establishing effective policies/procedures
Negotiating and getting desired results
Working closely and smoothly with others
Gaining trust and respect of key people
Making effective recommendations
Anticipating problems and issues and preparing alternatives
Taking the initiative when opportunity appears
Effectively overseeing a myriad of details
Handling details well without losing sight of the big picture
Responsive to others' needs
Finding and obtaining the resources necessary for a task
Making those above me look good
Getting people at all levels to support and implement decisions which have come down from the top
Implementing new programs
Working effectively with superiors and people in other work units
Gaining the cooperation of people or groups even when not possessing authority over them
Turning around negative situations
Obtaining allies

Supervising Skills

Getting maximum output from people
Understanding human motivation
Developing a team that truly works together
Training and developing staff
Encouraging people to seek personal and professional growth
Developing a smooth functioning organization
Effectively disciplining when necessary
Creating an environment for people to trust and respect each other
Supervising difficult people
Delegating work effectively
Knowing the strengths and weaknesses of others
Consistently recruiting and hiring good promotable people
Holding profitable meetings
Increasing morale
Staying in touch/Communicating with staff
Mediating
Effectively cross-training staff
Encouraging people to want to do their best
Helping people become all they are capable of
Reducing turnover
Minimizing complaining and backbiting

Persuading Skills

Influencing others' ideas and attitudes
Mediating between groups
Obtaining consensus among diverse groups
Effectively selling ideas to top people
Getting people to change their views on long-held beliefs

Getting people to value something not previously valued
Getting departments or organizations to take desired action
Getting people/clients/customers to reveal their needs
Really listening to people and sensing their true needs
Developing a strong knowledge base so questions can be answered
Selling products
Selling services
Selling ideas to others
Selling yourself
Closing a deal
Gaining support from those impacted by decisions/ changes
Helping people see the benefits of a course of action

Speaking Skills
Holding the attention of a group
Strong, pleasing voice
Clear enunciation
"Reading" a group
Impromptu speaking
Thinking quickly on your feet
Telling stories
Using humor
Handling questions well
Getting a group to relate to you
Coming across as sincere and spontaneous
Making convincing arguments
Providing clear explanations of complex topics
Presenting ideas in a logical integrated way

Numerical Skills
Solid ability with basic arithmetic
Multiplying numbers in your head
Figuring out "story" problems

Adding long columns of figures
Figuring out percentages
Recognizing patterns and relationships in numbers
Gaining lots of valuable information from graphs, tables, and charts
Quickly spotting numerical errors
Sensing when an answer or number could not logically be correct
Storing large amounts of numerical data in your head
Making decisions based on numerical data
Making rough calculations/estimates in your mind
Analyzing statistical data

Financial Skills
Developing a budget
Staying within a budget
Finding bargains
Estimating costs
Eye for a profit
Recognizing money making opportunities
Ability to buy low and sell high
Managing money/Making money grow
Setting financial priorities
Developing cost cutting solutions
Negotiating financial deals
Understanding economic principles
Gut feeling for financial trends
Ability to get financing

Office Skills
Making arrangements
Scheduling
Expediting
Concentrating on details
Efficient with paperwork
Using the telephone to get things done

Knowing how to get information
Organizing an office
Organizing records
Creating systems for data storage/retrieval
Memory for detail
Quickly spotting errors
Thorough understanding of regulations and procedures
Cutting through red tape to achieve a goal
Expert at using and manipulating the system to resolve a problem
Processing information accurately
Pleasant phone voice
Learning office procedures quickly
Operating business machines
Proofreading, correcting

Body Skills
Finger dexterity
Hand dexterity
Eye-hand coordination
Physical coordination
Quick reflexes/reactions
Walking long distances
Standing for long periods
Strong arms/legs/back
Running
Jumping
Throwing
Lifting/Carrying
Physical endurance
Steady hands
Sorting things
Depth perception
Sense of rhythm
Working quickly with hands and fingers
Sense of taste
Sense of smell
Sense of hearing
Sensitive touch

Able to see/spot things others miss
Skilled at sports
Control over your body
Enduring pain or discomfort

Mechanical and Tool Skills
Inventing
Improvising with a machine or tool
Assembling/Building/Installing
Precision work
Operating power tools
Using hand tools
Operating machinery/equipment
Driving cars, trucks, and equipment
Fixing and repairing
Troubleshooting/Diagnosing problems
Figuring out how things work
Drafting/Mechanical drawing
Understanding manuals/diagrams
Mechanical ability
Understanding electricity
Reading gauges/instruments

Idea Skills
Imaginative
Conceiving and generating ideas
Improvising
Innovative
Creative
Inventing
Conceptualizing
Synthesizing and borrowing ideas, and creating something new
Seeing the big picture
Developing new theories
Recognizing new applications for ideas or things
Open to new ideas from others

Able to look beyond the way things have been done in the past

Refusing to become fixated on a single idea and looking for better ideas

Seeing things others don't see

Finding ways to improve things

Bringing together two distinct concepts to produce something original

—Writing Skills

Overall writing ability

Writing clear concise sentences

Grammatically correct writing

Strong versatile vocabulary

Developing a logical, well organized theme

Vividly describing feelings, people, senses, and things

Stirring up people's emotions

Creating living, real, believable characters

Developing logical and persuasive points of view

Summarizing and condensing written material

Editing, strengthening, tightening someone's writing

Humorous writing

Simplifying scientific and technical material

Making "dry" subjects interesting

Writing
Letters
Memos
Reports
Position papers
Research reports
News articles
Speeches
Manuals
Proposals for funding
Poetry
Song lyrics
Fiction
Satire
Slogans
Advertising

—Planning Skills

Planning programs or projects

Setting attainable goals

Determining priorities

Forecasting/Predicting

Scheduling effectively

Making persuasive recommendations

Using facts while trusting gut feelings

Time management

Accurately predicting results of proposed action

Accurately assessing available resources

Anticipating problems before they develop

Anticipating reactions of people and sensing whether they will support a proposal

Finishing projects on time

Sensing whether a project or program will work and making appropriate recommendations

Developing alternative actions in case the primary plan doesn't work as expected-

Developing innovative methods and techniques

Predicting where bottlenecks can occur and preparing workable plans to get around the bottlenecks

Considering all the details of a project, even the smallest

—Problem Solving/Troubleshooting Skills

Anticipating problems

Solving problems

Untangling messes

Bringing order out of a chaotic situation

Determining root causes

Intuitively sensing where the problem is and usually being right

Recognizing and resolving problems while they're still relatively minor

Able to come in and take control of a situation

Selecting the most effective solution

Improvising under stress

Helping a group identify solutions

Not stopping with the first "right" answer that comes to mind

Handling difficult people

Staying calm in emergencies

People have confidence that now you're here, things will be ' aken care of

—Organizing Skills

Organizing/Planning events

Organizing offices

Organizing systems

Organizing people to take action

Organizing data/information

Making sure people are in the right place at the right time

Organizing enjoyable and memorable happenings

—Researching/Investigating Skills

Working on research projects

Researching in a library

Knowing how to find information

Able to sift important information from unimportant

Investigating

Tracking down information

Following up on leads

Organizing large amounts of data and information

Keeping an open mind

Summarizing findings

Designing research projects

Discovering new things or phenomena

Relentlessly seeking an answer

Developing new testing methods

Gathering information from people

Producing surveys or questionnaires

Identifying relationships

Detecting cause and effect relationships

Collecting data

Using statistical data

Weaving threads of evidence together

Developing hypotheses

Extracting pertinent information from people

—Analyzing Skills

Interpreting/Evaluating data

Evaluating reports and recommendations

Analyzing trends

Accurately predicting what will occur based on facts, trends, and intuition

Designing systems to collect or analyze information

Weighing pros and cons of an issue

Simplifying complex ideas

Exposing nonlogical thinking

Seeing both sides of an issue

Synthesizing ideas

Clarifying problems

Diagnosing needs/problems

Breaking down principles into parts

Constantly looking for a better way

Identifying more efficient ways of doing things

Getting to the heart of an issue

Artistic Skills

Excellent taste
Artistic
Sense of color combinations
Sense of beauty
Drawing scenes/people
Painting
Depth perception
Envisioning the finished product/ sensing how it will all come together
Sense of proportion and space
Envisioning in three dimensions
Spatial perception
Designing visual aids
Calligraphy/Lettering
Appreciating and valuing fine works of art
Capturing a feeling, mood, or idea through photography, drawing, sculpting, cartoons, music, etc.
Developing visually pleasing things (charts, reports, manuals, etc.)
Applied sense of color, shape, design
Conceiving visual representations of ideas and concepts
Sensing what will work and look right
Sensing what people will appreciate
Working well with artistic people
Producing high quality mechanical and line drawings
Sensing the difference between good and great art

Performing Skills

Poised and confident before groups
Showmanship
Responsive to audience moods
Making people laugh
Getting an audience involved with you
Getting an audience to relate to you
Powerful stage presence
Getting an audience enthusiastic or excited
Eliciting strong emotions from an audience
Stirring up an audience to take some type of action
Entertaining an audience
Playing musical instruments
Dancing
Acting
Singing
Modeling
Poetry reading

Observing Skills

Intuitive
Highly observant of surroundings
Long memory of scenes once observed
Hearing/seeing/feeling things others are unaware of
Perceptive/Sensitive/Aware
Picking up on people's feelings, reactions, and attitudes
Eye for fine/small details
Spotting slight changes in things
Recalling names and faces of people

PRINCIPLES OF
SALARY NEGOTIATIONS

Negotiating a salary is not difficult but it does require practice. By studying and then practicing these principles, you could increase your starting salary by five to twenty percent.

1. You owe it to yourself to get the best starting salary and benefits possible. Salary, respect, and authority are all tied together.
2. Employers generally have a salary range to work with. Your goal is to be offered the position and negotiate for the high end of the range.
3. Determine what the typical salary range is for the occupation and industry by asking people who are knowledgeable. The *Occupational Outlook Handbook*, found in most libraries, will usually give you a clue. Note the year for which the average salary is given and then figure in inflation.
4. Never (well, almost never) ask about salary. Discussing salary before a position has been offered is seldom beneficial.
5. You may be asked, "What are you presently earning?" Your response will depend on what you have learned about the salary range, whether you are currently underpaid, or whether you are making a career change and may be willing to take a lower starting salary. It is unfair that organizations would try to measure your worth to them based on your present earnings, nevertheless it happens all the time.
6. If you are earning below their range of, say, $28 thousand to $34 thousand, you might reply, "I'm earning $26 thousand. That's exactly the reason why I'm here." You are letting the employer know that you know you are worth more than what you are presently being paid.
7. If you are earning above their range, you might say, "I'm presently earning $36 thousand, but starting salary is not nearly as important as working for the right organization with good long-range opportunities."
8. Entry-level positions usually have fairly strict salary ranges.
9. Salary ranges are determined by several factors. You will earn less than your boss, more than those you supervise,

309

and about the same as those with equal responsibility. People usually earn ten to thirty percent more than those immediately under them.

10. If you have a good background and are seeking a job change rather than a career change, go for a twenty-percent increase in salary. The employer has decided to look outside rather than promote from within. She expects to pay a premium for your experience, fresh ideas, and potential. This explains why some employers ask about your present salary. They take that figure and add twenty percent to see if you are still in their range.

11. Employers are humans too. No one likes to be rejected. If they feel they cannot match your salary expectations, the employer may decide not to make an offer even though he would dearly love to have you. It is important, therefore, to have a feel for the range and let the employer know that you are very interested.

12. Sometimes an employer begins talking salary before a position has actually been offered. The employer may ask, "What is the minimum salary you would accept?" A good reponse might be, "Shall I assume you're offering me the position?" The employer may not, in fact, actually have determined to offer you the position, but more than one job seeker has received a somewhat startled "Yes" or "Yeah, I guess I am offering you the job." It may be just the push the employer needs. The employer may think in an instant, "Why not, I really don't need to interview any more people, this is the right person."

13. Employers use two main approaches for negotiating salaries—asking and telling.

14. In the asking approach the employer makes the job offer and then asks, "What kind of salary are you looking for?" or "How much do you feel you're worth?" or "What is the minimum you would accept?" You have several options. "The starting salary is important to me, but not nearly as important as a job that fits me and allows me to make a kind of contribution I know I'm capable of. I believe in three years I should be earning $42 thousand." This is a good response. You are giving the impression of being very realistic and flexible. Actually you have just put the interviewer in a corner. The interviewer may know that the best she can hope to do is get you a six-percent increase each year. Therefore,

to reach your $42 thousand in three years, the starting salary must be the $35 thousand you actually wanted. Surprisingly, it is easier for a supervisor to start you off high at the beginning than to obtain raises commensurate with your contributions later on.

If you believe the range is, say, $30 thousand to $35 thousand, you could present a range. "I would say based on my experience and potential, between $32 thousand and $37 thousand, depending on my responsibilities." Or you could turn the table—"How much do you think I'm worth?" Or you could state a single figure, about five percent above what you believe the top of their range is. If you thought the top of their range was $35 thousand, you can look the employer in the eye and say, "I was thinking about $37 thousand." The employer will probably reject that and say so in one way or another. Don't let it bother you. Simply ask, "What is the *best* you can offer me?" Because of your confidence and the potential you have demonstrated, the next figure will probably be very close to the top of their range.

Of course, the employer could respond, "We were thinking closer to $29 thousand." Perhaps you have misjudged the range. For this company $30 thousand may be the top of their range. Or you may not have completely sold the employer on your potential. Your response might be, "I feel I'm worth more than that. However, working for the right organization is really more important than the starting salary. Let's call it a deal at $32 thousand." The employer may still not go for it, or may come up to $30 thousand. You may have negotiated as far as you can.

15. The telling approach works like this: "John, we'd like to start you out at $30 thousand and then review your salary in six months." You must quickly decide whether you will negotiate, since you were expecting at least $32 thousand. You might try these:

"Mr. Russell, I'm glad I turned out to be your top choice. Although money is not the only factor, it is important. In fact, it's the major reason I have chosen to leave my job. When I started out I made a decision to take a job at twenty percent above what I'm now earning. I really don't see a reason to change that decision.

If there is any way you can adjust your budget, it would sure help. I never intended to accept anything below $34 thousand.''

The straightforward approach also works. ''Mr. Russell, based on my potential I really feel I'm worth $34 thousand, but if you would make it $32 thousand, the decision would sure be a lot easier.''

The creative approach should sometimes be tried. Remember, the offer was for $30 thousand. ''Mr. Russell, based on the duties you've described, I agree that the job is probably worth no more than $31 thousand. I'm sure you would agree with me, however, that I'm capable of handling much more. And when I began this job search, I never intended to accept anything below $35 thousand. But perhaps if the responsibilities were increased you could justify $34 thousand.'' Notice what has been done. The offer was for $30 thousand, and the interviewee is basically agreeing but says the job is worth $31 thousand. Even while agreeing, the interviewee is adding a little, and then asks if the responsibilities could be increased.

16. Use another job offer as leverage whenever possible. You may have received an offer where the salary is satisfactory, but the job is not what you really want. Then you may get an offer where the job is perfect but the salary is low. ''Mr. Stuyvesant, the job itself is perfect, and of course I would really enjoy working with you. The salary is below what I expected, and I already have an offer at three thousand a year more. If you could adjust your budget, it would make my decision a lot easier.''

17. How tough you negotiate depends on how strongly you feel about your worth.

18. Once you have negotiated for the best salary possible, other factors remain, particularly if their offer is below what you expect. If they offer a six-month salary review, ask for a three-month review. Other factors are cost of living increases, moving expenses, tuition reimbursement, flextime, an extra week of vacation without pay, or other factors that are important to you.

Salary negotiations are usually not long and drawn out. The whole process may take less than two minutes. Observe this typical negotiation:

Employer: Bob, I'd like to have you join us. I'll start you out at $25 thousand and then review your performance in six months.

Bob: I appreciate the offer. As I'm sure you could tell, I'm really quite excited about the position. I'll be honest though; I had thought the job would be worth considerably more. I had figured on something closer to $32 thousand.

Employer: (Pause) Bob, I know I'm not going to be able to match your figure, but I'll tell you what, let's start you at $26,500.

Bob: That certainly helps. I really do want to accept the position and money is not the only issue. I feel that there are going to be excellent opportunities with this company. I still feel the job is worth thirty-two, and I know I'm worth that much, but I would definitely consider thirty.

Employer: Bob, I'm sure you realize that any firm like ours has to place minimums and maximums on salaries at various levels to keep everything in the company balanced. I suppose I could offer you twenty-eight, but that's as high as I can go.

Bob: Make it twenty-nine and you've got yourself an employee.

Employer: All right, you've got a deal at $28,500. Agreed?

Bob: Agreed. Twenty-eight-five and a review in three months.

Employer: Do you really think you can prove yourself in three months?

Bob: I think so.

Employer: Okay, twenty-eight-five and a review in three months, but I'm not promising a high pay increase, you've got to earn it.

Bob: I understand. I think you'll be pleased with my results.

The ability to negotiate for a higher salary is one of the most valuable skills you can develop. Once you understand the principles, the practice is up to you.

APPENDIX A

THOUGHTS FOR JOB FINDING COUNSELORS

Resume Power was written to enable people to write top-quality resumes with or without professional assistance. I do believe, however, that virtually everyone can benefit from professional editing or advice.

I began writing resumes professionally in 1979 and was always bothered by the lack of agreement among job finding experts regarding what made successful resumes. I felt certain that someone somewhere must have thoroughly studied the subject, but a computer search in 1981 turned up only a few surveys which were of little help. About the same time I came across a private firm which had taken out a full page ad in the *Chicago Tribune* to tout their heavy-duty statistical research. They charged me forty dollars for their slim book. Unfortunately, they were producing only mediocre resumes. I concluded that either the research methodology was faulty (the book contained few details), the results had been misinterpreted, or they had lacked the creativity to apply the results and produce really effective resumes.

In 1982 I began my research using the Wilcoxon-Sign statistical method for determining significance. Four studies have been completed. By this time I had expected to complete at least sixteen, but the studies proved more difficult and time consuming than I had anticipated. As this book goes to press, I cannot offer the definitive work that I had hoped for, but as a start, I still feel good about what has been done. The studies were not as numerous, the samples as large, nor the randomness of the raters as rigorous as I would have liked, but it is a beginning.

If you, or any graduate students you are working with, would like to pursue this type of research, I will be glad to share my experiences and do what I can to ensure that reliable results are obtained. You can reach me at 1750 - 112th N.E. C-247, Bellevue, Washington 98004. My phone number is (206) 454-6982.

It is my hope that *Resume Power* will be used as a textbook in resume writing workshops. Naturally, I would like each reader to agree with every suggestion made in the book, but that would be unreasonable to expect. To use the book as a textbook, of course, does not require total agreement, and I would encourage your use of additional handouts to supplement the book.

Using *Resume Power* as a textbook will help you cover more points in more detail than can be covered in the typical three- to six-hour resume-writing workshop. You'll be able to concentrate on discussing major points, helping people get started on their resumes, and answering individual questions.

I welcome any advice you may offer. If you or any students find a section difficult to understand, please let me know. If you disagree with any advice, let me know what you would recommend and why. Several career professionals have reviewed the manuscript and offered some extremely valuable advice. This book is much improved because of them. With your help the book can be strengthened further.

APPENDIX B

RESUME RESEARCH METHODOLOGY

In the four studies completed to date I am not claiming the same rigorous standards one would expect for highly technical research. For randomness I tried to select people from different backgrounds, but anyone who agreed to take the time became a rater. Except for the college recruiters, there was no effort made to select only people who actually make hiring decisions. In each study some of the people had hired staff while others had not.

In each study the raters were given the same instructions. A set of six resumes was given to them and they were asked to rate the applicants according to how much they would like to interview them. One week after rating the first set, the second set of resumes was rated by the same raters. The matched resume pairs were identical except that one variable had been changed. If I was testing the effect of color of paper, resume #1 in set A was on white and resume #1 in set B was ivory. The Wilcoxon-Sign nonparametric technique was used to determine statistical significance.

The following chart shows the different variables studied and indicates which were found to be significant and at what level of significance. Two of the studies used the resumes of recent college graduates with business degrees. One group of raters were campus recruiters. The most significant finding in that study was that without one exception all ten campus recruiters preferred the resume without personal data to the one which included personal data. The other group of raters (sample size thirty) came from many backgrounds and they preferred the resumes with personal data.

The study using the resumes of secretaries utilized a wide variety of raters with a sample size of twelve. The study using the resumes of engineers utilized only engineers as raters, with a sample size of twelve.

For those not familiar with statistics, .01, .02, and .05 indicate that we have a high degree of certainty that the factor studied truly had a significant effect. In fact, they are referred to as levels of significance. In statistical studies .01 represents somewhat stronger evidence than .05 that the factor really had the effect. In the chart on page 285, wherever you see a dash, it means that the variables were studied, but any differences in the two variables were not considered statistically significant.

	College Grads (recruiters)	College Grads	Secretaries	Engineers
Accomplishments	-	.01	-	.01
No Accomplishments	-		-	
Typeset			-	
Not Typeset	.02	.05	-	
Personal Data		.02	.01	-
No Personal Data	.01			-
Two-Page Resume	-	-	.01	-
One-Page Resume	-	-		-
Qualifications Section	-	.01	.01	
No Qualifications Section	-			
White Paper				.05
Ivory Paper			.01	
Letter of Recommendation			.05	
No Letter of Recommendation				.05
Salary History			-	
No Salary History			-	
Interests/Activities Section			-	
No Interests/Activities			-	
Typed on Nylon Ribbon*				
Typed on Carbon Ribbon			.01	

*The resume typed on a carbon ribbon had much sharper type and was probably preferred for that reason.
A dash indicates the variable was studied, but was not significant.

APPENDIX C

CAREER AND JOB FINDING BIBLIOGRAPHY

Below are the best job finding, interviewing, and career planning books available. Each is a classic in its own right. Because they approach job-finding from different perspectives, you can benefit greatly from all six. There are other excellent books on the market, but these will give you the most valuable and practical advice.

JOB FINDING

Guerrilla Tactics in the Job Market, Tom Jackson, Bantam Books, 1978. Jackson has been helping job seekers for many years. This is his very practical and useful guide to the job search.

What Color is Your Parachute?, Richard Bolles, Ten Speed Press, 1987. After many years on the *New York Times* Best Seller list, *Parachute* continues to encourage and motivate people to do the things unsuccessful job seekers fail to do.

Who's Hiring Who, Richard Lathrop, Ten Speed Press, 1977. I believe this is the most practical book available on the job search. While excellent for managers, it is especially helpful for military people, career changers, those with little work experience, and those aspiring to management.

INTERVIEWING

Sweaty Palms: The Neglected Art of Being Interviewed, Anthony Medley, Ten Speed Press, 1984. A witty, highly enjoyable, highly enlightening book covering all important aspects of interviewing.

CAREER PLANNING

The Three Boxes of Life, Richard Bolles, Ten Speed Press, 1978. Through his humor and wisdom, Bolles takes the reader through the process of making decisions which lead to sound career choices.

Your Career: How To Plan It, Manage It, Change It, Richard Buskirk, Mentor, 1976. This classic is filled with case histories to give you practical ideas on how to start and build a career.